CHURCH BELLS AND BELL-RINGING

A NORFOLK PROFILE

New Year's Eve in the Bellchamber. Pen and water colour by Henry
Ninham c.1850. *Reproduced by kind permission of the Vicar of St Peter
Mancroft, Norwich.*

CHURCH BELLS AND BELL-RINGING

A NORFOLK PROFILE

Paul Cattermole

THE BOYDELL PRESS

First published 1990
The Boydell Press, Woodbridge

ISBN 978-1-84383-782-4

Transferred to digital printing

The Boydell Press is an imprint of Boydell & Brewer Ltd
PO Box 9, Woodbridge, Suffolk IP12 3DF, UK
and of Boydell & Brewer Inc.
668 Mt. Hope Avenue, Rochester NY 14620, USA
website: www.boydellandbrewer.com

A CIP record for this title is available
from the British Library

This publication is printed on acid-free paper

CONTENTS

I can make no other Apology *for this* Book, *than that it was written by* One *who took* Pleasure *in the* Composition; *and flatters himself there may be several of his* Taste, *who may like to peruse* Books *of* this Sort, *which hitherto have met with a* kind Reception. *He is truly sensible what an* ill-natur'd World *he sends* these Sheets *into,* (viz. *to be* criticis'd *and* censured *by every* One *that pleases :*) *But as there is not* one Paragraph *in the* whole Book *but what he can produce* authentick Vouchers *for, he is in hopes that the* candid *and* unprejudiced Reader *will approve of* this Performance: *If so, then let* Criticks *snarl, and* Censurers *cavil; it is the* Candid *and* Ingenuous *that I esteem, it matters not much what is said by the* Sneerer.

Benjamin Mackerell, 1737.

ILLUSTRATIONS

Swanton Morley, west facade of church begun c.1379 and finished c.1440.

Hilborough, west facade

Illington, early fifteenth-century tower.

Billingford by Scole, tower begun after 1507 and left incomplete.

Wood Norton, tower begun in the sixteenth century.

Denton, tower of c.1700.

Brockdish, tower of 1864 by F. Marrable.

Kimberley, tower begun in the sixteenth century.

Yelverton, tower c.1672 designed for a ring of five bells.

Between pp.144 and 145

Three bells from Forncett St Mary.

Fourteenth-century king-post frame, with later frame-heads, at West Newton.

Fourteenth-century scissors-braced frame at Thompson.

Detail of the braces of the West Newton frame.

Detail of the frame at Bedingham.

Seventeenth-century bell-house at Wood Rising.

The Field Dalling bells in their eighteenth-century fittings.

Detail of the Field Dalling bell-frame.

Ground pulley, 1754, at Fundenhall.

Headstock, 1577, at Illington.

Removal of bells from disused churches.

Early fifteenth-century bell by Thomas Potter, at Boxford, Suffolk.

Disused bell probably cast by Richard Brasyer I, at Ufford, Suffolk.

Bell cast by Richard Brasyer II, at Tacolnestone.

Wedged ironwork supporting the treble bell at Wacton.

Bell cast by William Brend of Norwich, 1615, at Great Ellingham.

Bell cast 1721 by John Stephens, hung with its contemporary fittings at Seething.

Bell cast 1671 by Edward Tooke for Norwich, St Peter Parmentergate.

Bell cast 1599 by Thomas Draper of Thetford, at Illington.

Early fourteenth-century bell cast by Thomas de Lenne, at Long Stratton.

Fifteenth-century cast by John de Guddinc (or Godyng), at Wendling.

Lettering and marks used by Thomas de Lenne.

Lettering and marks used by Thomas Derby of Lynn, from a bell at Ampton.

TEXT FIGURES

FOREWORD

John L'Estrange published 'Church Bells of Norfolk' in 1874 when archaeology was still in its early stages – Tyssen's 'Church Bells of Sussex', the first of such books, was published only ten tears previously. Today archaeology is an exact science, its methods constantly becoming more and more accurate – and no end to the process is in sight.

Dr Cattermole's work is a monumental example of the contemporary historical and archaeological method at its best. Unlike earlier campanologists, he has visited every tower about which he writes. He has really looked at, perceived and investigated, every relevant matter, concerning modern scientific changeringing – of which he is himself an expert practitioner – its origin and development, in the 16th and later centuries, the organisation of ringing and ringers, the evolution in tower after tower from a few 'great bells' to a larger number of smaller bells to facilitate changeringing, the origin and development of bell towers and the organisation of the freemasons and other craftsmen who built them, the development of bell-frames and fittings, the relevant literature – churchwardens' records and other material, wills and other documents, and the Norfolk bell-founders.

He has drawn many fascinating and original deductions from the evidence he has amassed. Truly a definitive work destined to become a classic.

Gilbert Thurlow
Dean Emeritus of Gloucester

AUTHOR'S PREFACE

This study of the church bells of Norfolk began in 1977, when the Norwich Diocesan Association of Ringers decided in its centenary year to record the contents of the church towers which formed its territory. The writer agreed to collate the results of the survey, as well as collecting information from the church towers in his immediate neighbourhood; and it soon became clear that there were many interesting bells to record, and a wealth of documentary material relating to them. Notes made during his visits to numerous churches, and a study of some of the documents relating to them, formed the basis of a thesis presented in the University of London in 1984; and this book explores the same material in a rather less specialised context. Although much of the evidence is drawn from Norfolk churches, there are many issues which have a wider relevance.

Writing in 1929 A. R. Powys, Secretary of the Society for the Protection of Ancient Buildings said: 'there has been an increasing trade in the re-hanging of church bells in the last thirty years, and during that time fine old bell-cages which could have been repaired have been destroyed and replaced, old bells have been mutilated by the removal of their cannons, and others – rare works of the sixteenth and earlier centuries – have been melted down.' The great restorations of bells which took place in more prosperous counties during the nineteenth century passed many Norfolk villages by; and it is a sad fact that a large number of churches have peals of five or more bells which are no longer fit to be rung; but from an antiquarian standpoint we may be considered lucky in what has survived. Local bell-hangers working during the 19th century – such as the Hurrys of Norwich and Day of Eye – were very conservative in their approaches; and this has meant that old bells and bell-frames have been preserved. There are also many towers in rural Norfolk where the bells have been swing-chimed for generations with nothing more than occasional maintenance.

This book is intended as a general introduction to the historical background of church bells and bellringing, rather than a specialist gazetteer of churches and bells in Norfolk. At the beginning of his *Church Bells of Norfolk* (published in 1874) John L'Estrange wrote: 'I had no idea that there was so much to be done'; and the present writer could only agree that any attempt to write up the results of a complete survey of each tower, with a critical interpretation of documentary evidence, would be time-consuming indeed. It is, however, intended eventually to publish a detailed description of the contents of individual church towers, to revise and update L'Estrange's monumental work.

In publishing a work of this kind, thanks are due to so many individuals who have helped in a variety of ways, not least to incumbents and churchwardens who have allowed the writer to inspect the bells in their charge. It would be impossible to recall in print the names of all those local people – and especially fellow ringers – who have helped with arranging visits to their churches. Many have gone out of their way to gain access to awkward places, either by providing ladders, or even by laying floor-boards. A particular debt is owed to Charlie Banham of Caston and Alf Foreman of Garboldisham who helped on some early visits to difficult towers; and to Harold Turner of Tacolnestone, who has been the means of getting into a number of otherwise inaccessible belfries. Church architects, especially Andrew Anderson, Neil Birdsall and Keith Darby, have been kind enough to let me know when scaffolding was in position which might offer a rare opportunity to inspect a bell that was otherwise out of reach; and builders have been very cooperative.

Miss Jean Kennedy's staff at the Norfolk Record office could not have been more helpful, in providing documents for study and suggesting likely sources for research; and the writer is especially grateful to Paul Rutledge, Susan Maddock and Diane Clews for their patience over several years. Sadly Professor R. Allen Brown, my supervisor at King's College London, died before I could thank him properly for his expert and amiable help, without which this book would not have been written.

David Cubitt of Norwich, who has communicated a wealth of material from his own researches, was kind enough to read the first draft of the book; and his comments have been particularly helpful. I also owe a considerable debt to Ranald Clouston of Hartest, who has shared so much of his knowledge of bells and bell-ringing with me. Welcome advice in specialised areas has been received from Simon Cotton, John Eisel, George Elphick, Christopher Pickford: and the encouragement of old friends such as Frank Arnold, Nolan Golden and Frank Phillippo has made the work all the more enjoyable. Christopher Dalton, whose particular interest in old bell-frames is shared by the author, has kindly supplied excellent photographs. Aubrey Forster, whose valiant efforts to reduce the number of unringable bells in the county are greatly appreciated, has also been a constant source of encouragement and assistance. Lastly I record with gratitude the patience of my family who have accompanied me on so many expeditions to inspect bells, and who have spent countless hours in windy churchyards and chilly churches.

Paul Cattermole
Tharston, 1989

Chapter One

BELL-RINGING IN NORFOLK

EARLY RINGING

It would be difficult to imagine East Anglia without her churches and their bells. Many of the buildings are landmarks whose tall flint towers can be seen across the open countryside, and whose bells can be heard two or three villages away. The ancient importance of bells is so easily underestimated now that we can communicate news quickly by electronic means; and it is worth remembering that the purpose of Athelstan's decree in A.D. 937 – that each thegn should build a bell-tower on his estate – was to provide adequate warning against invasion.[1] But the most obvious use of bells in the Middle Ages was to announce the times of the various services and offices in the churches of towns and villages; and quite elaborate sets of instructions for ringing survive from sources as early as the 10th century at some of the great monastic churches, where there would be as many as ten or twelve services each day. Perhaps more important than announcing the times of church and civil occasions, though, is the place which church bells have long held in the affections of

The following abbreviations are used throughout to identify sources.

ANF Wills proved in the Norfolk Archdeaconry Court (Norfolk Record Office).
CBC J. J. Raven, *The church bells of Cambridgeshire*, 1881.
CBE C. H. Deedes and H. B. Walters, *The church bells of Essex*, 1909.
CBN J. L'Estrange, *The church bells of Norfolk*, 1874.
CBS J. J. Raven, *The church bells of Suffolk*, 1890.
DCN Manuscripts belonging to the Dean and Chapter of Norwich (Norfolk Record Office).
NCC Wills proved in the Norwich Consistory Court (Norfolk Record Office).
NCR Records belonging to the City of Norwich (Norfolk Record Office).
NED Deeds enrolled in the Norwich City Court; among the records of the City of Norwich (Norfolk Record Office).
NRO Norfolk Record Office.
OFB Old Free Book of the City of Norwich; among the Norwich City records held at the Norfolk Record Office.
PRO Public Record Office, Chancery Lane, London.

[1] E. A. Fisher, *The greater Anglo-Saxon churches*, 1962, p. 319.

A BELL IN HER USUAL POSITION

a. Stock
b. Stay
c. Slider
d. d. Blocks
e. Wheel
f. Groove of Wheel
g. Fillet
h. Ball of Clapper
i. Flight of Clapper
k. Cannons
l. Timber of Cage
m. Gudgeons
n. Lip of Bell

A BELL SET AT HAND STROKE.

The dotted line denotes the position of the rope in the groove of the wheel.
The arrow shows the direction in which the bell will move when the rope is drawn downwards.

FIG 1

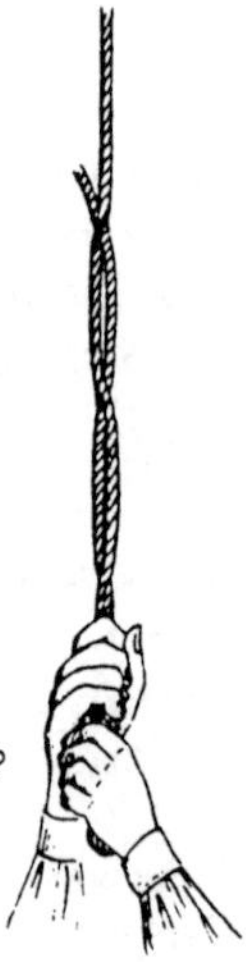

FIG 2

N.B. The figure of the Ringer is drawn considerably too small for the size of the bell on account of space.

Diagrams showing a bell hung for full-circle ringing.
Reproduced from: Changeringing, an introduction to the
early stages of the art of church or hand bell ringing for
the use of beginners, *by Charles A. W. Troyte, 1872.*

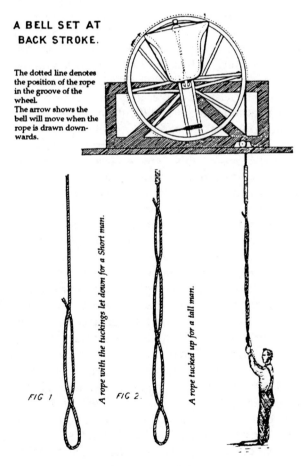

**A BELL SET AT
BACK STROKE.**

The dotted line denotes
the position of the rope
in the groove of the
wheel.
The arrow shows the
bell will move when the
rope is drawn down-
wards.

A rope with the tuckings let down for a Short man.

A rope tucked up for a tall man.

FIG 1

FIG 2.

N.B. The figure of the Ringer is drawn considerably too
small for the size of the bell on account of space.

ordinary people. It has been the writer's happy experience in rural Norfolk to hear people's great appreciation when bells are restored to use,
perhaps after very long periods of silence; or when it has been possible to
arrange ringing for special occasions at churches which have no ringers of
their own. For centuries we have celebrated joyful events with bell-
ringing; and mediaeval wills show the tremendous importance attached
to proper ringing in commemoration of the dead. Ringing at weddings,
for example, is a natural expression of happiness; and many sad people
have been comforted by the solemn notes of half-muffled bells.

At this point a paragraph is probably necessary to explain to those who
are not acquainted with bells a few technical details of bell-hanging, as
well as the basic principles of bell-ringing in the English tradition. In
some places abroad large bells are commonly hung stationary and
sounded by iron clappers or hammers which are pulled directly by ropes.
Whilst the bells which hung in a tree at North Lopham c.1400 must have
been rung in this way,[2] it has long been the practice in England to mount a
clapper inside the bell, which is then fixed to a stout beam (or 'headstock')
mounted on axles (or 'gudgeons'). The whole assembly is then swung so
that the bell speaks as the clapper strikes it. Because bells of varying sizes
swing at different natural speeds it is difficult to control them precisely;
and there can be no doubt that the earliest form of ringing was little more
than the indiscriminate jangling regularly heard from towers on the conti-
nent of Europe at the present time, where large bells of fine tone are
swung at random to produce an impressive, if not very orderly, effect. As
a bell is swung higher the clapper hits it harder to produce a loud and
resonant note, bringing out partial tones which give bell-music its unique
quality. The simplest mechanism for swinging a bell is a lever fixed to the
headstock, with a rope tied to the end of the lever: by this means the bell
can be swung high enough to speak adequately, but the lever eventually
rises to a position where the pull of the rope becomes ineffective. The
problem can be solved if the lever is replaced by a curved channel, forming part of the rim of a wheel whose centre is in line with the gudgeons.
A bell with a half-wheel can be swung through at least a right angle on
either side of the vertical, to produce a very satisfactory note; while a
three-quarter-wheel allows a bell to be swung up to the vertical point, and
a complete wheel adds greatly to the strength of the assembly. The English method of ringing involves swinging a bell through a gradually
increasing sweep until it reaches an upside-down position, when the
ringer adjusts his pull to allow the bell to come to rest just beyond the
point of balance. A very small tension in the rope is then sufficient to
prevent the bell from continuing over the balance and completing a sec-

---

[2] See the entry for North Lopham in the Norwich Domesday, held in the
     Cathedral Library.

ond circle. A movable bar called a 'slider', which is attached to the bell-frame just below the bell, engages a timber 'stay' fixed to the headstock, and this device allows the ringer to rest his bell just over the balance. As the bell swings up in one direction a length of rope is taken up on the rim of the wheel, and it is necessary to pull on the 'tail-end' to recover the rope. If the pull is judged correctly, the bell reverses its swing, returning exactly to balance point; and a coloured hand-grip (called the 'sally') is carefully positioned to allow the ringer to catch the rope in the right place. A considerable degree of expertise in handling the bellrope is needed to achieve this type of ringing, but when sufficient skill has been acquired a ringer can make his bell speak at any predetermined moment. This cycle, known as 'full-circle' ringing, consists of two strokes (called 'whole-pulls'), and is quite distinct from 'swing-chiming' where the bell only rocks back and forward through a small arc. It seems likely that full-circle ringing was being practised in Norfolk by the second half of the 15th century, but there are many examples of half-wheels which have been fitted to bells at much later dates. Particularly good examples of half-wheels can be seen with difficulty at Great Dunham, and more easily at Eccles and Little Melton; while the earliest surviving complete set of fittings for full-circle ringing appear to be those of 1707 at Ashwellthorpe, last restored in 1796.

Very detailed records of ringing in the 13th century survive at Lincoln to show that various combinations of bells were used to announce the canonical hours; and it appears that the only extended period in which the bells were completely silent was during the small hours of the morning. Mr J. R. Ketteringham, in his book on the bells and ringers of Lincoln Cathedral,[3] remarks that: 'the life of Lincoln Minster revolved around the sound of the bells which enabled those whose duty it was to attend service to be there at the proper times, and those who worked within the sound of the bells to tell the time of day according to the way in which the bells were rung. The importance of the bells in the daily routine of the Cathedral and in the life of the City is reflected in the high status of those who had the responsibility of ensuring that they sounded at the correct time and that they were maintained in order to do so'. There are very few East Anglian sources which tell how church bells were used in the Middle Ages; but at Norwich we are lucky in the survival of a monastic Customary[4] dating from about 1300. This is not a service book of the usual kind which contains the words of offices said and sung in the Cathedral, but is more in the nature of a guide to the way in which various services and

---

[3] J. R. Ketteringham, *Lincoln Cathedral, a history of the bells, bellringers and bellringing,* 1987, pp. 39, 41.

[4] J. B. L. Tolhurst, *The monastic Customary of Norwich,* Henry Bradshaw Society, 1926.

ceremonials should be conducted. Directions are given for placing candles and lights, for the ordering of rituals and the movement of processions, for the types and colours of vestments to be worn; and there are
numerous other details of organisation which include *inter alia* the instructions for ringing the Cathedral bells. Using the book it would be
possible to recreate the programme of ringing at the Cathedral for a
complete year, and the complexity of the arrangements shows why it was
necessary to appoint officers with special responsibility for ringing and
maintaining the bells.

The Sacrist, one of the obedientiaries[5] (or executive officers) of the
Norwich Cathedral priory, was responsible for the provision and maintenance of bells in fit condition to be rung; and it is in the rolls which
survive from his department that we find a number of useful references,
not least to the rebuilding c.1300 of the great detached Belfry, or 'Clocher',
which stood west of the Cathedral church and in which hung five large
bells. There are many references to oil, ropes, tallow and the various
necessaries for the smooth going of the bells, and occasional amounts
paid for more major work. The Sacrist was responsible for the repairs to
the Cathedral church following the great fire which was started by a
lightning strike in 1463: new bells were cast and hung in the central tower,
and the 15th-century bell-frame can be clearly seen in an 18th-century
drawing which shows a section of the tower. This bell-frame is very
similar in design to other contemporary frames which survive in a few
local churches, and it can be seen that the trusses are built without king-
posts, giving a structure which would be quite stable for bells to be rung
in full circles. An account of 1521 refers to making a new wheel for the
third bell in the central tower and repairing the frame [*in factura nove rote
ad terciam campanam in choro iiij s. et in reparacione le belframes ij s. iiij d.*],
and it seems more than likely that the bells in both towers at the
Cathedral were regularly rung 'up' by the end of the 15th century.

The Norwich Customary[6] details many offices and occasions which
were to be announced by single bells from the central tower; and there
were other times when different combinations of bells were used. Sometimes a pair of bells was rung; or on occasions such as the Vigil of St John
Baptist, the three lightest of the five bells in the central tower were rung
before Vespers [*pulsentur tres parve campane ad vesperas utrasque*]. More
elaborate ringing was ordained for the principal festivals such as All
Saints' Day, when all the bells were to be rung together and the candles
lighted before the office of Matins [*Ante matutinas pulsentur simul omnia
signa et illuminentur cereoli ut mos est in principalibus festis*]. On the Commemoration Day of the founder of the Priory, Herbert de Losinga, there

---

[5] About 100 rolls relating to the Sacrist's department (1272–1537) survive among
the records of the Dean and Chapter, now at NRO.
[6] See note 4.

are instructions for ringing all the bells in the Clocher [*Et magister celarii faciet pulsandum in magno campanili et potum et cibum ministrabit eis*]. The heavy peal in the detached tower seems to have been reserved for use only on the most important occasions; and it is noteworthy that the ringing was at the behest of the Master of the Cellar (who was second in importance only to the Prior) rather than the Sacrist. The organisation of the complicated schedule of ringing was left in the hands of a specialist, a *campanarius*: like John de Rudham, whose name has come down to us through a property transaction which he made in Norwich in 1290.[7] It is fairly certain that this particular man was also trained in the law, being employed on various legal causes by the Convent. Since few payments to ringers have been traced in the Sacrist's accounts it is likely that the actual pulling of the ropes was left to the 'four servants of the church' who received regular salaries, or even to such of the poor bedesmen living in the Almonry as were able to help. Henry VIII's Statutes[8] tell us how the ringing was to be provided c.1540, and it is likely that earlier practice was modified to take account of the smaller number of services and offices which would take place after the priory had been dissolved. The new Dean and Chapter were to appoint two honest and industrious men under the control of the Sacrist, whose duties were to assist in preparing the altars, lights and vestments, in sweeping the church and causing windows to be kept cleaned and glazed, and in ringing the bells at the hours prescribed by the Dean or Vice-dean. These two Subsacrists were enabled by the Statutes to call upon the services of as many of the bedesmen as were needed to ring the bells: but it is doubtful how much help these pensioners could have given since they were described as 'oppressed by poverty and afflicted by destitution, wounded or broken by war, or come to the debility of old age'.

Among the Cathedral Priory muniments is an interesting document[9] which relates to ringing in 1521. In consideration of a sum of £20 given towards the reparation of the Cathedral church, the Prior and Convent grant to John Flowerdew of Norwich the appointment of the two clerks commonly called the Bell Ringers [*officium duorum clericorum vulgariter nuncupatorum le Belle Ryngers*]. An annual salary of £3. 17s. 4d. was to be paid in four instalments by the hand of the Sacrist, and the perquisites of the office included a robe of the livery of the Prior containing four yards of cloth worth 4 shillings per yard, and each evening they were to receive a measure of monastic beer from the Master of the Cellar. The post of Bell Ringer seems to have been one of prestige, since lesser servants received very much cheaper livery, and their victuals were provided by the Cellarer, an inferior officer to the Master of the Cellar. It seems likely that

7   NRO NCR Roll 2, membrane 28.
8   NRO DCN 29/2 fo. 23.
9   NRO DCN 38/4.

John Flowerdew was in effect being appointed as Ringing Master at the Cathedral, where his deputed ringers would draw their salaries from the Sacrist and ensure that the daily bells were faithfully rung, and where Flowerdew would be responsible for raising a full company to ring on greater occasions. Payment was generally made for funeral ringing in parish churches, and it is very likely that other occasions not directly connected with the regular services of the Cathedral would be similarly rewarded. The salaries which supported the regular bellringers were safe-guarded by a condition which allowed John Flowerdew to enter the Rec-tory manor of Bawburgh (which belonged to the Sacrist) and seize the profits if at any time the wages or perquisites of the bell-ringers were in arrears. It is noteworthy that Flowerdew appears to have been a local landowner of some substance, with property in Wymondham and Hethersett; and it seems likely that Henry VIII's subsacrists replaced Flowerdew's bellringers c.1540.

Ringing in the villages would not have followed such a complicated pattern, but it was customary even in lesser churches for there to be special ringing on festival days. Jeffery Elyngham's will of 1493[10] shows that in the small church at Fersfield the bells were sometimes rung during the course of processions, and that it was necessary to move the ringers up from the ground floor to an elevated gallery 'so that the processions on festival days may pass easily beneath the bellringers'. We get an impress-ion in an early account[11] at Dereham (1419–1421) of some of the special occasions which merited ringing, when the clerks were paid 6d. for ring-ing the three bells in Easter Week on the anniversary of commemoration of benefactors [*solutis clericis pro pulsatione in anniversario pro benefactoribus in septimana Pasche*]. Forty years later the churchwardens paid regularly for ringing on three occasions: 'Itm payed to the ryngers for ryngyng for alle crysten Sowlys on Estern Tuesday iiij d. Itm payed to the ryngers on holy thursday [Ascension Day] iiij d. and on corpus christi day iiij d. for ryngyng the tyme of precession as it hath been of old usage.' By the 1460s there were at least five bells at Dereham, and it appears that the ringing on special occasions was no longer done by the parish clerks, although they presumably retained the responsibility for regular ringing for the daily offices.

A surprising sidelight is thrown on bell-ringing by the proceedings against heretics in the Diocese between 1428 and 1431, when sixty sus-pected Lollards were examined before the Bishop of Norwich or his offi-cers.[12] Among the charges laid against Margery Baxter, who appears to have been the formidable wife of a leading heretic, was that she had

[10] NRO NCC wills, Awbreye 141.
[11] NRO Phillips MS 40, 973; and P 182 D.
[12] N. P. Tanner, *Norwich heresy trials 1428–1431, Camden fourth series*, 1977, *passim.*

taught that all bells should be taken down from churches and destroyed, and that those who had charge of ringing should be excommunicated. Four leaders of another thriving school of heresy at Earsham were delivered to the Bishop by the Justices in 1429. Among then was one John Skylly of Flixton who in 1427 had removed an image of the patron saint from St Andrew's church at Trowse, taken it to Bergh Apton and burnt it with some ceremony. In the instrument by which he abjures his heresy, John Skylly states that he had 'held taught and afermed that ryngyng of belles in churches availeth to nothyng but oonly to gete money into prestes purses'. Others had gone further, claiming that 'ryngyng of belles be but Antecristis hornes'. These statements support the suggestion in the East Dereham accounts, that ringing was controlled by the clergy during the early years of the 15th century; but it would be surprising if ordinary people felt quite as much resentment as did the more zealous Lollards.

We can be sure that bells were rung on many occasions other than those recorded in Churchwardens' accounts, which show only the payments for ringing ordained by the church authorities. Ringing at funerals[13] is well-documented, and testators felt it necessary to give careful instructions in their wills for ringing on the day of burial as well as on various anniversaries (called *obits*). James de Heyham, Rector of Quidenham, requested in his will of 1400 that the ringers should have 12d. on his burial day; 6d. on the seventh day after; and a further 6d. on the thirtieth day [*lego pulsantibus in die sepulture mee xij d. et in septimo die vj d. et in trigint' die vj d*]. Simon Kede's will, written at Bunwell in 1530 requests: 'An obit to be doon for my sowle my fathers sowle and all christen sowles that is to wete placebo and dyryge songen the bellis rongen as the custome is and masse of Requiem saide or songen'. It is clear in wills such as that of John Dannok, Parish Priest of St Peter Mancroft in 1514, that the ringing requested was more than the tolling of a single bell: he makes a bequest to Shotesham All Saints church with the condition 'that the parishe ther Ring a pele with iiij bells and the curate to say placebo dirige and masse of Requiem'. Another early use of the word 'peal' to describe ringing is found in the will of William Bodye of Poringland (1520), who asks that there should be 'at the day of my obit a dirige in the said church and a ppele rang with the belles'. In similar vein Thomas Chapman of Barnham Broom writing his will in 1490 provides for ringing as follows: 'I will that every creature shall have at my dedeit day at the first dirige bread

---

13 The following wills are cited in this paragraph: James de Heyham, NRO NCC wills, Harsyk 268; Simon Kede, NRO NCC wills, Platfoote 99; John Dannok, NRO NCC wills, Coppynger 114; William Bodye, NRO NCC wills, Robinson/Fedymont 117; Thomas Chapman, NRO NCC wills, Wolman 69; John Cowall, NRO NCC wills, Spyltymber 255. See also The Red Register of Lynn, quoted in D. M. Owen, *The Making of King's Lynn*, British Academy, 1984, pp. 63, 141.

and chese and drink and the same tyme iiij ryngers yche of them j d. and so continnyng to nyte after ryngyng eche of them iiij ryngers j d'. The refreshment of the bellringers also concerned John Cowall Rector of Stratton St Michael in 1509, when he requested 'dirige and a masse with iiij d. in brede and ale to the Ryngers'. There was so much ringing of this kind at King's Lynn during the latter years of the 14th century that the Assembly restricted ringing for anniversaries and obits to a maximum of one hour with breaks, because of the serious damage to the bell towers of all three churches. The same ordinance (1391) allowed the 'great bells' to be rung only for deceased brothers of the Trinity Gild and their wives, as well as the prior and monks of St Margaret's Priory. Much of the evidence for funeral ringing has survived in wills; and it is inconceivable that other important personal events – especially weddings – would not have been marked by a 'peal' on the church bells. There are a few references to ringing for secular occasions in pre-Reformation church accounts, and it seems that ringing for royal occasions was a requirement rather than a courtesy. When Queen Catherine of Aragon went to pray at the shrine of Our Lady of Walsingham for Henry VIII's safe return from his French campaign in 1513 she passed through Shipdham,[14] where the churchwardens were fined 12d. 'for fawte of ryngyng qwhan the qwenne cam throw the contre'.

The regular chiming of church bells for services was also used to regulate secular business; since most people had no other method of telling the time of day. There are accounts for building a sophisticated mechanical clock at Norwich Cathedral in the Sacrist's accounts for 1322–24; and others were probably in use by the beginning of the 14th century in a few Norfolk churches. A striking clock in the Clocher at Norwich Cathedral was repaired in 1486, and there are contemporary references to a clock at East Dereham. New clock bells were bought for Swaffham in 1538, and the mediaeval clock bell at Hingham is heavily indented on the outside of the soundbow. Benjamin Mackerell[15] records that chimes were first set up in King's Lynn in 1566 (at St Margaret's church), and it is likely that these played simple tunes on the five bells. St Nicholas' Chapel also had 'Five good Tunable Bells . . . The first Chimes upon them were erected in the Year 1631 . . . These at first play'd but one tune; but in this year, the Chapel-Wardens have caus'd the former to be disanull'd and for the more Variety of Musick have order'd some new ones to be added to them'. At St Margaret's church 'the first Chimes upon the Eight Bells were set up: By the Gift and at the Charge of Sir John Thorowgood' in 1667. St Peter Mancroft, Norwich also acquired a set of chimes, in 1678.

---

[14] NRO PD 337/85.
[15] B. Mackerell, *The history and antiquities of the flourishing Corporation of King's Lynn*, 1738, p. 227.

As long as bells were used mainly as instruments to give notice of various religious services, it was important to have distinctive modes of ringing for different occasions. A listener could easily tell the difference between the tolling of a single small bell and that of a large bell; or perhaps between a pair of bells and a trio: but the tunefulness of larger numbers of bells rung together 'in peal' was probably not considered to be particularly important. It is only after about 1450 that we find many references[16] to the need for bells to be 'tuneable', or to 'accord' with each other; while the more musically apposite names 'treble' and 'tenor' seem to supplant the older descriptions of the 'little' and 'great' bell on occasions. In 1498 William Nycoll bequeathed to Tivetshall St Margaret 'a belle clepyd a tenor to the bells hangyng in the steple now at this tyme', and William Tedar made a similar gift in 1504 when he wished 'to have anoder belle acordyng tenor to the tweiyn bells beyng in matsalborough [Mattishall Burgh] forseid upon my coste and charge and all thyngs Redy to Rynge with the said ij bells withinne the space of j annum next after my decesse'. The new bell bequeathed to Wilby church in 1504 was described as *'una campana quattuor trebull'*; and Robert Pyrle of East Harling in 1519 went to some lengths to provide funds for an additional bell: 'I wyll and command that my close callyd Wodcokkys with ix acres of fre land leyng in the feld of Estherlyng after this croppe be sowlde by the syght of the parson of Esyherlyng and my executors and the mony therof becumyng schalbe geven to the makyng of a treble bell in the chirch of Estherlyng'.

A bond[17] made on 18 July 1521 between John Aleyn, brazier of Norwich of the one part and Stephen Betryng, William Brown and Robert Myller of Hanworth of the other part, concerning a new treble bell for Hanworth church, shows something of the careful negotiations which took place between a bell-founder and his clients:

> The condycyon off this oblygacion is suche that where the wythin bownde John Aleyn hath yeten made & delyveryd to the within named Stephen Betryng Wylliam Brown & Roberd Myller & for the Chyrche of Hanworthe withyn wretyn a new trebyll bell yff the same bell after it be sett up & hangyn in the Steeple off Hanworth aforeseid be & contynue off suffycyent accorde perfyght tewne hoole trebyll sownde and swete ermony in tewne & Warkemanship to the other bellys now hangyng in the stepyll aforeseid by the space of on hole yere & a daye aftyr it be hangen in the same stepyll by the seid Stephyn Wylliam Roberd or one off them or off ther assygnes so that no defawte be founde in warkemanschyppe nor metal theroff in the meane tyme in the only defawte of the seid John Aleyn wyche seid belle yff it be

---

16 The following wills are cited in this paragraph: William Nycoll, NRO ANF wills, Shaw 46; William Tedar, NRO NCC wills, Ryxe 40; Robert Pyrle, NRO ANF wills, Gedney 153.

17 NRO AYL 145.

founde defectyffe in the necglygence of the seid John Aleyn by too or thre Credabyll persons of musyke indeferently chosen within the seid yere Than the seid Stephyn Wylliam & Roberd schall do stryke the seid bell provyd defawlty & recary it to the Workyng howse of the seid John Aleyn in Norwych

Than yff the same John Aleyn after resonabyll warnyng so theroff to hym made do newe yote & make the seid belle of a suffycyent accorde & perfight tewne in every condicyon as is above seid and delyver or cawse to be delyverid the same belle at hys workyng howse Immedyately as it can be goten to the seid Stephyn Wylliam & Roberd Wyche belle so delyverid to be & contynue in perfight tewne as is above seid by the space of on hole yer & a daye as is aforeseid Provyded allweys that iff the same John Aleyn schall more the seid belle in yotyng of the same over and abowght the weight wyche it berith the day of the date within wretyn That than the said Stephyn Wylliam & Roberd schall alowe to the seid John Aleyn xxx s. for a hundyrth weight and yff the same John Aleyn mynysche the same bell than grawntyth the foreseid John Aleyn to alowe the seid Stephyn Wylliam & Roberd xx s. for a hundyrthweight and yff the same John Aleyn well and trewly holde & performe all the premyssys aforeseid than that thys present oblygacion to be voyde or ellys to remayne in full streynght and effecte.

Musical considerations were important at Hanworth, and one hopes that the new bell fulfilled the promise of perfect tune and sweet harmony with the other bells, and that its whole treble sound was acceptable. The matter was to be judged by three credible persons of music, chosen impartially, and if the bell did not please them, then it was to be carried to and from the bell-founders for recasting until such time as it was found to be suitable. Unfortunately neither the contemporary churchwardens accounts, nor the bell, survive at Hanworth, but a similar process is well-documented at East Dereham. In 1486 we find evidence that a bell was carried between Dereham and Norwich several times, suggesting that it was recast or exchanged more than once before it was considered suitable as the third in the ring of five; and there is no indication that it was defective in anything other than its musical quality: 'the bell that servyd not'.

It is surprising to find that, whilst early-16th-century churchwardens' accounts (such as those at North Elmham, Denton and Shipdham) show the considerable effort which went into keeping the bells in order, payments for ringing were few and far between. At North Elmham, for example, the only recorded payment for ringing between 1539 and 1547 was 'to the Ryngers whan we kept for our late Soverayn Lord kyng Henry the viijth'. This may be taken to suggest that, whilst the simple ringing of one or two bells by the parish clerk sufficed for the regular services, companies were certainly available to ring 'peals' on special occasions.

The popularity of bell-ringing as a secular pastime was growing; and ringers who practised at various churches made themselves available to the churchwardens when required.

Bell-ringers would probably not have been greatly concerned when Henry VIII, who had received the title of 'Defender of the Faith' from Pope Leo X in 1520, proclaimed himself head of the Church of England in 1535, cutting the ties with Rome. Services, however, continued along the familiar lines until the great changes which took place during the reign of Edward VI. In some places there is evidence that bells were transferred to parish churches from religious houses suppressed between March 1536 and March 1540, when approximately 250 houses in the Diocese of Norwich were dissolved.[18] The Court of Augmentations had given instructions for the rapid dismantling of the monastic buildings; and the sale of bells, together with lead from roofs and other building materials, probably took place on the spot after the surrender of each house. St Andrew's church, Norwich acquired the great bell from the tower of the Dominican friary in 1538, and the churchwardens of St Lawrence's church in the same city bought four bells from the College of St Mary in the Fields. At Walsingham in 1538 the Guild of the Blessed Virgin Mary had given 40 shillings 'in part payment for the great bell of the late Friars Minors', presumably to hang it in the tower of the parish church, where the pre-Reformation bell-frame (removed in 1986) showed clear signs of having been adapted to take a much heavier bell than any of those for which it was designed. Towards the end of his reign it is likely that the king was keen to get his hands on some of the valuable property belonging to the parish churches, in much the same way as he had done when the monasteries were suppressed a few years earlier; and it appears that the first steps towards diverting valuables belonging to the parish churches into the royal treasury were taken before the accession of Edward VI. The 1552 Inventory for Roudham tells us 'that ij belles were carried away by Hugh Blye and William Faconer and Richard Coste and Sir francis Lovell Knyght wayenge by estimacion viij c.and this was done in the xxxviij[th] yere of Kyng Henry the viij[th] without the consent of the parisheners'.

After Edward VI's accession, congregations would have noticed that services which had been said or sung in Latin were now in English, and that much of the equipment used before the Reformation was no longer needed by a Protestant congregation. Churchwardens may have wondered about the future of their bells, particularly when the king's officers began making enquiries. A definite instruction dated 15 February 1549 appointed Commissioners to summon incumbents and churchwardens, and to require from them inventories of remaining church valuables; and

---

[18] See P. Cattermole, Ph.D. Thesis, London University, 1985, pp. 346–349.

it was ordered that any church property sold should be restored, unless it could be shown that the sale had taken place with the agreement of the parishioners and that the proceeds had been used charitably.[19] A typical return from such an enquiry remains for Woodton church, dated 3 Edward VI, in which the churchwardens stated that they had sold a bell weighing 11 cwt for £10 and had used the proceeds to recast the lead on the south side of the church, to whitewash the church and mend certain windows, to make a poor-box and to mend a bell-clapper: two paraphrases were purchased and half the cost of a new bible was provided.

It would appear that the instructions of 1549 were not carried out with sufficient speed to satisfy the King's advisers, and further Commissioners were set to work in the autumn of 1552 to produce inventories[20] for all 690 churches in Norfolk. These give, in addition to the list of church goods, a schedule of the plate and bells which would be allowed to remain after the Commissioners' work had been carried out in full. Many inventories survive, to give us our first definite record of the goods and valuables (including bells) in Norfolk churches. It is worth printing a copy of a typical inventory from a small Norfolk village, such as the document which was presented on 29th April 1552 by the chief inhabitants of Hapton[21] to Edward VI's Commissioners gathered at Norwich. Peter Martyn, Thomas Perman, George Whitefoot and John Hette made the following return:

> In primis one chales with a pateyn of Sylver parcell gylte
> weying viij ounces the unce valewed at iij s. viij d. xxix s. iiij d.
> Item thre belles in the steple by estimacion of xv C. in weyght
> wherof the one vj C. the next v C. the thirde iiij c. valewed at
> xj li v s.
> Item iij Belle Clappers valued at ij s.
> Item ij hande belles ij s.
> Item one vestment of blew bryges satten valewed at iij s. iiij d.
> Item one other vestment of grene satten vj s. viij d.
> Item one Cope of blew bryges satten valewed at iij s. iiij d.
> Item one other vestment of dornekes valewed at ij s. viij d.

Some of the inventories show that churchwardens[22] had hurriedly sold bells and other church goods in order to convert the property to local

[19] *Ibid.*
[20] *Ibid.*
[21] H. B. Walters, Inventories of Church Goods, *Norfolk Archaeology*, Vol. XXVII, 124.
[22] Churchwardens' accounts cited here include the following:
Wymondham Abbey, in the Muniment Room at the Abbey, by kind permission of Mr D. Wright; A. G. Legge, *The ancient churchwardens' accounts of the parish of North Elmham . . .*, 1891; Bunwell accounts, at the church (by kind permission of Messrs. C. F. W. Phillippo and F. C. J. Arnold).

uses, rather than allow the Commissioners to realise its value. At Wymondham, for example, where the parishioners had bought the bells from the Abbey tower at the Suppression, six bells were sold to an Ipswich merchant for £62, leaving only two bells in the parish tower in 1552. At places such as Bunwell, however, life went on as usual after the first contact with the 'visitors' on 3 April, 1552. The wheel of the great bell was mended in May, and two clappers were refurbished in July of the same year, just a month before the Inventory was delivered at Norwich; so we may assume that bell-ringing continued as it always had done. In January 1553 the Commissioners were ordered to collect all the outstanding inventories and to bring in to the King's treasury all the ready money, plate and jewels certified as remaining in the churches; but other less valuable items, such as vestments and altar cloths, were to be sold in the parishes, as were other metals remaining, with the stated exceptions of 'great bells' and 'saunce bells', which were to remain in the churches until the King's pleasure in the matter was known. The actual confiscation of the church goods from North Elmham is recorded thus: 'Item for our Costs and other Comanded to bryng the Chyrche Goods with their Inventarye of the same, Bells and a Payer of chalyce onlye excepted, before the Kyngs Mayesties Commissioners at Lenne the iiijthe day of June in the vijth yere of hys gracs Reygn vj s.' The Commissioners clearly intended to confiscate all but a single bell from most churches; but the date when the more easily available goods were delivered from North Elmham (4 June 1553) was close to that of the death of Edward VI, 6 July, 1553. It is frequently stated (in guide books to churches, and in other places) that Edward VI's Commissioners removed bells from church towers, leaving only the smallest; but the existence of so many towers containing more than a single pre-Reformation bell shows that this practice was not widespread. In a few places (such as Old Buckenham and Hilborough for example) the Commissioners, anticipating the King's command, had seen to the removal of church bells before the 1552 inventory was made; but the destruction was nothing like as extensive as is sometimes supposed. Whilst there is no doubt that a few bells were lost during the upheavals of Edward VI's reign; most seem to have survived, simply because it was so difficult to remove them.

Most churches in the county whose 1552 Inventories have been traced had rings of three or four bells, and while the recorded weights should be treated with some caution, the fact that many towers contained heavy bells is confirmed by the size of surviving pre-Reformation bell-frames, several of which are designed for rings of bells with tenors weighing 20 cwt or more. While we know that Norwich Cathedral had a light five (tenor about 12 cwt) in the central tower and a very much heavier five in a detached belfry in the Close, it is difficult to find information about other city churches since their 1552 inventories have not been found, and only a few earlier certificates have been traced. St Peter Mancroft would surely have had five bells after the tower was completed c.1510, and the inscriptions on the old bells at St Gregory's church suggest another early ring of five. A very few Norfolk churches (mainly those without towers) had only a single bell or a pair of bells in 1552; and the following towers in the Norfolk are known to have had more than four 'great' bells in 1552:

Aylsham	5	30 cwt
Banham	5	14 cwt
Blofield	5	18 cwt
Bressingham	5	12 cwt
Brooke	5	15 cwt
Carleton Rode	5	16 cwt
South Creake	5	15 cwt
Cromer	5	18 cwt
Hickling	5	21 cwt
Hingham	5	20 cwt
King's Lynn St Margaret	5	28 cwt
Norwich Cathedral (Central tower)	5	12 cwt
Norwich Cathedral (Clocher)	5	weight unknown
Norwich St Andrew	6	24 cwt
Norwich St Gregory	5	9 cwt
Norwich St Michael at Plea	5	11 cwt
Norwich St Peter Mancroft	5	23 cwt
Norwich St Stephen	5	11 cwt
Redenhall	5	24 cwt
Salle	5	41 cwt
South Lopham	5	20 cwt
Terrington St Clement	5	20 cwt
Tibenham	5	22 cwt
North Walsham	5	28 cwt
Worstead	5	16 cwt

There are other towers which had rings of bells in the 1500s, but where the Commissioners found only one or two in 1552. East Dereham had a ring of five by the 1460s (returning only a single bell of 40 cwt in 1552), Swaffham had five bells by c.1520 (two bells were taken down in 1548, leaving only three in 1552), and Wymondham had at least eight bells after the transfer of the Abbey bells in 1538 (only a pair of bells weighing 18 cwt and 26 cwt were recorded in 1552). Thus it seems that there were about 30 rings of five or more bells in Norfolk before 1552, significantly fewer than the 45 rings recorded in Suffolk.[23]

It must have been very confusing to return to older religious practices during Mary's short reign; but it is probable that the vestments of green

---

[23] Information from Mr R. W. M. Clouston.

satin and blue Bruges satin mentioned in the 1552 inventory were brought
into use again at Hapton church, that the tower bells rang out as before,
and the small handbells were used to let the people know when the most
solemn part of the Mass was taking place at the altar. During Elizabeth's
reign the English Prayer Book was revived – with a more liberal brand of
Protestantism than her half-brother's; and the Church of England returned to more settled times. There is no doubt that bell-ringing continued to be a popular pastime, although there were few dramatic
developments in the provision of new and augmented rings of bells in
Norfolk before about 1600.

Towards the end of the 16th century there are echoes which suggest that
bellringing was carried to excess. When Queen Elizabeth visited Norwich
in 1578, Blomefield records that she was greeted at St Stephen's gates by
the City Waits, 'who chearfully and melodiously welcomed her Majesty
into the city'. The music was 'marvellous sweet and good, albeit the
rudeness of some ringers of bells did somewhat hinder the noise of the
harmony'. Edmund Spenser hints at protracted ringing to celebrate a
wedding in his poem, *Epithalamium*:

> Ring ye the bells, ye young men of the town,
> And leave your wonted labours for this day:
> This day is holy; do ye write it down,
> That ye for ever it remember May.'

And an enigmatic statement[24] in Mackerell's *History of Lynn Regis* relates
to the year 1582: 'About this Time certain Lusty Young Fellows began to
set up Ringing again, which for some Time had been disused; divers of
the Aldermen meaning to silence them, occasion'd a great Disturbance,
which turn'd to the Mayor's Disadvantage, and was the cause of Spending a great deal of Money.' Whatever happened then, a new bell-frame
was provided for the heavy five at St Margaret's church, King's Lynn in
1595. Little Walsingham bells became five in 1569; and at Norwich, St
Giles's bells became five in 1593; and St Peter's Mancroft bells were increased to a ring of six in 1602. By the end of Elizabeth's reign there were,
perhaps, no more than forty churches with rings of as many as five or six
bells, but it is certain that full-circle ringing was enjoyed in these towers,
as well as on the multitude of rings of three or four bells scattered across
the county. The secular nature of ringing is emphasised by an entry in the
Parish Register of Itteringham,[25] which shows that there was considerable
enthusiasm for ringing on the three bells there: 'Memorandum that the

[24] Mackerell, *op. cit.* p. 229. The writer has not so far been able to trace Mackerell's
source for this statement, which he suspects is among the archives of the
Borough of King's Lynn.
[25] NRO PD 439/1.

4th day of december in the morning 1601 et Eliz[abeth] 44 the bell Sallars were burnt downe, how it came no man could rightly tell, but by great presumption as after was well knowne it was knowne to be downe by negligence of certayne ringers be candlelight for joy that Ashley Wood Gent was returned home from London. The sayd Bell Sallers were set up the 21 Aprill, and the 23 the same month the bell frames and the bells were set & hangd up with great care in the yere of our lord God 1602.'

Paid ringing, as shown in churchwardens' accounts tended to be done for state occasions, such as at Swaffham[26] in 1575 when the churchwardens paid 4s. 4d. 'to William Bysshopp and his company on the memory-all day of the queenes majesties coronatyon'. The only other ringing recorded in the churchwardens' accounts there is the ringing of the Day bell. In Norwich the St Gregory's churchwardens[27] regularly paid 12d. 'to the Ryngers the xxvijth day of August for Ryngyng in the remembrance for the deliverye of the Cittie from the miserable Rebellyon of Kett'. Apart from such occasions, payments for ringing remain fairly rare items; and there is no hint of ringing for services.

Elizabethan churchwardens' accounts, in common with those written towards the end of the reign of Henry VIII, invariably show sums of money spent on the regular maintenance of the church bells, often in preparation for ringing on special occasions. At Tibenham[28] the bells were looked after by a regular bell-wright, who had the occupation of a house in the village for his pains; and a contract[29] dated November 1593 for the maintenance of the Swaffham bells is of interest.

> It is covenanted and agreed between the township of Swaffham and Robert Bisshopp that the said Robert Bisshopp (for and in consideration of foure nobles of good and lawfull money of england yerely and every yere to be paide unto him the said Robert Bisshopp by the handes of the churchwardens of Swaffham afor saide untill the full ende and terme of five yeres next and immediately ensewing after the date above written) shall kep and maintaine the bells of this towne in good and suffi-cient caste to be runge and all things to them necessary yerely during the said terme of five yeres and at the end of the said five yeres shall leave the bells and ropes and all other thinges to the same belonging in as good caste and reparation as they are at the day of the date hereof provided if that anye of the bells shall chance to rive and to break that then the same is to be repaired at the costes of the said township of Swaffham aforsaid. Pro-vided likewise that the said four nobles shalbe quarterly paid to

---

[26] NRO PD 52/71.
[27] NRO PD 59/54.
[28] Cambridge University Library, Buxton MS (Tibenham Churchwardens' ac-counts).
[29] NRO PD 52/70.

him the said Robert the quarter to begin at the Feast of all Soles last past for Consideration whereof the said Robert hath received foure nobles in hand and as a full discharge for the first whole yere next ensueng after the date above written and over and besides he hath received uppon good wille by the consent of the town iij s. iiij d.

It appears that the Swaffham bellwright provided the labour and materials for the running repairs to the bell installation, while the churchwardens were to carry the cost of any major work, such as recasting. This seems to have been a relatively common practice, and explains why there are no payments for individual small items such as nails, timber for stays, oil and tallow in some parish accounts.

One of the great fascinations for ringers, in addition to the physical exercise, is the delight in the sound of precise and rhythmic striking. It is the writer's experience that many non-ringers, too, who listen to church bells are acutely aware of the difference between good, rhythmic ringing and a piece of ragged and careless striking; and it must always have been so. In the very early days of full-circle ringing it would have taken considerable effort to produce the simplest form of orderly ringing, where the bells sound in sequence down the musical scale from the lightest bell (with the highest note) through to the heaviest bell (with the deepest note). In musical notation this sequence, called 'rounds', would appear on a ring of five tuned to the key of G as follows:

DCBAG

It has, however, long been the convention among ringers to refer to the number of a bell rather than its note, and their notation would be:

1 2 3 4 5

The earliest efforts at orderly full-circle ringing must have been repeated attempts to ring 'rounds' accurately; and once this had been achieved ringers would surely have sought more interesting patterns. The simplest means of producing variety is for the ringers to change the sequence in which the bells sound every few minutes, as instructed by their conductor. This type of ringing is still regularly heard from church towers, and is the preferred method of ringing at many places in Devon and Cornwall. A typical 'touch' of 'call-changes', which might still be heard on a Sunday morning in rural Norfolk could be arranged as follows, with each sequence (or 'row') sounding for a minute or so:

1 2 3 4 5	Rounds
2 1 3 4 5	Bells 1 and 2 change places

2 1 4 3 5	Bells 3 and 4 change places
2 4 1 3 5	Bells 1 and 4 change places
4 2 1 3 5	and so on . . .
4 1 2 3 5	
1 4 2 3 5	
1 4 3 2 5	
1 3 4 2 5	
3 1 4 2 5	
3 1 2 4 5	
1 3 2 4 5	
1 2 3 4 5	Rounds

It is conventional for ringing to start and end with rounds, and the conductor would probably dwell on sequences such as 2 4 1 3 5, 1 4 2 3 5 or 3 1 4 2 5 for longer than others, since certain rows are thought to be more tuneful than others. The effort needed to change place between the rows depends on the weight of the bells, how well they are hung, and how carefully they have been maintained. It should be possible for each change to take place without any alteration of the rhythm, but it would not be until bell-frames were relatively steady, and bells well-hung, that any precision could be achieved. There is little doubt that this form of bell music has survived from the early days of full-circle ringing.

THE RISE OF CHANGERINGING

As the design of bell-frames and bell gear improved during the late 16th and early 17th centuries, and with the provision of generally lighter sets of bells, it became possible to change the sequence of the rows more frequently during ringing; and the ultimate development was for the rows to be rung as a continuous sequence, sounding successively and without interval at each 'half-pull'. For this to be possible it was necessary for ringers to develop a rather more sophisticated physical approach, relying on careful coordination of hand and eye, as well as the facility to memorise their places in the sequence of changes, and to strike their bells accurately in quick succession. Heavy sets of three and four bells which had survived from pre-Reformation days, and on which call-changes might be rung relatively easily, gave way in the early years of the 17th century to rings containing generally larger numbers of lighter bells which were more suited to changeringing. Developments in the design of bell-frames were also influenced by a demand for more manageable bells. Many of the oldest surviving frames for three and four bells have trusses which were designed for bells to be swung high, but not through a full circle; and in the plan of many old bell-frames the order in which the ropes fell in the ringing room was apparently of no particular consequence. With the advent of changeringing, it was much more convenient for the bell-ropes to fall in numerical order; and although there are many recorded instances of complicated peals being rung on bells where the ropes do not fall logically, it is very noticeable that a great many pre-Reformation bell-frames have been adapted at a later date to bring the ropes into an acceptable circle. These developments, seen in the towers of many Norfolk churches, suggest that peals of bells were augmented and adapted to make half-pull changeringing easier and more rewarding.

The earliest printed book[30] on the art of changeringing, Richard Duckworth's 'Tintinnalogia', was published in London in 1668. Early in the book he remarks on the speed with which changeringing had become popular, remarking that 'within these Fifty or Sixty years last past, Changes were not known nor thought possible to be Rang'. It seems that he is referring to the introduction of half-pull changeringing, since it is inconceivable that this method could have arisen without a previous tradition of ringing call-changes. In his book he goes on to derive the number of possible rows on all numbers of bells from 3 to 12; and gives various methods for writing out the extents of 24 changes on four bells, and 120 changes on five bells, with directions for producing the extent of 720 changes on six bells. Several of the methods published in Duckworth's book are still regularly rung in towers with five or six bells.

Duckworth's statement that the 'Cambridge Eight & Forty' was 'for many years was the greatest peal that was Rang or invented' is of some importance in understanding how changeringing may have spread to Norfolk. It would appear that even if the full extent of 120 rows possible on five bells had been discoved during the early years of the 17th century – as it must have been by mathematicians of any competence – no method of producing them consecutively in a form which could actually be rung on tower bells had been discovered. The important constraint on the sequence in which the rows can be rung is the physical effort needed to alter the speed of particular bells between successive rows.

It is usual to ring about 30 rows per minute on an average ring of five bells with a tenor of about 10 cwt, where each bell has an interval of about 2 seconds between its successive strokes. Thus when rounds are rung consecutively

```
1 2 3 4 5
1 2 3 4 5
1 2 3 4 5
1 2 3 4 5
```

each ringer has to cause his bell to turn through a full circle once in every

[30] *Tintinnalogia, or the art of Ringing*, Printed by W. G. for Fabian Stedman, London, 1668. Reprinted Bath, 1970. I am grateful to Dr J. C. Eisel for helpful comments on early printed books, made in advance of the publication of *Change Ringing – the history of an English art* by the Central Council of Church Bell Ringers (1987).

two seconds, and with well-hung bells this requires little effort. To ring a change between two consecutive rows such as

1 2 3 4 5
1 2 3 5 4

requires the ringer of No. 5 bell to shorten his interval and the ringer of No. 4 to lengthen his: the effort required to do this is significant, but not excessive. To attempt to ring a change such as

1 2 3 4 5
1 2 5 3 4

would, however, require the ringer of No. 5 bell to shorten his interval very drastically; the physical effort would be quite considerable, and the strain on the bell wheel and fittings would be great.

In printing the figures of the 'Cambridge Eight & Forty' in 1668, with another set of changes called the 'Twenty all over', Duckworth remarks: 'I will insert two or three old peals on five bells which (though rejected these days, yet) in former times were much in use, which for Antiquity sake I here set down.' Thus it seems that the 'Cambridge Eight & Forty' was for some time the longest sequence of changes which it was possible to arrange for practical ringing. There is no doubt that in the 17th century, as now, the production of changes suitable for ringing was a fascinating pastime for those with mathematical interests; and numerous scraps of paper containing written changes must have passed between composers and ringers. Mr R. W. M. Clouston and Mr G. J. W. Pipe believe that the earliest surviving written changes[31] are those in an account book belonging to the Launce Charity at Halesworth which begins in 1611, where a column of figures for the 'Plain Changes on four bells' is written opposite a page dated 1621. They very reasonably link the appearance of these figures in the account books with the work done on the Halesworth bells by William Brend of Norwich between 1611 and 1621.

In Norfolk no such written treasure has so far been discovered in surviving churchwardens' books, but it is very likely that the spread of changeringing through the county was assisted by the specialist activities of William Brend and his son John Brend II, who cast bells for many Norfolk churches during the first forty years of the 17th century. A significant piece of evidence for early changeringing appears in the vast collection of documents known as the Aylsham Collection,[32] which was until recently in the hands of a local solicitor and is now in the Norfolk Record Office. A large part of the collection consists of papers dating from the late

[31] R. W. M. Clouston and G. J. W. Pipe, *Bells and belllringing in Suffolk*, 1980, p. 35. and *Changeringing* (1987), plate 13, p. 41.
[32] NRO AYL 175. Illustrated in *Changeringing* (1987), plate 15, p. 45.

The Hanworth Changes, probably written early in the six-teenth century by William Doughty. Notice how the paths of individual bells are marked.

By permission of the Norfolk Record Office, (NRO, AYL 175).

16th century and the 17th century, relating to the Doughty family of Hanworth. Some of the papers concern Robert Doughty's activities as a Justice of the Peace, while others refer to his father's and his own management of their large estate in Hanworth and adjacent villages.[33] Among the papers is a single sheet on which are written down various sequences of changes including the 'Cambridge Eight & Forty', and an attempt (which fails at 20 changes) to produce the extent of changes on four bells with a fifth bell ringing always last. The 'Cambridge Eight & Forty' has been written down with the paths of particular bells marked out in exactly the way that present-day ringers do when they set about learning a method of half-pull changeringing. Duckworth's remarks about the 'Cambridge Eight & Forty' suggest that it was current during the first quarter of the 17th century, and the handwriting of the figures bears out a date in the same period. Other papers in the collection show that there was a considerable interest in mathematics in the family, and various early handwritten tables of sines and cosines are present, as well as methods for estimating the area of a circle and the volumes of irregular solids; of more practical importance to a country landowner are numerous calculations of the area of various parcels of land.[34] One particular set of calculated areas, apparently in the same hand as the 'Cambridge Eight & Forty', is written on the back of a letter from Robert Doughty, then studying at Cambridge, 'to his lovinge Father Mr William Doughty at his house at Hanworth'. The letter was subsequently used as scrap, presumably at Hanworth; and the most likely author of the calculations on the back would be William Doughty. It seems most probable that this early realisation of the 'Cambridge Eight & Forty' was written out by William Doughty at Hanworth,[35] and it is interesting to observe that the ring of five bells at Hanworth appears to have been completed between 1612 and 1635. Inscriptions on the bells at nearby Aylsham show that the Doughty family were interested in the bells there towards the end of the 17th century. It is likely that the science of writing out changes, and the art of half-pull ringing, might have become popular in local churches through one or two generations of young Norfolk men who went up to Cambridge to study, as did William Doughty and his son Robert (1631–1633 at Christ's), bringing back their new-found hobby with them. At Woodton we find an inscription to the effect that 'Mr Robert Suckling with others gave this bell 1641' when a ring of bells was cast by John Brend for the church; and there is evidence

---

[33] See: James Rosenheim, 'Robert Doughty of Hanworth, a Restoration Magistrate, *Norfolk Archaeology*, Vol. XXXVIII, 296–312.

[34] Especially NRO AYL 190.

[35] The writing, which is not that of Robert Doughty, seems to be from the same hand as the many calculations ascribed to William Doughty, relating to the measurement of land. See also *Ringing World*, 1987, pp. 446, 508 for further discussion of the document.

Ketteringham, Sir Arthur Heveningham's tower completed in 1609.
Lithograph by J. B. Ladbroke, c.1820.

that many other rings were augmented by public subscription at about
this time. The long list of subscribers to the new bells at Ketteringham in
1610 shows that ringing was popular with a wide cross section of rural
society.

The work at Ketteringham,[36] which is worth examining in detail, must
be typical of many similar but unrecorded happenings in other parishes.
According to the parish register: 'Ketteringham steeple fell in the night
season, being a very calm night, the 20 of July, 1608. The whole foot of the
font was removed a foot breadth from his place: the cover of the font was
stroken off, and the upper part of the second stone likewise stroken off,
and nothing of them hurt; yea all the bells were whole and not one of
them broken. The masons, namely Osborn and others, began to build it
up again, and the first stone was laid the 28th of August, 1608. They
ceased their work a little after Hallowmas, and began their work again the
4th of April, 1609, and finished all the steeple the 22nd of June 1609; at
which time the plummer laid the lead above and there was wanted of
lead 3 hundred, which cost £3. The porch was trimmed and all the rest
done the first of July, 1609; and the townsmen carried all the rubbish and
stones in the church and the church-yard the 6th of July, 1609. The Lord be
praised for all such good works. Amen. This was registered by me,
Richard Parker, minister of Keteringham.' The parish clerk has added: 'He
might have put in that the steeple fell, and he lying in the Vicarage heard

---

[36] Churchwardens' accounts NRO PD 42/13, Registers lost, but selections published in *Norfolk Archaeology* III.

it not.' A further note recorded that 'The carpenter, one Dymond of Norwich began the work for the bells the 23rd day of April 1610. The irons for the stocks of the bells were made at Norwich, and the week after brought home. The frame was carried into the steeple and the bells set up the 7,8,9,10 daies of May 1610 were rung the 10 of May 1610.' The Churchwardens' accounts for 1609 contain a subscription list for the restoration of the tower and bells, and we find that the project was keenly encouraged by the Lord of the Manor: 'Geven by Sir Arthur Hevenyngham Knight All the tymber and plancke for the two Solleres, and all the tymber for the top of the Steple, And lickwise all the tymber for the Belle frames, And besydes he did give: 3000 of Bricke the Carpenters had all ther meate and drincke all the tyme of ther making the Solleres and Belle frames And he did give the Masons all ther drincke all the tyme that they were of Byldinge up parte of this Steple All this was well worth twentye marke at the Leste.' The County Treasury gave £13. 6s. 8d. towards the work of rebuilding the upper part of the tower, and the decision was taken to recast the tenor of the old ring of three bells and add two trebles to complete a ring of five. We find 'Sir Arthur Hevenynghams Children and Frendes' heading a long subscription list towards the new bells and frame, and the sum of £4. 10s. 10d. was 'Geven Willingelye by Sir Arthur Hevenynghams sarvinge men in the house towards the makinge of these two Littele Belles'. On three of the bells, which were first rung on 10 May 1610, was inscribed *ex gratia et favore arthuri hevyngham militis domini manerii de Kettryngham anno domini 1610'*. It may be worth observing that the three sons of Sir Arthur Hevenyngham were at Cambridge between 1592 and c.1605, and their keenness for the bells at Ketteringham might well have been inspired by contact with changeringing while up at the University; and correspondence in the Aylsham Collection reveals strong connections with the Doughtys of Hanworth. Their enthusiasm was clearly shared by others in the village outside the squire's immediate circle: many local inhabitants gave freely to the work, and it is recorded that other townsmen worked voluntarily in carting lime, stone, sand and brick for the work, while the husbandmen bought the bellropes.

The ring of five at Ketteringham, with a tenor weighing about 9 cwt, was created by splicing two pre-Reformation bells in with three bells newly cast by William Brend of Norwich; and the frame and fittings were made by Thomas Dymond of Norwich. The bells were ideally suited to changeringing, and the record in the parish register shows that the ringers could hardly wait for the work to be completed. The back five of the present ring of six remain just as William Brend left them, but Dymond's frame has been replaced. The founder and carpenter had worked together when St Peter Mancroft bells were rehung and increased to six in 1602, and again in 1608 to provide a peal suitable for changeringing at St Stephen's Church, Norwich where the bells were funded by a large public subscription.[37] The St Stephen's bell-frame which remains (now sadly without its ring of five), shows how the bell-hanger reconciled the requirements of protecting a rather flimsy tower with the need to produce a sensible rope circle. The basic design of this timber frame at St Stephen's church, Norwich has not been significantly improved upon, and there are many similar structures in churches throughout Norfolk.

It is difficult to trace the early history of many rings of bells because few relevant parish documents have survived from centuries before the 18th, and later recastings have often made it difficult to ascertain exactly when particular bells were introduced to a tower. The following list includes towers where there is strong circumstantial or documentary evidence for the provision of new bells completing rings of five or six between 1552 and 1645: defective though it almost certainly is, the list shows the great period of activity during the early years of the 17th century.

Little Walsingham	5	21 cwt	1567	
Norwich St Giles	5	14 cwt	1593	
Forncett St Peter	5	16 cwt	1602	
Norwich St Peter Mancroft	6	23 cwt	1602	increased from 5
Ketteringham	5	9 cwt	1610	
Oxborough	5	10 cwt	1610	
Martham	5	16 cwt	1611	
Pulham St Mary	5	15 cwt	1611	
Aslacton	5	8 cwt	1614	
Great Ellingham	5	13 cwt	1615	
Shotesham All Saints	5	12 cwt	1615	
Thetford, St Mary	5	10 cwt	1615	
Norwich St Lawrence	5	15 cwt	1615	or earlier
Barton Turf	5	11 cwt	1616	
Loddon	5	15 cwt	1616	
Ranworth	5	12 cwt	1616	
Shipdham	5	12 cwt	1616	
Ashill	5	14 cwt	1617	
Attleborough	5	13 cwt	1617	
Kenninghall	5	24 cwt	1617	
Mattishall	5	23 cwt	1617	
Norwich St John Timberhill	5	8 cwt	1617	or earlier
Saxlingham Nethergate	5	8 cwt	1617	
Shropham	5	13 cwt	1618	
Ludham	5	19 cwt	1619	
East Dereham	5		1619	weight not known.

[37] St Stephen's churchwardens' accounts at the church, extracts among the Rump Mss. at Norwich School.

Hingham	6	20 cwt	1619	increased from five.
Norwich St George Tombland	5	10 cwt	1619	
Starston	5	12 cwt	1619	
Pulham Market	5		1620	weight not known.
Lyng	5	9 cwt	1621	
Saham Toney	5	14 cwt	1622	
Cawston	5	15 cwt	1623	or earlier
Paston	5	11 cwt	1623	
Holme Hale	5	15 cwt	1624	
King's Lynn St Margaret	6	28 cwt	1626	increased from 5
Kirby Cane	5	7 cwt	1626	
King's Lynn St Nicholas	5	13 cwt	1628	
Norwich St John Sepulchre	5	10 cwt	1628	
Stratton Strawless	5	12 cwt	1629	
West Walton	5	11 cwt	1629	
Catfield	5	10 cwt	1630	
Acle	5	10 cwt	1632	
Hevingham	5	12 cwt	1632	
Thurlton	5	11 cwt	1632	
Wilby	5	9 cwt	1633	
Norwich Ss. Simon & Jude	5	8 cwt	1634	
Swaffham	6	16 cwt	1634	
Hanworth	5	12 cwt	1635	
Happisburgh	5	11 cwt	1637	
Wiggenhall St, Mary V.	5	8 cwt	1638	
Fakenham	5	19 cwt	1639	
Broome	5	9 cwt	1640	
Norwich St Mary Coslany	5	10 cwt	1640	
Winfarthing	5	14 cwt	1640	
Southrepps	5	14 cwt	1641	
Woodton	6	8 cwt	1641	

Some of the above rings were created by casting one or two new bells and splicing in older bells, thus providing the basis of many surviving rings which have a mixture of pre-Reformation and later bells. At other towers it seems likely that bells already in stock at the bell-foundry were tuned to accord with each other, forming rings of five such as those at Hanworth and Aslacton, where there are bells of mixed early-17th-century dates. In some towers, such as Paston (1623), a heavy ring of three or four was recast into a new ring,[38] and there is strong evidence that complete rings were originally cast for Shipdham (1616), Ludham (1619), Stratton Strawless (1629), Catfield (1630), Acle (1632), Thurlton (1632) and Happisburgh

---

[38] Confirmed in PD 264/22 and PD 264/23, documents relating to Paston. Thanks to Mr D. Cubitt for pointing these out.

(1637). Ludham's new five, cast from the metal of a heavy four, was apparently financed by Samuel Harsnett in 1619, his first year as Bishop of Norwich: the inscription on the second bell *'Musica Campanarum Cor Hominis Consolat'* (The music of the bells soothes the heart of Man) shows that the undertaking was to provide a tuneful set of bells to be rung together in peal. The increase of the bells from four to five is well-rehearsed in the Catfield Parish Register,[39] where it is recorded that the 'fower olde bells of Catfield were changed and cast into fyve sweete and tuneable well tuned bells'. It is interesting that the rhyming account of the work (printed by L'Estrange) makes several puns on the word 'change'. The work of recasting the 'unsorteable bells' into 'fyve newe tuneable and consortable belles' was undertaken by voluntary subscription, and was agreed to by all except three or four parishioners. The bells were 'fitted for Stocks and Wheeles' before being hung in the steeple in a new bell-frame on 10 July 1630. The only complete ring of a single date to survive intact is that of 1632 at Thurlton, where five excellent bells were probably cast in the village under the supervision of John Brend II of Norwich.

When these new rings are added to those which survived from before 1552, it is clear that there were many towers in Norfolk where changeringing could have been practised during the first decades of the 17th century. A few of the older rings were very heavy, and it is likely that little scientific changeringing was done on the five bells at Salle,[40] where the tenor weighed 41 cwt: the ringers would probably have needed the meat and drink bequeathed to them in Robert Sendall's will of 1584, even if they only rang call-changes. There is no doubt that the heavy five at Wymondham (tenor 26 cwt) were being rung to changes when a competition was advertised there in 1731,[41] and changeringing may well have flourished much earlier at towers such as Lynn St Margaret (where a man was drawn up and killed by the rope of the 28 cwt tenor, presumably while ringing it, in 1621[42]), Redenhall (24 cwt), Tibenham (22 cwt) and North Walsham (28 cwt). Some of the lighter fives would have been ideal for changeringing, such as that at Banham, where the tenor was recast[43] in 1597 to be 'good parfett and tuneable to the other bells aforsayd'. The impression gained from the large number of new bells cast during the first half of the 17th century is that there was considerable interest in ringing, and especially scientific half-pull changeringing.

While the effects of the Civil War and the consequent disruption of church life are reflected in the very small number of bells cast between 1641 and

---

[39] CBN pp. 114–115.
[40] W. L. E. Parsons, *Salle*, 1937, p. 227.
[41] D. Cubitt, 'Henry Cross Grove extracts', *Ringing World*, 1971, p. 948.
[42] Mackerell, *op. cit.* p. 233.
[43] Banham parish documents seen at the church.

c.1650, there is no evidence that bell-ringing was discouraged; and churchwardens' accounts such as those at Banham and Norwich St Stephen show that ringers were paid on a variety of civil occasions. A few examples from the St Stephen's accounts[44] show that there was no break in the tradition of ringing; and that the activity was encouraged by the civic authorities. In 1644 'Ringing for the great Victory at York' marked the Royalist defeat at Marston Moor, and this was followed by 'ringing upon two days of triumph', presumably for the Parliamentarians. Lord Fairfax, commander of Cromwell's New Model Army, visited Norwich in 1648 to the ringing of the St Stephen's bells, and they rang again in 1651 'when Worcester was taken, by command of the Mayor'. As the tide turned in 1659, they rang 'when General Monk and the Londoners were agreed for a free parliament', and a little later 'upon the King being voted by both houses, and also when he was proclaimed on 10th May' 1660. When the Earl of Arundel was restored as Duke of Norfolk, the Mayor ordered every parish to ring their bells 'to testifye this cities rejoicing for the same, out of their respect to that noble family', and the St Stephen's ringers obliged. Two other noteworthy ringing days where when Bishop Reynolds entered the city to take up his throne in the Cathedral, and 'when the charter came home'.

Although there is no surviving evidence to show that the Parliamentary Visitors destroyed or removed bells during the Visitations of 1643 and 1644, they were concerned to remove 'superstitious' inscriptions. An example of the mutilation of church bells is found in the churchwardens' accounts for 1644 at Bressingham:[45] 'Item paid vij of May to Captaine Gilley for the viewing of the church for abollishing superstitious pictures vj d. Item paid to John Nun for 2 dayes work and for taking down of glas and pictures about the church and the letters about the bells iij s. iiij d.' Although the inscriptions on the Bressingham bells were defaced, L'Estrange was able to make out the form of two of them as 'Sancte Johannes Ora Pro Nobis' and 'Sancta Anna Ora Pro Nobis'. It is clear from the record of William Dowsing's itinerary through Suffolk that such inscriptions would have been offensive to a Puritan conscience. Captain Gilley seems to be identified by entries in 1643 in the churchwardens' accounts at Banham:[46] 'to Cracknell of Diss for glasing work at the Church when the Imagerie Glass was taken down by order of the Parliament by the view of Mr Gillie of Hopton in Suffolk being imployed by the Parliament for the same purpose £02-13-01.' While Mr Gillie's instructions relating to the glass at Banham seem to have been carried out effectively, it is surprising to find four fine pre-Reformation bells in the tower which retain invocations to St Anne, St Peter, St Nicholas and the Archangel Gabriel. There

---

[44] See note 37.
[45] NRO PD 111/69.
[46] Seen at the church.

Wacton, tenor bell. Partially obliterated inscription on fifteenth-century
bell. The legend, '+ AVE GRACIA PLENA [] DOMINVS TECVM', was probably
defaced in the 1640s.
Photograph by the author.

are several bells in other churches, most of them in the south of the
county, whose inscriptions were probably spoiled at about this time.

Duckworth's 'Tintinnalogia' shows that the years following the Restoration of Charles II saw a great national expansion in the art of changeringing,[47] and it seems very likely that Norfolk ringers, and particularly those
in Norwich, were in the forefront of the activity. It is clear from the
number of new rings completed in Norfolk during the second half of the
17th century that six-bell ringing was gaining in popularity. In addition to
the earlier rings at Norwich St Andrew, Norwich St Peter Mancroft,
Swaffham, Hingham and Woodton, rings of six were completed at Holme
Hale (1652), Great Yarmouth (by 1670), Attleborough (1671), Worstead
(1675), Norwich St Michael Coslany (1676), Aylsham (by 1677), Bergh
Apton (1678), Loddon (1680), Diss (1691), Norwich St Mary Coslany
(1696) and Stratton Strawless (1696). By c.1700 there were certainly other
sixes at Cawston, Norwich St Giles, Tivetshall St Mary, Salle, Scarning and
North Walsham; and at a few other places where records have not been
traced. Many celebrations must have taken place along the lines of those
at King's Lynn[48] in 1686 when a statue of James II was set up in the
Market Place: 'N.B. The King, Queen, and the rest of the Royal Family's
Healths were drank; and the Day was concluded with the Ringing of
Bells, Bonfires, all Sorts of loud Musick, Fireworks, discharging the Great
Guns, with all other Demonstrations of Joy and Loyalty.' Bell-ringing was
certainly popular.

[47] *Tintinnalogia, or the art of Ringing*, Printed by W. G. for Fabian Stedman, London,
    1668. Reprinted Bath, 1970. *passim.*
[48] Mackerell, *op. cit.* p. 254.

Duckworth gives directions for ringing[49] on a full octave of bells, and the churchwardens of St Margaret's church at King's Lynn appear to have contemplated adding to their ring of six just before the end of the Commonwealth. There were considerable dealings with Mr Thomas Norris in 1659–1660, involving the transport of bells to Gunworth Ferry, presumably on their way to the foundry at Stamford, and the accounts entered in 1664 show that the work involved increasing the bells to eight.[50] It is clear that the exercise was seen as providing bells for the amusement of the ringers rather than as a necessity for the church, and the parish was not prepared to accept a rate for the upkeep of the new bells. 'It is further agreed and declared by the parishioners here present that their giving their consent and approbations to what the Churchwardens have done in reference to the new casting of the bells be no ways binding to the parishioners to be made lyable to an assessment for the same, the work being begun and carried out by a voluntary Contribution of some of the inhabitants'. Not far behind Lynn was St Peter Mancroft at Norwich where the octave was completed in 1672. If Duckworth's advice was followed, early adventures on these new octaves would probably have consisted of ringing old five-bell and six-bell methods on various selections of bells, with the remaining bells striking in fixed positions behind the changing bells: he recommends that· 'the most complete and musical Peal that ever was Rang on eight Bells is Grandsire Bob . . . on 123567 the fourth and tenor lying behind every change'. This would begin as follows:

1 2 3 4 5 6 7 8	
1 2 3 5 4 6 7 8	The fourth bell moves up
1 2 3 5 6 4 7 8	
1 2 3 5 6 7 4 8	. . . until it reaches 7th place.
2 1 5 3 7 6 4 8	The first six bells are now
2 5 1 7 3 6 4 8	ringing the sequence known
5 2 7 1 6 3 4 8	as Grandsire Bob, while bells
5 7 2 6 1 3 4 8	4 and 8 ring consistently
7 5 6 2 3 1 4 8	behind the changing bells.
7 6 5 3 2 1 4 8	
6 7 3 5 1 2 4 8	And so on . . .

As the 18th century progressed, changeringing became an ever more popular pastime, whose most significant development was the interest in eight-bell ringing. Teams were now confidently ringing seven changing

---

[49] See note 47.
[50] Mackerell, *op. cit.* p. 9 in 1738 refers to 'five very large Bells . . . the Biggest and the least of these were purposely broken, and with some Addition cast into others, to make a Ring of Eight, which was effected in in the year 1663, as they remain to this day.' The churchwardens' accounts (NRO PD 39/72) seem to record this work in 1659 and 1660; and the number of bells is first given as eight in a reference dated 1663/64.

bells with the eighth bell covering, as well as methods where all eight bells were involved in the changes.

Seven-bell work with covering tenor:	Eight-bell work
1 2 3 4 5 6 7 8	1 2 3 4 5 6 7 8
2 1 4 3 6 5 7 8	2 1 4 3 6 5 8 7
2 4 1 6 3 7 5 8	2 4 1 6 3 8 5 7
4 2 6 1 7 3 5 8	4 2 6 1 8 3 7 5
4 6 2 7 1 5 3 8	4 6 2 8 1 7 3 5
etc.	etc.

While the extent of 120 changes on five bells takes about 4 minutes, and the 720 changes on six bells can be completed in about 25 minutes (depending on the weight of the bells), there are enormous possibilities for changeringing on the larger numbers. The first recorded full peal[51] of 5040 changes on seven bells (in 3 hours and 18 minutes with a covering tenor) was rung by the Norwich Scholars at St Peter Mancroft in 1715, and it is a measure of local enthusiasm that Norwich should take pride of place when changeringing was popular in other centres such as London, Cambridge and Oxford. The history of ringing in Norfolk and Norwich during the 18th and 19th centuries is worth a book on its own, and it is sufficient to remark that many performances of national interest were recorded in Norfolk during this period. Rings of eight were completed in most of the more important towns and villages in Norfolk by c.1800, and the chronological list of early octaves is as follows:

Lynn St Margaret	probably 1659/1660
Norwich St Peter Mancroft	1672
Aylsham	1700
Norwich St Andrew	1705
Norwich St Michael at Coslany	1726
Great Yarmouth	1726
Alburgh	1737
Redenhall	1737
Swaffham	1737
Norwich St Giles	1738

[51] This peal, recorded on a painted board in the ringers' gallery at Norwich, St Peter Mancroft, has long been accepted as the first performance of the extent of changes on seven bells with a covering tenor. Articles in the *Ringing World* from time to time have cast doubts, suggesting that there had been an earlier performance at St Sepulchre's church, Snow Hill, London. W. Cook, in his article 'The College Youths 1637–1987', *Ringing World*, 1986, however, dismisses the suggestion; and it is hard to imagine the London ringers allowing the Norwich claim to stand for so long without questioning its validity.

Diss	1741
Hingham	1742
Kenninghall	1743
Fakenham	1746
Wells	1749
East Dereham	1754
North Elmham	1757
Downham Market	1771
Lynn St Nicholas	1766
Hilgay	1779
Thetford St Peter	1790

Ringing also flourished at the many churches with five and six bells; and the chief record of this activity is found in the advertisements for ringing competitions, which appear in local newspapers. In 1711[52] ringers were invited to compete for five pairs of gloves at Catfield, and in the following year we read that: 'On Monday 28th Instant [January] there will be Five Pairs of Gloves rung for at Acle in Norfolk, and Seven Ribbs of Roast Beef given for the Ringers Dinners at the Kings-head in the said Town'. County ringers were also invited to try their hand in a five-bell competition at St Martin at Palace, Norwich in June 1732; and many similar open competitions were advertised. Although engaged in ever more impressive performances at the three eight-bell towers in the city, the Norwich Ringers could not resist a challenge made by the five-bell ringers from Garboldisham in January 1733. When they met at Bunwell in the spring of that year to ring for a wager of five guineas, the Norwich Ringers were victorious; 'and what redounds too to their Credit, was the treating each other with the utmost civility'.

Ringing on ten bells must have seemed an inviting prospect when two new trebles were added to the octave at St Peter Mancroft in 1724. The work seems to have been a speculation by John Stephens, a bell-founder who had fairly recently removed from London to Norwich; but the two bells were only in the tower for a matter of months, since the expected subscriptions for purchasing them seem not to have materialised. A further attempt was made to increase the number of bells in 1735, this time to twelve, but subscriptions were again not sufficient to achieve the target. Two lighter bells were added to the octave instead of four; and a board high up in the present ringing chamber records that 'This ring was made a peal of ten by the Addition of two Bells, Subscribed for by Gentlemen in the Parish, and Rung for the first time on the 20th of June 1736'. Mancroft did not achieve a ring of twelve before the celebrated heavy ring was

---

[52] D. Cubitt, 'Henry Cross Grove extracts', *Ringing World*, 1971 has provided much of the material for this and the two succeeding paragraphs. Grateful thanks are here recorded to Mr Cubitt for information relating to ringing in 18th-century Norfolk and Norwich freely communicated over a long period.

installed in 1775, eleven of which bells remain in the tower. Aylsham bells were also augmented in 1736, and a long peal on all ten bells was recorded there in March of that year.

Much other unrecorded ringing was enjoyed at towers with five and six bells, and the activities of bell-founders in Norfolk during the 18th century were considerable. Thomas Newman seems to have had a good working relationship with local ringers, as his advertisement in the Norwich Gazette of 8th September 1711 shows: 'Mr Tho. Newman Bell-founder of this City, having cast Six new Bells for the Parish of Market Deerham the same are now fixing, and will be rung on Thursday next by the Six best Ringers in Norwich; where will be a very great Appearance of that Society to give their Judgement of that new peal.' The Norwich ringers duly replied: 'Whereas we the Society of Ringers were invited to Market Deerham in this County, to ring and give our Approbation of the new Peal of six Bells, cast by Mr T. Newman Bell-founder of this City, at which Time of Invitation we did attend, and do allow and approve of them to be a good harmonious Peal; and that the said Peal gives a general satisfaction not only to Us, but to all those that have yet heard them.' Newman had spent some time casting bells in various places before settling in Norwich, and in his early days he seems to have established a good working partnership with Simon Oates, a carpenter from Hautbois, and a blacksmith from Horstead.[53] There are numerous instances of churchwardens replacing cumbersome heavy sets of three and four bells with lighter rings of five and six which were more suitable for change-ringing. At Ashwellthorpe, for example, a faculty petition[54] from the Rector and churchwardens requests that 'your Lordship would be pleased to grant your licence for the casting of the biggest bell into two small bells – viz. a treble and second to the other three and to dispose of the overplus of the Mettal towards the charge of new running and refitting them that they may have five bells of good size'. The bells still hang in Ashwellthorpe tower, almost untouched since Newman and his bellhangers left them.

A common method of augmenting a ring in the 18th century was to remove the heaviest bell and cast two or more lighter bells from the metal, and the town-reeves' accounts at Alburgh[55] show that this was the method by which the bells were increased from four to six in 1730. When a bell of approximately 12 cwt at Long Stratton[56] provided the metal for two bells weighing approximately 3½ cwt and 4 cwt, the exercise was almost self-financing; since the bell-founder was able to take the excess

[53] See churchwardens' accounts for Scottow, NRO PD 145/43 and Tunstead, NRO PD 285/38.
[54] NRO FCP/1.
[55] NRO PD 193/58.
[56] NRO PD 122/33.

metal in payment for his work. Such activities did not always meet with the approval of parishioners, who were attached to the deeper notes of their heavier bells. The inscriptions on the 1741 bells at Banham show that the ringers were not universally popular when the tenor bell of the old ring of five was sacrificed to provide two smaller bells to make up a ring of six:

> 'PULL ON BRAVE BOYES IM METTLE TO THE BACK
> BUT WILL BE HANGED BEFORE ILE CRACK'
>
> WE TREBLES CAM BY SMALL CONSENT
> OUR BIRTH I HOPE WILL BRING CONTENT
> TWINS FROM OLD TENOR OUR LOST OLD DAD
> SOME WE MAKE MERRY BUT SOME ARE MAD
> THOMAS NEWMAN OF NORWICH MADE ME
> MR. WM. LEECH 1741

Duckworth[57] gives directions for tuning rings of bells in his *'Tintinnalogia'*, preferring a diatonic scale. A ring of five should sound the lowest notes of the scale (G, A, B, C, D for example), and additional bells should be of higher pitch (using an E to augment to six, and F sharp, G to complete an octave). There is little doubt that new rings of bells cast by many early founders came from the moulds in reasonable tune with each other, but the addition of bells to an existing ring, even in comparatively recent years, often posed a problem. Late in the 18th century the Gloucester bell-founders introduced a tuning machine,[58] which consisted of a donkey-powered vertical lathe in which a bell was turned against a cutting tool; but before this refinement was introduced the only method of removing metal from a bell which needed tuning was by means of either a file or a cold chisel. When a bell is tuned metal is removed from inside the soundbow to flatten the note, or from the outside of the lip to sharpen the note, the latter process having a notoriously bad effect on the tone of the bell. It is interesting to note that a contract for a new bell required in 1691 to increase the Diss bells from five to six required that the work should be done without recourse to any chipping or tuning.

Once hung in the tower, hand-tuning is the only possibility short of removing the bells to the bell-founder's yard, and we can follow the activities of an itinerant bell tuner in south Norfolk. In 1740 the Dickle-

---

[57] *Op. cit.,* pp. 3, 4.
[58] Mr R. W. M. Clouston informs me that the brothers Hemony in Amsterdam, working there in the period 1655 to 1680, had a tuning lathe driven by 5 or 6 men to pare off metal from the lip to the crown. *Vide* Andre Lehr, *De Klokkengieters Francois en Pieter Hemony*, 1959, p. 46. The Hemonies understood harmonic tuning, and Canon Simpson only rediscovered what they had been doing. The Rudhall machine seems only to have covered the lip and soundbow, not the waist and crown.

burgh churchwardens had their bells tuned, when John Kemp was paid 6s. 'for the board of Mr Collet', and the churchwardens paid 6s. 8d. 'for mending Mr Collet's chisels'. Thomas Newman's octave at Diss, installed in 1741, included older bells, and John Collett was paid £2. 2s. 0d. 'for Chiping the Bells' to bring them in tune.[59] When the tenor bell was removed from the diatonic ring of four bells at Long Stratton in 1724 the character of the bells was greatly altered, and a ring of four sounding the notes F, G, A, B flat was altered to a ring of five sounding G, A, B flat, C, D. The doleful key of G minor was clearly not appreciated by the churchwardens, who paid Mr Collett £2. 0s. 0d. for tuning the bells in 1743.[60] The bells at both Stratton and Dickleburgh, in common with many others in Norfolk show the signs of the bell-tuner's activities; and a reference in a letter[61] about the Weybread bells shows that itinerant bell-tuners, using chisels, practised as late as 1879.

THE LOSS AND DESTRUCTION OF BELLS

Although the growth of changeringing caused an increase in the number of bells in certain towers, there are many churches which have fewer bells in the 20th century than they had in 1552; and the increase in the number of towers containing but a single bell is significant. The Diocesan records give a very good account of the way in which many bells were lost, and the Faculty books[62] are full of instances where dilapidated churches were put into repair using valuable bell-metal, or the lead from the roof, to cover part of the expense. At Sparham, for example, the petitioners reported that the roof of the south aisle was ruinous, decayed and in danger of falling; a new roof was needed as well as two new buttresses to support the wall. The total cost of the work was estimated at £95, of which £75 was raised by the sale of the lead from the aisle roof (blue pantiles were substituted), and £35 from the sale of the two smallest bells. Only fifty years previously John Stephens had cast a splendid five for the church, but by 1776 one of the trebles was cracked, and it seems that the ringers were not able to oppose the reduction of the bells to three. At Barton Turf the sale of two cracked bells enabled the churchwardens to use stone rather than timber when they replaced crumbling window frames in 1793;

---

[59] See NRO PD 122/33 (Stratton), PD 100/62 (Diss) and the Dickleburgh accounts at the church.
[60] NRO PD 122/33.
[61] Norfolk and Norwich Archaeological Society, Garsett House Collection, Candler Mss.
[62] Much of the information in this section is from the Faculty Books (Class FCB, beginning in 1633) and the Faculty Papers (Class FCP, beginning in 1660) at NRO.

and at East Tuddenham bells were sold to reroof the church, and provide a ceiling with a 'Handsome cornish'. While it is possible to feel sympathy for the 'seventy poor journeyman weavers' who could not afford to repair Swanton Abbot church, or the churchwardens at Runhall who found 'no help forthcoming from the wealthy landowners'; one cannot help feeling that the bells in some churches were seen as a resource, ready to be plundered if the need arose.

There is no doubt that many churches were in a deplorable state of repair during the 18th century, as at Great Hockham where 'the inhabitants cannot assemble together for the hearing of Divine service without apparent danger to their lives', or at Flordon where the steeple fell 'suddenly and unexpectedly' in April 1774. Not all bell installations were kept in good order, and we find that an inspection at Great Moulton in 1674 had revealed 'That all the tymber (being the foundation and support of the weight of the Bells within the Steeple of that sayd Moulton) together with all the frames and stockes of their sayd belles are rotten and utterly useless for anything but the fire And that the biggest Bell within the said steeple is Broken'. A number of towers where the bells were regularly rung had become rather shaky, and the ringers who were paid for their efforts at Carleton Rode up to 1755 must have been a little surprised when part of the tower fell away early in the following year. The Faculty Books suggest that it was relatively easy for churchwardens in parishes where there were only two or three bells to persuade the parishioners to part with some of them, but there are several instances of the destruction of complete peals of five or more bells. Where towers had collapsed, as at Great Moulton (1747), Burston (1754), Carleton Rode (1756), Bawdeswell (1763), Costessey (1768) and Foulden (1791), or where there had been a disastrous fire, as at Foulsham in 1770, one might expect bells to go: although the North Walsham churchwardens kept six of their seven bells from 1724 – when the tower fell – until 1836. At Garboldisham two churches, each with a ring of five in good order, stood close together until 1733; and when All Saints' was dilapidated one of the redundant bells was used to increase the ring at St John's to six. The short-lived rings such as the six at Blickling (1703–1751) and the fives at West Harling (1726–1756) and Sparham (1726–1776) are remarkable. Other 18th-century losses include the fives at Gunton (1742), Gunthorpe (1762), Felbrigg (1778), Barton Turf (1793) and Ingham (1799), as well as innumerable bells from smaller rings; but one might have expected places such as Lynn, where five bells at All Saints' church were reduced to one in 1765, and Cromer, whose ring of five was decreased in 1767, to have found other ways of keeping their churches in repair. Blakeney lost its ring of five in 1802, and as late as 1868 the Langham bells were reduced from five to three.

But perhaps there is another side to the story, since it is well-known that the ways of some bell ringers offended many clergy and churchwardens.

In the preface[63] to *Campanalogia Improved* there is more than a hint of the low estimation in which the Exercise was generally held during the early years of the 18th century. We read that the art was 'esteemed by the Generality of People to be a mean and mechanical Exercise'; this because it was 'followed and practised by Persons whose Course of Lives (as reported) has been infamous; and also by Persons whose Subsistence for themselves and Families is gained by painful and hard Labour; and therefore not a fit and commendable Exercise and Recreation for one that has been genteely and handsomely brought up and educated'. The hold which bell-ringing was seen to gain on some of its practitioners 'withdraws and alienates Mens Minds from the Business by which they obtain and procure Subsistence for their Families, making them Drunkards, neglective of their Occupations and Trades, and consequently the utter Ruin and Impoverishment of themselves and all that depend upon, and receive a Livelihood and Maintenance from them'. The author recognises that ringers had been known to 'fail and come to Want', but infers that their condition was in many cases due not so much to the pursuit of bell-ringing itself, as to 'following Gaming, Horse Races, Cock-fighting, or some such Mischief'. In some cases where good rings of bells were lost, it may have been the quality of the bell-ringers which persuaded churchwardens that it was no bad thing to sell some of the bells. Not all bells sold by Faculty were lost, and many secondhand bells were purchased by bellfounders and later incorporated into newly formed rings, such as the octaves at Diss (1741) and Kenninghall (1743). The Swaffham churchwardens bought bells from North Pickenham and South Pickenham in 1737; and the Mr Tomling who bought the Blickling bells in 1753 was in business with Joseph Mallows, the Dereham bell-founder.

BELFRY REFORM

The poor condition of many Norfolk church buildings, revealed by the Faculty books between c.1740 and c.1840, is a symptom of the parlous state of the church at large during those years, when local conditions were notoriously bad. Dr Jessopp[64] wrote that 'The Georgian era in the diocese of Norwich was a period of such deadness as had never been known before, and which we may well pray may never be known again'. He also remarked[65] that 'The pluralists, of whom there were many more than is

63 J. D. & C. M. *Campanalogia improved*, 1702.
64 A. Jessopp, *Diocesan Histories: Norwich*, 1884, chap. XII *passim*.
65 Dr Augustus Jessopp, Rector of Scarning and sometime Head Master of Norwich School, wrote much that did not find favour with contemporary churchmen. This quotation from *Arcady, for better for worse*, (1887) is typical of his perception; and the writer is grateful to Mr D. Cubitt to bringing it to his attention.

generally thought, could not be resident in all their livings. What they, and other absentee incumbents, did was not so much employ even a poorly paid curate to be resident, but appoint a neighbouring resident incumbent to do the additional duty at a rate considerably less than paying a curate'. Churchwardens were more concerned with pressing parochial matters such as the relief of the poor and the maintenance of the highways to bother too much about the church fabric. Bell-ringers, together with the orchestras and choirs which operated from the west galleries in many churches, had gained a strong reputation for their irreverence and independence from authority. Most of the formally constituted ringing societies, such as the Norwich Scholars, were secular rather than religious organisations, their ringing being more of a sporting pastime than a service to the church. It is not surprising that most companies enjoyed their ringing almost independently of the clergy, ringing for church services only very occasionally, and reserving their energies for times of their own choosing.

Many towers were originally designed with a gallery, often level with the cill of the west window, from which the bell-ringers were intended to perform; and this seems to have been a convenient arrangement as long as the ringing was closely associated with church services. Nothing symbolises the ringers' alienation from the church more clearly than the many instances where they removed themselves from view, to perform from a small chamber high in the tower. Although in some towers the shorter ropes would have made the bells easier to handle, there are many places where ringing takes place in small, badly-lit chambers immediately beneath the bells, which are inconveniently loud. Ringing chambers have been formed in other churches by filling the tower arch with panelling, or screenwork; and there are several places where a doorway has been cut through the wall of a stair turret to allow the ringers to get to and from the ringing chamber without needing to pass through the church itself. Enthusiasm for ringing on eight bells was very strong, and it was not uncommon for ringers from remote villages to walk several miles if there was a chance to ring on a full octave; and the inevitable consequence of this trend was that many ringers deserted towers with smaller numbers of bells.

During the second half of the 19th century there were moves by the clergy to gain what they considered to be proper control of the ringing at their churches, and there are many well-documented clashes between bell-ringers and incumbents. The Reverend B. J. Armstrong of East Dereham was not pleased by his ringers: 'Among the numerous characters difficult to manage with whom a clergyman has to deal – such as clerks, schoolmasters, singers and organist – the bellringers are often conspicuous. With so fine a peal as ours, I have long sought ineffectually to organize, properly, these worthies by means of rules. To this they would never submit till I hit on the plan of declining to bestow my Christmas Box till they did. After much vapouring and fuming and threatening not to ring out the old year with the usual muffled peal, they have succumbed, and to-day (January 4th 1855) brought their rules signed by them all. Nothing like determination in such cases.' The Dereham ringers were, however, 'very angry and rebellious' when the Vicar stopped them from ringing in June 1858 to celebrate the controversial decision that the Corn Hall should not be pulled down.

The Reverend G. A. Poole, writing in 1873,[66] observes that 'some five or six generations ago Bellringing was a fashionable exercise among gentlemen', but that in his time 'we want a higher moral standard, and in some of them [ringers] at least (so as to afford some security for decorum) a higher social position'. Perhaps he was recalling competent gentleman-ringers such as Theodore Eccleston of Crowfield Hall, Suffolk – who rang at Coddenham, and was instrumental in having Stonham Aspall bells augmented from five to ten; or the Reverend Samuel Parr, Headmaster of the Norwich Grammar School 1779–1785 – who was a useful change-ringer on six-bells, even if he could only ring rounds on the higher numbers. Poole advocated 'the formation of a Society of change-ringers in every parish; and if he is young and active, I would have the clergyman not only the principal authority among them, but the best ringer'. There were moves to this end by Norfolk clergy a few years earlier; and we read in Armstrong's Diary of a dinner for forty ringers from Norwich, Swaffham, Thetford and Lynn at the inauguration of a recast bell at Dereham in July 1864: among the party was 'The Reverend A. Sutton, son of Sir Richard, who is famous for bell-ringing, clock making, and organ playing'. The occasion seemed to Armstrong 'a good opportunity of putting the Company of Ringers on a better footing'. He accordingly 'drew up some rules and induced them (the Dereham Ringers) to meet the churchwardens and myself in vestry', where the rules were agreed.

Largely at the instigation of the ringers at Redenhall and Alburgh, and with strong clerical support, the Norwich Diocesan Association of Ringers[67] was founded in 1877. At a meeting at Dereham, in February 1878, 'Deputations came from the companies at Diss, Norwich, Redenhall, and various other places. The Rev. Mr Harris of Tunstead attended, also Sutton of Tofts and Legge of Elmham. Between forty and fifty sat down to dinner. They were very civil, and seemed heartily engrossed with their hobby'. The establishment of a ringing organisation, under the patronage of the Bishop of Norwich, did much to spread interest in changeringing,

---

[66] Quoted in T. North, *The church bells of Northamptonshire*, 1878, pp. 159–160. See also J. R. Ketteringham, 'The Lincoln Correspondence', *Ringing World*, 1988, p. 969.

[67] Reports of the Norwich Diocesan Association from 1877 are available at the Norwich Public Library.

as well as encouraging clergy and ringers to take greater care of their bells. The Dereham ringers, and probably others like them, still had opinions of their own about the conduct of ringing; and another clash of wills is recorded by Armstrong in April 1879: 'In consequence of my forbidding the bells to be rung in Lent, even on the occasion of a Royal Marriage, and a threatened strike of the ringers, it seemed for a long time that there would be no joyful peal this Easter. The uneasy and jerky motion of a single bell or so intimated that there was a commotion among the ringers. However, at 9–30 – out they went.'

Although 'Belfry Reform' was one of the principal objects of most diocesan and other territorial ringing associations founded during the last quarter of the 19th century, it was not a completely unqualified blessing, as Dr Jessopp[68] observed in 1887, just ten years after the Norwich Diocesan Association of Ringers was formed: 'But of all the sad things that have happened to our villages, two of the saddest and most to be regretted are, first, the decay of all instrumental music among country people; and secondly the decay of bellringing . . . How has this deplorable effacement of our rural music been brought about ? There is only one answer – It has been brought about by the general deluge of smug and paralyzing respectability which has overrun our country villages. And for this I am bound to say that the clergy and their families are in great measure answerable.' Jessopp was a near neighbour, at Scarning, of the redoubtable Benjamin Armstrong.

Many parsons who controlled early territorial ringing associations linked improvement in the quality and behaviour of ringers with the promotion of scientific changeringing, making call-change ringing something of second-class pursuit. There is no doubt that the mathematical skills required for scientific changeringing are harder to acquire than proficiency in call-change ringing; and it is much more difficult to recruit and maintain an efficient company, the problem being more acutely felt in the smaller parishes. Most formal associations of ringers would only allow competent scientific change-ringers to become members; and for some call-change ringers the pressure to aspire to that respectable state was sufficient for them to lose interest. Keen ringers tended to travel to centres where changeringing was practised, leaving many of the smaller villages without companies of ringers; and it is sad to record the very large number of towers in Norfolk where rings of five and six bells have, over the years, been neglected in favour of the higher numbers.

A great deal of work was done in church towers between 1860 and 1920, and many rings of bells were rehung and augmented during this period. Conservative restoration schemes have preserved ancient bells, and we in

[68] Jessopp, *op. cit.*, 1887.

Norfolk are spared the monotony of the numerous rings of very good, but uniform, bells which abound in some other parts of the country. It can truly be said that no two rings of bells in Norfolk sound alike; and the fine modern peals, such as Hethersett, Gaywood, Wymondham and Great Yarmouth are heard in interesting contrast to the many older rings of bells which remain.

The fact that there are now (1988) fewer really efficient changeringing companies in rural Norfolk than there were 60 years ago is a reflection of the changing pattern of village and family life; but there are still several towers, mostly in the towns and larger villages, where keen changeringers continue to achieve a high standard. The signs for the future are, however, more hopeful than they might appear; and there are indications that the efforts of a wide range of ringers are appreciated. The Norwich Diocesan Association of Ringers takes a positive interest in the more loosely organised companies which maintain ringing at a surprisingly large number of country churches, often ringing call-changes for Sunday services. In recent years there have been ringing competitions for both scientific and call-change ringers; and a more liberal qualification for membership has been accepted. Perhaps the most encouraging feature of recent years has been the great determination and interest shown by many small communities in bringing back to life some of the derelict rings of bells in the county. Practical work in the tower has been supported by the Diocesan Association of Ringers and complemented by local fundraising; and encouraging grants for bell restoration work in Norfolk have been made by local and national charities. It is to be hoped that the church bells which have for so many years been an important part of parish life in Norfolk will continue to be rung and appreciated in the future; for theirs is one of the oldest man-made sounds which can still be heard, and their message is as relevant today as it ever was.

Com all ye that feare the lord
Com with care to heare his word
Com with zeale and good behaviour
Com to knowe thy god and saviour.

(Inscriptions at Great Ellingham, 1615.)

Chapter Two

CHURCHES AND THEIR TOWERS

Large bells like those which hang in church towers at the present time must have been used in England at least as early as the 7th century; and a number of early towers which were clearly designed for bells survive in various parts of England. Norfolk churches, such as Bessingham, Great Dunham and Aslacton have very early towers with large sound-windows, and there is no doubt that bells were widely heard from Anglo-Saxon times onwards. The former parochial chapel of St Mary, near New Buckenham castle, has on the west gable the remains of an early bell-cote designed for two small bells; and it is likely that many other churches originally had similar arrangements. There are still several bell-cotes where a sanctus or sacring bell once hung on top of the gable between the nave and chancel. The provision of larger bells in greater numbers made it necessary to construct suitable towers in which to hang them; and the purpose of the massive bell frame is to transmit the large forces due to bellringing with as little hazard as possible to the tower fabric. Church building in pre-Reformation times, as now, was an expensive business, and towers were often seen as a luxury. Many Norfolk churches were rebuilt piece-meal during the period c.1350–c.1550, with a new tower as one of the last refinements to the plan; and there are not a few instances where an old and unfashionable tower has been allowed to remain after a fine new church was built.

Apart from the dark brown Carstone which occurs in the north-west of the county, flint is the only valuable building stone found in Norfolk. The chalk which lies under most of the county contains layers of flint which have been quarried for various purposes since Neolithic times; and the beaches provide cobbles. Flint appears in nodules of varying size and colour depending on where it is found; and there were pits in most parishes from which parishioners might take available building materials such as flint and sand. Many parish pits were confirmed in the inclosure awards made during the early years of the 19th century. The chalk itself was burned at kilns in a large number of villages to make lime for mortar; and there was a flourishing trade in quicklime between Norwich merchants and builders working in various parts of Norfolk and Suffolk, such as the Broadland, where the underlying chalk was deeply buried.

Most tower walls have a core of small pieces of broken flint, bedded in hard mortar, between an inner and an outer skin. Small flint nodules and broken stones are often used to provide a good key for a plaster rendering on inside walls, while the treatment of outside walls varies considerably. It is clearly important for tower walls to be weatherproof, and to require a minimum of maintenance; and some 15th-century towers are only now receiving their first major repointing. Some towers are faced with un-broken flint nodules pointed with a hard lime mortar, while others have the flints split in halves and placed so that the fracture planes are on the outside: in both types of facing the joints are necessarily wide, and small flint gallets are inserted in the mortar to provide a more durable surface. Carefully selected flints can also be used for the jambs and voussoirs of quite large arched openings. It appears that when an arch was made the voussoirs were put in place first; after which a mortar infill, aggregated with rough flints, was poured over a centering and allowed to set. Most centerings were made of timber boards whose outlines still remain in the hard mortar, whilst at Hales it can be seen that osiers were used to form the round openings. Many large round-headed tower arches through to the nave of a church are constructed almost entirely of flint and mortar, a remarkable example, 18 feet high and 6 feet wide, surviving at Tasburgh. The corners of several naves are constructed from very large flints, but only a few square towers such as Guestwick, Hethel and Ketteringham have flint quoins, which at Hethel rise to a height of about 40 feet. A very few churches in Norfolk have buttresses entirely of flint, and one or two stair turrets have corners made of flint. The main problems associated with building in flint are its hardness, which prevents any carving; the awkward shapes; and the impermeability which makes it difficult for mortar to get a 'key'.

Carstone is rather more manageable, but less durable than flint. Like many soft sandstones it is easily eroded by rubbing, and does not stand up well to the effects of the weather. Seen in the coloured layers of the cliffs at Hunstanton, carstone was quarried during the Middle ages at pits such as that at Snettisham, where the churchwardens' accounts record the sale of quantities of 'le Carstone'. There were other quarries at Bexwell, near Downham Market. A few churches at a distance from Snettisham, such as Bessingham and Beeston St Lawrence, have carstone in their walls; but most examples are in a confined area. Fine towers built of carstone in combination with brick, flint and limestone occur at Middle-ton, East Winch and West Winch. Clunch, a somewhat harder form of chalk found also in north-west Norfolk, is occasionally used in building. This relatively soft material is readily carved, as can be seen in the fine tower arch at St Thomas' Chapel, Wymondham. Very easily eroded, clunch is usually employed for internal details such as window openings and doorways. A few towers have their walls built mainly of clunch, with a facing of carstone and limestone details: Sandringham and West Newton are good examples.

Limestone for use in building was, necessarily, imported. In Norman times, much of it came from quarries in Normandy, but during the 14th, 15th and 16th centuries stone was also imported from quarries in Lincolnshire, Northamptonshire and Yorkshire. The Norwich Cathedral Priory rolls show that Weldon and Barnack stone was brought from the quarries by water, landed at Brandon, and carried to Norwich by road. There are also references to building stone from Caen and Quarr (Isle of Wight) coming by sea and river through Yarmouth to Norwich; and it is not unlikely that stone from Yorkshire bought by the North Repps churchwardens in 1470 also came into Norfolk by sea. Transporting limestone by road was expensive: one ton-tight of Weldon stone cost 3s. 4d. at Brandon in 1479, and the cost of carrying it to Norwich doubled its price. Apart from the Marshland churches, only a few expensive towers such as Norwich St Peter Mancroft, Lynn St Margaret, and Cawston are faced entirely in limestone. The main use of limestone is for the architectural details of buildings: in quoins and voussoirs, in tablements and weatherings, in the formation of moulded arches and piers, for vaults and shafts and, almost universally, for the traceries of windows. 14th and 15th century accounts at St Giles's Hospital, Norwich, show that many of the limestone details for buildings could be purchased ready-made in Norwich from various masons, from 'skews' for buttresses to copings for parapets, and even a finial cross for a chancel gable.[1] When traceried windows were required for the new chancel at Hardley, the limestone, bought in Yarmouth, was taken to a Norwich yard, where the details were cut, and then taken by cart to Hardley. The rough masons had prepared openings in the walls to receive the limestone details, which were fitted by a Norwich freemason.

Roman brick has been identified in several churches, a particularly good example being at Caistor-by-Norwich, where the Roman town has been suggested as the obvious source. There is no doubt, however, that locally made brick was in use as a building material from at least the 14th century. The Cathedral church at Norwich was floored with brick tiles in 1290 and the walls of Norwich, begun in 1294, show considerable use of

Much of the material in this chapter is distilled from a thesis presented in the University of London (1985, P. Cattermole, *Church towers, bells and bell-frames*, especially pp. 287–345) where there are copious references to original sources. The footnotes given here refer to material not included in the thesis. For building dates see: P. Cattermole and S. Cotton, 'Mediaeval parish church building in Norfolk', *Norfolk Archaeology*, 1983. Particular thanks are recorded to Dr S. Cotton for helpful communications over a long period, and for his comments on the draft of this chapter.

[1]   NRO NCR Case 24c, Costessey rolls.

brick. The circular Cow Tower, built towards the end of the 14th century as part of the Norwich defences, has a flint core and is faced entirely with brick. An account of 1398/99 confirms that many loads of flint were carried from various pits, and bricks were purchased in quantity.[2] Although doubts about the durability of brick as a facing material (and a preference for flint) are expressed in a will of 1463 relating to the rebuilding of Risby Gate at Bury St Edmunds, the Cow Tower has survived. Brick appears in a number of churches and towers in Norfolk from the late 14th century onwards. The earliest examples show its principal use as an alternative to limestone for forming internal details, such as the corners of the tower and the jambs and voussoirs of arched openings. Brick was almost invariably used to form the soffits of arched openings, and in most cases where these are regularly seen the details are concealed either by plaster, or by thin limestone arrises.

The earliest complete towers to be constructed almost entirely of brick are probably at Gaywood and Walpole St Andrew, and there are fine 16th-century brick towers at Carleton St Peter, Shotesham St Mary, and Wheatacre. The structural brick of the Shotesham tower is faced with knapped flint, while at Wheatacre we have the only major use of brick as a decorative facing material. Window traceries of brick are noted in a number of late 15th- and 16th-century towers; but perhaps the most sophisticated use of the material is found stairways such as that at Bixley, with its careful detailing and neatly vaulted head. The reticence shown by masons in using brick as a facing for churches and towers is surprising, and is not paralleled in local secular buildings. At Norwich, for example, none of mediaeval churches has brick-faced walling, despite its early use in the Cow Tower. The fabric of the large church at Loddon, which was built by Sir James Hobart in the late 15th century, is almost entirely of brick, but it is faced with knapped flint: in his own manor-house at Hales, however, Hobart built extensively and unashamedly in brick, as can be seen in the remaining brick-faced range of Hales Hall and in the great barn across the courtyard there. There is little doubt, from the different colours and textures seen, that bricks came from a wide variety of sources. In the 19th century there were a large number of brickyards in the area, and there is every reason to suppose that the local brickearths were exploited during the earlier period when many of the churches were built.

In parts of the country where freestone is readily available, decoration is achieved by carving; and the towers of Somerset and Gloucestershire are, perhaps the best of those which rely on fine sculpture for decoration. In East Anglia the contrast between building materials is of considerable decorative importance, where patterns are sometimes formed by inserting a filling of dark coloured flint in a framework of limestone. Simple chequered and lozenge patterns are often used for the facings of buttresses,

2   B. Ayers, *Digging deeper*, Norfolk Museums Service, 1987, pp. 16–21.

while larger areas are sometimed panelled. Another treatment of large areas is to form tracery patterns: where in some cases the limestone mouldings are carved in relief, while in others the tracery is faced level with the flint to form 'flushwork'. Some of the most intricate flushwork is seen in the decorative monograms on the buttresses at New Buckenham. The tower at Redenhall has its entire west face executed in flushwork, and flushwork parapets form an impressive crown to many towers, that at Bunwell being particularly fine. Brick is also used decoratively, especially in the voussoirs of alternate brick and flint seen above windows and doorways; and a few churches have chequered brick and flint parapets.

The usual position for a Norfolk church tower is at the west end, on the central axis of the nave. Older towers were often left untouched when naves were widened, or aisles added. Masonry in the west walls of churches such as Bedingham and Tasburgh shows clearly that symmetry was preserved when the nave was widened on both sides; while towers such as Hardley, Norton Subcourse and Pulham St Mary were left off-centre when the nave was widened on one side only. Occasionally when an arcade was opened into a new aisle, or a new nave was built between an older tower and chancel, discrepancies in measurement made it necessary to lay out one bay wider or narrower than the rest: the curious design of the nave clerestory at Great Ellingham, and the narrow arches at the west end of the aisles at St Peter Mancroft, Norwich may have come about in this way. Early towers at Cley and Lynn St Nicholas remain at the corners of large and impressive churches, and at East Tuddenham the original nave became an aisle when a wide nave was built to the north of it. Later aisles have encroached on both sides of the west towers at Beeston-next-Mileham and Norwich St Andrew; while at Swannington and Swanton Morley arches to the north and south open into contemporary aisles to form a lofty space at the west end of the nave. Other churches have towers which are built inside the west end of an earlier nave. At Bramerton – where the church was substantially reconstructed c.1463 – the small tower is supported on one side by the older west wall of the church and on the east side by a newer wall built across the full width of the nave; while the north and south sides of the tower are supported by wide brick arches. The spaces at ground level on either side of the tower have squints which suggest that they might have been used as small chapels. A similar tower at Thurton c.1514 has solid north and south walls which leave small enclosed chambers on both sides, that on the north divided by an internal floor to form a first-floor chamber which could have been used for the accommodation of either a sacristan or a parochial chaplain. Perhaps the best example of a tower of this type is at Thuxton (c.1416), and a very fine clunch arch across the nave of the parochial chapel of St Thomas, Wymondham formerly supported a small tower of the same type. It would appear that this method of constructing a new

Shimpling: typical church in a small Norfolk village. *Photograph by the author.*

Ketteringham, tower. The lowest stage is probably Anglo-Saxon (see the large erratics used in the corners, and the narrow south window). Sir Arthur Heveningham's work of 1609, which replaced the 15th-century upper stage after its collapse, was rebuilt by Sir Francis Boileau in 1870. *Photograph by the author.*

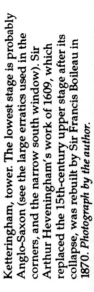

West Newton, church and tower of carstone with limestone dressings, typical materials used in north-west Norfolk. *Photograph by the author.*

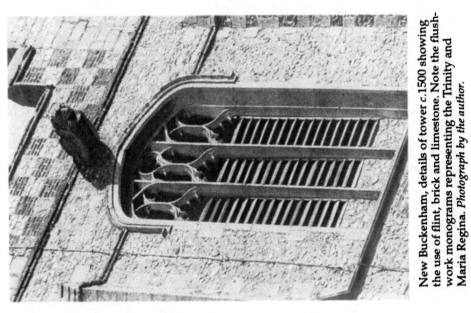

New Buckenham, details of tower c.1500 showing the use of flint, brick and limestone. Note the flush-work monograms representing the Trinity and Maria Regina. *Photograph by the author.*

Newton Flotman, interior of tower c.1450 showing typical rubble walls, and window opening with brick details. *Photograph by the author.*

Claxton, tower built of flint with brick dressings. Note the niches, or tabernacles, provided for statues of saints to watch over the graveyard. *Photograph by the author.*

Great Dunham, square Anglo-Saxon tower. *Photograph by the author.*

Hethel, Anglo-Saxon square tower with tall flint quoins and later bell-chamber. *Photograph by the author.*

Burnham Ulph, church with gable-cote for a pair of bells. *Etching by J. S. Cotman, 1817.*

Thurton, sixteenth-century tower built inside an earlier church. *Photograph by author.*

Wymondham, twin towers. The square west tower was built by the parishioners, and the octagonal central tower by the convent. *Photograph by the author.*

Aldeby, cruciform church of former priory, now the parish church, with central tower. *Photograph by the author.*

Howe, early Anglo-Saxon tower with round and double-splayed windows. *Photograph by the author.*

Tasburgh, round Anglo-Saxon tower with fourteenth-century bell-chamber. Note the shallow arcaded decoration. *Photograph by the author.*

Topcroft, early round tower with octagonal upper stages. Note the fourteenth-century sound-windows below the fifteenth-century bell-chamber. *Photograph by the author.*

Forncett, Anglo-Saxon round tower. *Photograph by the author.*

Pulham Market, early fifteenth-century tower. *Photograph by the author.*

Deopham, fifteenth-century tower. *Photograph by the author.*

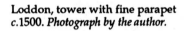

Loddon, tower with fine parapet c.1500. *Photograph by the author.*

Tharston, small tower c.1490 with buttresses, stairway to bells and pinnacled parapet. *Photograph by the author.*

Hilborough, late fifteenth-century tower with exceptionally fine detail.
Photograph by the author.

Tivetshall, 'inexpensive' unbuttressed fifteenth-century tower, whose
stairway rises only to the first floor. *Photograph by the author.*

Great Cressingham, small tower with fine west facade. Notice the crowned 'M', for St Michael, and the blank shields which would have carried painted blazons. The tower is probably the work of the Norwich mason, James Woderofe. *Photograph by the author.*

Broome, west facade of small early fifteenth-century tower showing distinctive tracery in the west window. *Photograph by the author.*

New Buckenham, ceremonial tower entrance with carved frieze of shields above, and arms in the spandrels. Note the flush-work panelling and the fine carved base course. *Photograph by the author.*

Swanton Morley, west facade of church begun *c.*1379 and finished
*c.*1440. The high quality of the design suggests that the architect may
have been Robert Wodehirst of Norwich, who was probably also
responsible for the towers at Broome, Illington and Wickhampton.
Photograph by the author.

Illington, early fifteenth-century
tower, showing large 'sound-holes'.
Note the 'Decorated' motifs in the bell-
chamber windows, and the strongly
'Perpendicular' lines of the west
window. *Photograph by the author.*

Hilborough, west facade. *Photograph
by the author.*

Billingford by Scole, tower begun after 1507 and left incomplete. The high quality is typical of early sixteenth-century work. *Photograph by the author.*

Wood Norton, tower begun in the sixteenth-century, with bell-chamber added *c.*1700. *Photograph by the author.*

Denton, tower c.1700, with later clock-chamber above the bell-chamber. *Photograph by the author.*

Brockdish, tower of 1864 by F. Marrable. Victorian towers like this, although found in great numbers elsewhere, are very unusual in Norfolk. *Photograph by the author.*

Yelverton, tower c.1672 designed for a ring of five bells. *Photograph by the author.*

Kimberley, tower begun in the sixteenth century, the upper stage dated 1631. *Photograph by the author.*

tower would have been much less expensive than building it outside the west wall of the church in the conventional way.

Modernisation of a church meant that the nave was often increased in height and width, or a clerestory was added; making an older tower look disproportionately small. At Ashwellthorpe the late 14th-century nave dwarfs the very short tower; and at Shelton the brick church (building c.1497 and hallowed c.1504) is tall enough to obscure part of the east sound-window of the tower: at St Peter Parmentergate, Norwich a finely carved tower ventilator is now below the pitch of the nave roof. Many towers such as Beeston-next-Mileham and Pulham St Mary were heightened to improve their relationship with the mass of an enlarged church, as were almost all of the round towers. Conversely a tall tower sometimes dwarfs an older church, as at Tibenham; and in some places, such as Bixley and Arminghall, structural provision was made inside a newly-built tower to open a taller arch if the nave roof were to be raised at a later date. In many cases where a major rebuilding scheme for a church was undertaken the lower part of the tower appears to have been built at the same time, and the addition of the bell-chamber was often left to follow as a second campaign. In such cases it was possible to make an arch giving full support to the tower, which was itself a structural unity; and the buttresses were carried down to ground level at all four corners of the tower, as at Worstead and Bunwell.

Although most Norfolk churches have their towers at the west end of the nave, there are exceptions. Anglo-Saxon churches at Great Dunham and Newton-by-Castleacre are built on the 'three-cell' plan, with a square tower placed axially between nave and chancel. Both towers stand to their full heights, with semi-circular arches to the nave and chancel, and two-light sound-windows as distinctive features. Towers of similar age at Weybourne and Guestwick were once centrally placed, and that at Bawsey is still an impressive feature of the deserted church. Norman builders followed the tradition with their towers at Burnham Overy, Castle Rising, Fundenhall, Gillingham, and a particularly fine example at South Lopham. None of these seems to have been designed as a lantern tower providing light in the centre of the church, since their first-floor chambers have such small windows. Transepts added to an axial tower produce the cruciform plan favoured in some of the larger Norman monastic and collegiate churches, such as Norwich Cathedral, Great Yarmouth and Attleborough (where the chancel has been lost); and the large parish church at East Dereham has a fine lantern tower above the crossing. Smaller central towers of Norman origin are found at Aldeby, Flitcham, Gressenhall, and Melton Constable. The twin towers at the west end of the cruciform church at Lynn St Margaret are an unusual feature, and similar towers formerly existed at Castle Acre Priory. At Wymondham we have the monastic tower at the former crossing, and the parochial tower at the west end of the church.

South Lopham, axially placed tower: a fine example of Norman work in
a village church.
Lithograph by J. B. Ladbroke, c.1820.

A few towers are built onto the side of a nave or aisle in such a way that
the ground floor chamber serves as a porch. Holme-next-the-Sea is a fine
example of this arrangement, which also allows large west windows to
light the naves at West Bradenham, Hardingham, Mileham and Norwich,
St Stephen. Smaller churches at Briningham, Little Ellingham, Reepham,
Sculthorpe, Whinburgh and Wicklewood also have towers attached to
their south sides. The unusual position of the tower at Chedgrave probably arose when a west tower fell, and a new bell-chamber was built
above a small Norman chapel attached to the north wall of the chancel.

Detached towers are rare, but there are fine examples at West Walton
and the Terringtons in west Norfolk. The East Dereham clocher was built
to take the bells removed from a weak central tower; while small bell-
houses are shown in early 19th-century lithographs of the churches at
Hapton and Southburgh where towers had fallen. The thatched 'temporary' bell-house at Woodrising probably dates from the 17th century. The
round tower at Little Snoring, unlike the only other detached round tower
at Bramfield in Suffolk, has a tall eastern arch which suggests that a
church attached to it was pulled down and rebuilt further to the north.

Spires are exceptional in Norfolk; but there is documentary evidence
for their existence at churches such as West Harling, Pulham St Mary and
Whissonsett, which now have none. Ancient stone spires remain at

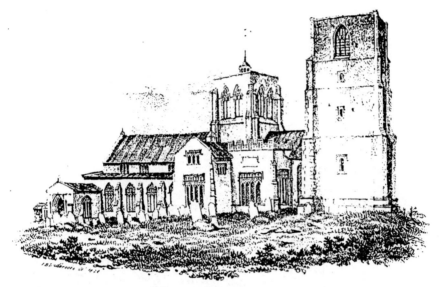

East Dereham, detached tower built in the sixteenth century to house
bells removed from the weaker central tower.
Lithograph by J. B. Ladbroke, 1824.

Norwich Cathedral, Snettisham and Wilton (that at Oxborough having
fallen this century), with large lead-covered timber-framed spires remaining at Banham and Little Walsingham. Fine Victorian spires top older
towers at Beeston-next-Mileham, Cranworth, King's Lynn St Nicholas
and Quidenham, and there are many churches with smaller 'needle'
spires. The Victorian towers at Framingham Pigot, Norwich Holy Trinity
and Southburgh have tall spires, and that on the slender brick tower at
Thorpe Episcopi was removed for the sake of safety. The elegant mediaeval timber fleche at East Harling inspired the Victorian finial at Norwich St Peter Mancroft, and west Norfolk churches at Necton, Shipdham
and Swaffham provide interesting variations on the theme.

There are a few oddities among Norfolk towers, none more curious
than the diagonally-placed twin towers at the west end of the strange
Victorian church at Booton, unless it is the unique brick tower of dimin-
ishing stages at Burgh St Peter. Unlike the other flint regions such as
Hampshire, there are very few timber bell turrets of any size in Norfolk,
but that at Sisland is rather like those found in counties near the Welsh
border. When the towers fell at Little Fransham and Thurgarton, the bells
were rehung in small chambers built above the south porches; and
Twyford has a neat cupola on the porch roof.

Although most of the surviving Anglo-Saxon towers are round; there are
a few exceptions, such as the central tower at Great Dunham and the west

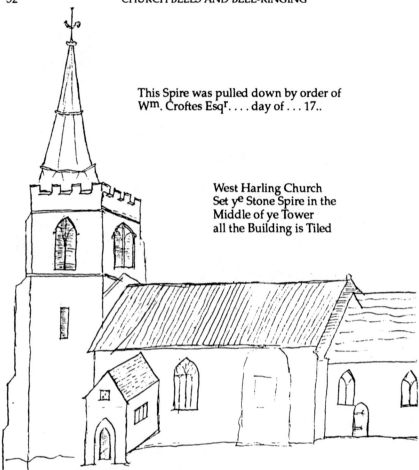

This Spire was pulled down by order of
W^m. Croftes Esqr. . . . day of . . . 17. .

West Harling Church
Set y^e Stone Spire in the
Middle of ye Tower
all the Building is Tiled

West Harling, 18th century drawing of former spire, pulled down c.1756.
*Sketch from Frere Mss (DS 594 352x3) by permission of the Norfolk Record
Office.*

tower at Hethel. The great Norman tower of Norwich Cathedral, one of
the finest in the country, clearly inspired towers like those at Castle Rising
and South Lopham; and many other large Norman churches must have
been swept away on the tide of church-building which resulted from the
great wealth of the county during the later Middle Ages. The west towers
of Lynn St Margaret are supported by fine Norman arches; and the interior of the crossing tower at Attleborough has two levels of arcading
inside the ringing chamber.
    The Normans built many churches in East Anglia, and it is worth
recording that round towers in Great Britain are almost entirely confined

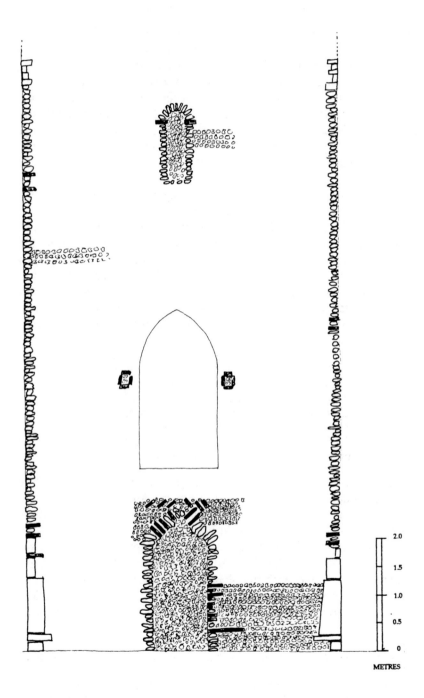

2.0

1.5

1.0

0.5

0

METRES

Hethel tower.
Diagram showing early features.

to Norfolk and Suffolk. Messent records 124 in Norfolk, 42 in Suffolk, 6 in Essex, 3 in Sussex, 2 each in Berkshire and Cambridge and a single modern tower in Dorset.[3] The writer has noticed one at Penpont in Breconshire, one at Dervaig on the Isle of Mull, and a very remote example on the Isle of Canna – and there are probably a few more. The main reason that most of the round towers are found in Norfolk is almost certainly the lack of a good local stone suitable for forming corners. Although large pieces of flint, and glacial erratics are used to form the corners of church buildings, they are quite unsuitable for the very tall corners of a square tower.

The round towers present a particular dating problem which has been considered by a number of researchers, some of whom have suggested more or less tight dating, while others have been less dogmatic. Munro Cautley observed that the majority of round towers dated from the Norman period, and that a certain number belonged to the 9th and 10th centuries. Messent stated that most of the round towers were built during the period A.D. 1000 to A.D. 1150, during the Saxon, Saxo-Norman and Norman periods, while Pevsner considers the majority to be Norman with, perhaps, about 20 Anglo-Saxon towers. The most pertinent comment seems to be that made by E. A. Fisher:

> It is difficult to justify any strict separation of these towers into groups. They are so alike in general, and often in specific, characteristics that the phrase 'sui generis' can be applied appropriately to them. They can be studied only as a group, regardless of chronology. To chose a few which are supposed to be pre-Conquest, either wholly or in part, often on unconvincing grounds, is to say the least arbitrary, and perhaps not really meaningful.

Some early towers such as East Lexham are very roughly built, while others have much more sophisticated masonry; and several show the accepted hall-marks of Anglo-Saxon workmanship alongside features which are unmistakeably Norman. At Forncett St Peter, for example, two sets of sound-windows have triangular heads and two others have semi-circular heads; while at Gissing Anglo-Saxon round windows with double splays are found with the obviously Norman sound-windows in an apparently uniform tower. Appearances are deceptive and flintwork is hard to date accurately.[4] The best that can be said is that there are fine

---

[3] C. J. W. Messent, *The round towers to English parish churches*, Norwich, 1958. *passim.*

[4] The round tower at Runhall is a case in point: Pevsner calls it 'Norman', Messent 'Norman and Early English' and Cautley 'Norman and 13th-century'; all based on the evidence of small deeply-splayed window openings, formed entirely from flint. From the inside it can be seen that there is a straight joint with the west wall of the nave, which cannot be earlier than the 13th-century

Swainsthorpe, externally featureless round tower (bell-chamber c.1500)
with typical Anglo-Saxon details inside.
Photograph by the author.

towers with Anglo-Saxon features, such as Aslacton, Bessingham,
Gissing, Forncett St Peter, Haddiscoe and Roughton which stand to their
full heights unaltered, except for a later parapet; and apparently complete
Norman towers at Burnham Deepdale, Burnham Norton, Kilverstone,
Merton, and Titchwell.

It is difficult to subscribe to Cautley's view that the round towers were
originally defensive,[5] like the pele towers of the Northumbrian border,
and the brochs of the Western and Northern Isles. His argument was
based on the frequency with which he found straight-sided doorways cut

and which has re-used Norman masonry in the jambs of the west door. The
upper part of the tower, which shows much brick inside, can be fairly securely
dated by bequests in the 16th century.
[5] H. Munro Cautley, *Norfolk churches*, Ipswich, 1949, pp. 2–5.

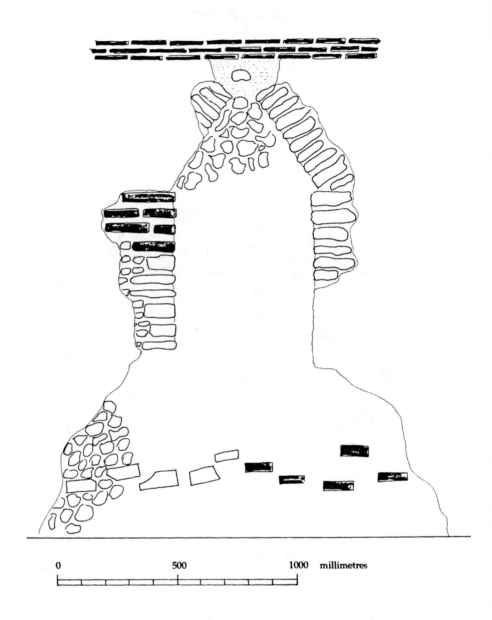

0   500   1000   millimetres

The blocked, gable-headed, opening at first floor level
in the east wall of the tower.

Swainsthorpe, Anglo-Saxon details inside the tower.

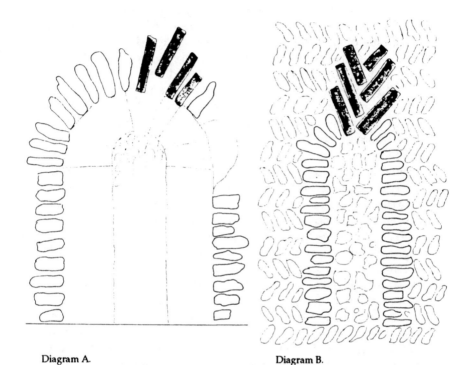

Diagram A.

Diagram B.

0   500   1000   millimetres

Diagram A: The blocked, round-headed, opening at first floor level
                    in the north wall of the tower viewed from inside.
Diagram B: The blocked, round-headed, opening at first floor level
                    in the south wall of the tower viewed from outside.

through the east side of the tower at high level, which he assumed were the original entrances. He could 'think of no other purpose than that of effecting an entrance by means of a ladder, as this could be pulled up after the last defender had climbed into the tower when they would be safe against even an army of assailants.' Cautley suggests that large ground-floor arches were only cut through the walls of these towers to increase the floor area of churches which were later attached to them. There are, indeed, many straight-sided high-level doorways in round towers: but the fact that all of them face eastwards would be a most unlikely coincidence if they were made without reference to an adjoining structure. It would also be very difficult to pierce a large arch through the stout flintwork of a round tower, and almost impossible to finish the masonry neatly without obvious infilling: the inside of Swainsthorpe tower shows some of the problems encountered when a tower arch has been altered. A few round towers, such as Forncett, Howe and Aslacton have small west doorways at ground level, further contradicting the defensive argument. Some east-facing doorways must have been made to connect with a gallery or enclosed room high in the west end of the church, while others must have given access to the space between the nave roof and a plastered ceiling. The east tower wall at Toft Monks has openings at two levels which must once have served both purposes.

Most round towers have been increased in height at some time, usually when a church was enlarged and a loftier nave roof built. While apparently Anglo-Saxon sound-windows remain open below the very much later octagonal belfry at Beechamwell, the inside walls of many round towers show that large sound-windows at a lower level have been blocked when a new bell-chamber has been added. Those at Norwich St Mary Coslany were only revealed when a later belfry was removed. Perhaps towers such as Howe, Tasburgh and Thorpe next Haddiscoe, which show no signs of sound-windows in the older parts, originally had thatched conical roofs: rather like the present tiled roofs at Little Snoring and Welborne, where sound of the bells escapes through louvred dormers.

Round Norman bell-chambers appear on earlier towers at Gayton Thorpe, and Thorpe next Haddiscoe; and there are many later examples; but the considerable difficulties of arranging a bell-frame in a round tower may have been the reason why so many round towers have been extended by adding octagonal bell-chambers. Brick is used extensively in most octagonal belfries for forming corners, and making the details of arched openings. These octagonal extensions to round towers are usually aesthetically very pleasing, as well as being functional; and towers such as that at Topcroft, where there are two additional octagonal stages on a round tower, are very impressive. A delightful chequered belfry completes the tower at Breccles; while lancet sound-windows beneath stepped flushwork parapets are found at Acle, Hassingham and Raveningham. Another common decorative feature is the use of limestone and

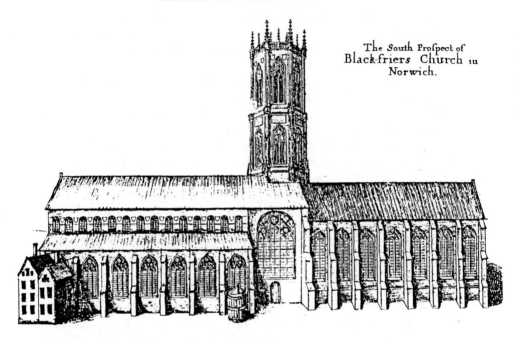

The South Profpect of Black-friers Church in Norwich.

Norwich, Dominican Friary, former octagonal tower.
Engraving from Dugdale's Monasticon Anglicanum.

knapped flint flushwork to produce traceried patterns on the faces of a tower between the sound-windows, good examples being found at Bedingham, Potter Heigham and Thorpe Abbots. Perhaps the most attractive of these octagonal belfries are at Quidenham and Shimpling, where they act as foils to Victorian spires.

Some towers such as Heckingham and Sidestrand have octagonal stages which are rather taller than the original round sections; while the elegant towers at Rollesby and Topcroft, where the circular part is almost reduced to insignificance may have been the inspiration for the towers at Billingford (near Elmham), Buckenham (near Cantley), Old Buckenham, Kettlestone and Toft Monks, which are octagonal from the ground. Octagonal towers rising above a central space between nave and chancel were favoured by the 15th-century designers of the Franciscan friars' church at Lynn and the Dominicans' church at Norwich; sadly the Norwich tower fell in 1712. Upper octagonal stages rise from square towers at Scoulton, Thuxton and very impressively at Wymondham. Towers at Methwold and Upwell in west Norfolk also have octagonal sections. It should be remembered that polygons were fashionable architectural forms during the middle ages, used for chapter-houses in monastic churches, and for porches in important churches such as Ludlow and

Bristol, St Mary Redcliffe. The octagon at Ely Cathedral (built in the 1320s) must have been the inspiration for some of Norfolk's humbler towers, as also for the timber lantern tower at Lynn, St Margaret (which fell in 1741).

Early English work abounds in the Marshland, with characteristic towers at Tilney All Saints, West Walton and Walsoken; while the tower of Lynn St Nicholas is almost engulfed by the vast 15th-century church. Towers such as Elsing, Rushford and Snettisham appear to be genuine 14th century Decorated work, and that at Aylsham is impressive in size and detail. There are other smaller towers showing good Decorated work at Ashill, Caston and Thompson. Another large Decorated tower is that at Hingham, probably begun during the incumbency of Remigius of Hethersett (1316–1359) and still under construction in 1375, when John de Ufford left money towards its building. Pride of place should perhaps go to Worstead tower, whose fine proportions and ornament were probably the result of the close ties between the village and Norwich Cathedral Priory.

Once Early English and Decorated motifs begin to appear in Norfolk churches, care needs to be taken in dating them, since many features which fell out of fashion in other parts of England were used in Norfolk throughout the period when the Perpendicular style was popular. Heckingham tower (c.1487–c.1507) has lancet sound-windows, as does the impressive 15th-century octagonal casing of the tower at Toft Monks, where all openings are of this type. Several towers have two-light windows with 'Y' tracery, or three-light windows with intersecting tracery which might be stylistically dated to c.1300; but in many instances the openings are constructed in sophisticated brickwork. Fabric bequests suggest that such traceries were relatively common in Norfolk throughout the Perpendicular period. Another very common treatment of tracery in a two-light window opening is to form an oculus at the head, enclosed either by a curved or straight-sided hexagon: this motif, which is found in Decorated church buildings as early as Norton Subcourse (c.1319) continues in popularity through to the 16th century, as at Thorpe Abbots. One of the most striking examples of mixed style is found in the tower at Hindringham, which was probably rebuilt shortly after the recorded collapse of an earlier tower in 1387. The slender proportions and neat diagonal buttresses look forward to the design of later Perpendicular towers, as does the fine west window with its strong verticals and dagger motifs in the outer lights; while the sound-windows have traceries which are strongly reminiscent of Decorated work in the Norwich Cathedral cloister.

Two of the earliest Perpendicular towers, at Bintree and Mattishall, were probably finished in the 1380s. Castle Acre tower, another fine structure with massive paired buttresses, was also begun towards the end of the 14th century, and many other towers of various sizes were built in the same style during the next 150 years. The importance of the tower at the

Great Hospital,[6] which has features found in many other local towers, is that it can be firmly dated to the 1390s. Salle and Cromer are two of Norfolk's largest towers, both probably dating from the 1420s and very similar in many broad respects, but the detailing of both is highly individual. Tracery in the west window at Salle has much in common with contemporary work in Swanton Morley church, as do traceries in the smaller towers at Broome, Illington and Wickhampton. Another small tower of the same date, and of excellent quality, is that at Great Cressingham, another parish which had strong ties with Norwich Cathedral Priory: there are good reasons for suggesting that James Woderofe, master mason at Norwich, was the designer. Two roughly contemporary towers in west Norfolk, Docking and Holme next the Sea, probably represent the efforts of Lynn masons during the first two decades of the 15th century. In Norwich itself, work had probably begun on the tower at St Peter Mancroft in the 1390s, and the fabric had reached a level where a bell could be hung c.1431. St Michael at Coslany tower was probably begun in the 1420s, as was St Giles, which perhaps waited until the 1450s for completion.

In the south of the county, Tibenham tower, which was probably finished in the 1430s has more in common with Suffolk towers; and there is an interesting trio of almost identical towers of excellent design and detail at Pulham Market (where bells were hung in 1438), Bressingham (c.1431) and Occold (c.1426). The large towers at Blofield and South Repps, together with the smaller, but related tower at Brisley, were probably begun in the 1430s: all have west facades with fine west windows, of which Brisley is particularly nicely detailed. The foundations for the great west tower at Wymondham were cleared in the 1440s, and the unusual octagonal buttresses are found also in contemporary towers at Bungay and Laxfield in Suffolk, and a little later at Redenhall in Norfolk.

---

6   NRO NCR Case 24a, Great Hospital Accounts 1306–1398. The building work
     on the tower appears as follows:
     Item in petre libere, in calion, emptis et tegulis preter iiij^{xx} carrectis de calyon datis per
     Rogerum de Eton person de Yelverton, ix. li. xvij s. viij d. ad campanile:
     Item in meremio empto pro factura novi campanilis: vli. viij s. xj d.
     Item in zabulo empto pro eodem: xv s. x d.
     Item in (   ) empto pro balks et speres pro eodem: jli. vj s. v d.
     In stipendio carpentarii reparantis dictum meremium: iij s. ij d.
     In poles emptis pro stagyng: iij s.
     In hirdeles emptis pro eodem: ij s. vj d.
     In skutellis et bollis ligatis cum ferro emptis pro eisdem: j s. iiij d.
     In boss' empto: viij d.
     In stipendiis diversorum cementariorum operantium super dictum campanile hoc
     anno: x li.
     In stipendiis diversorum daubatorium tegentis dictum opus erga tempus yemalis: j s.
     vj d.

Happisburgh, exceptionally tall fifteenth-century tower.
Lithograph, 1824, by J. B. Ladbroke.

Redenhall and Wymondham are expensive towers which stand apart
from the general run. Bradfield ('new' in 1451), Barton Turf and Coltishall
are typical of the more ambitious village church towers in north-east
Norfolk, their design having parallels in towers begun perhaps ten years
later at North Burlingham and Norwich St Lawrence. Westwick is a smaller tower of excellent quality, which was probably also begun in the 1460s.
There are apparently contemporary but very differently designed additions of upper stages (with 'Y' tracery in the sound windows) to towers in
south Norfolk, at Banham, Besthorpe, Tacolnestone and Wilby.

A later generation of towers includes those at Heydon (1460 onwards)
Foulsham ('new' in 1473) and perhaps Happisburgh. An unusual tower at
Deopham, which has similar proportions to the neighbouring tower at
Hingham but many details with no local parallels, was probably com-
pleted in the 1470s, and the fact that the church was a rectory belonging to
Canterbury cathedral may account for the 'foreign' details and styling.
Another highly individual tower in the extreme south of the county was
begun at Garboldisham c.1463, where the display of flushwork on the
buttresses and parapet is remarkable: here again there is a strong Suffolk
influence, possibly exerted by the architect of towers at Badwell Ash,
Elmswell and Ixworth.

The 1480s probably saw work begin on the two similar towers at North
Lopham and Kenninghall, with related bell-chambers added to the towers at New Buckenham and Saham Toney. The two latter towers were

probably inspired by slightly earlier work at Hilborough, where the bells were apparently hung c.1474. The similarity of these towers with work in the north aisle of Wymondham Abbey suggests a common source for their design, shared by other towers such as Ditchingham and Larling, and the unfinished work at Billingford by Scole. The lower part of Swaffham tower is probably contemporary with the above work, but its completion during the early years of the 16th century was contemporary with the building of Dereham's detached tower, and the old tower at Necton.

All the round towers, and a few of the square towers, rise from the ground with no definite plinth, or base course. Apart from the structural advantage of a thicker wall at the lowest part of a building, a plinth can add much to the appearance of a tower. This was realised by the designers of several of the 15th and 16th century towers, who turned a useful feature into a very definite embellishment. The absence of a base course is particularly noted in the less 'expensive' towers.

Some towers have very simple, undecorated base courses; while flushwork decoration may range from simple panelling to exuberant patterning such as that at Thurlton, where the base course has a band of flushwork lozenges beneath a delicately-patterned arcading with trefoiled heads and pierced spandrels. Decoration of the older base-course beneath the late-18th-century brick tower at Burgh St Peter is achieved by brick headers set out in a diaper pattern in the flint facing. Bunwell tower has a deep limestone base, whose bareness suggests that it was probably intended for carving at a later date; and at New Buckenham a very fine base-course surrounds the south aisle, porch and tower. Redenhall tower has carved shields contained in quatrefoils, and Ditchingham has an impressive array of limestone shields alternating with carved lozenges in a similar position.

In most square towers the thickness of the walls diminishes with the height of the tower. This is usually visible inside, where a series of off-sets at the levels of the tower floors may reduce a typical wall thickness from say 4 ft 6 inches at ground level to 3 ft in the upper stage. Although the addition of buttresses adds greatly to the strength of a tower, about one-third of square towers are built without buttresses. The external width of most unbuttressed towers does not vary from bottom to top; but there are a number of small towers (such as Arminghall, Bramerton, Hedenham, Rockland St Mary and Trowse) where a distinct batter provides considerable strength in the absence of buttresses. The usual form of buttressing consists of a pair of diagonal buttresses at the north-west and south-west corners of the tower, with occasionally a pair of buttresses at the junctions with the nave walls: these latter are often in the same line as the west wall of the nave, rather than set diagonally. The massive tower at Redenhall has octagonal buttresses, a feature noted in roughly contemporary towers at Bungay (Suffolk), Eye (Suffolk), Laxfield (Suffolk) and Wymondham.

Paired buttresses at the corners of a tower provide great strength, and those at Diss allow a very heavy ring of bells to be rung in a small tower. In a few cases structural evidence shows that buttresses were added to an earlier unbuttressed tower, and there is documentary evidence for this process in an Alburgh will of 1504. It is, perhaps, significant to notice that few of the unbuttressed towers have an expensive masonry stairway to the upper floors, access being as a rule by movable ladders. One has only to compare the very similar towers at Tivetshall, which is unbuttressed, and Tharston, where there are handsome panelled diagonal buttresses, to see that there is a distinct aesthetic advantage in well-designed buttresses.

Although not strictly a structural necessity, a parapet adds much to the appearance of a tower; and the gaunt, unfinished appearance of the otherwise fine towers at Kenninghall and Felmingham contrasts sharply with that of towers such as Loddon or North Repps which are finished with parapets. The most common form of parapet is a simple coping, which may have applied decoration as at Thurlton; or an embattled parapet of brick or limestone, sometimes faced with flint. One of the most impressive embattled parapets is that at Loddon, where bequests between 1501 and 1504 almost certainly refer to the very fine parapet which remains: there are three merlons on each side with diagonally set pinnacles at the corners and small crosses on the central merlons; the parapet is constructed of a mixture of brick and flint, its faces panelled in fine traceried flushwork, with the initials 'S' and 'T' apparently referring to the dedication of the church to 'Sancta Trinitas', the Holy Trinity. The embattled and pinnacled parapet at Ditchingham is decorated with lozenges of limestone, reflecting the decoration of the base course, in a design which closely resembles the parapets of a number of churches in, and to the north of Norwich; and on towers such as Honingham the embattled parapet has, in place of pinnacles, carvings of the symbols of the four evangelists in an impressive array. A particular form of parapet which seems to have found favour in south-east Norfolk, and which has more in common with the Suffolk towers, has stepped and embattled merlons. The usual form of decoration, as seen at Ellingham for example, is flushwork panelling to the merlons with carved limestone inserted below the embrasures: the decoration often includes formal patterns and shields. Pinnacles vary from the rather squat, diagonally-set pinnacles at Ellingham to the elegant, thin pinnacles, supported by small flying buttresses, at Alburgh. Burnham Westgate has a remarkable limestone parapet carved with figures; but the finest parapets are perhaps those at Redenhall and Bunwell, both 16th century, which seem to echo something of the effect of the fretted parapets seen in the towers of Somerset churches.

Churchwardens' accounts show that frequent attention was needed to keep bells in fit condition for ringing, and it is for this reason that access to the upper floors of a tower was important. A masonry stairway, usually in the form of a vice, was a distinct advantage over ladders; and it is usually accommodated partly in a projection on the outside of the tower and partly in the thickness of the tower walls. This causes structural weakness; and in a number of taller towers, such as those at New Buckenham, Cawston and Deopham, the sections of stairway connecting different levels are in different corners of the tower. In towers such as Rushall, Stratton St Michael and Scoulton the weakness associated with a stairway has resulted in its being filled with rubble, to preserve the tower structure; and there are relatively few towers like Langham where a masonry stairway rises from the ground-floor through to the level of the tower roof. In many towers the vice provides access only as far as the second-floor chamber which usually houses the bells, further height being gained by ladders. There is a remarkable, early timber stairway in the round tower at Forncett St Peter, where the stair treads are formed from triangular pieces of oak fixed to a pair of parallel beams by large iron spikes, the whole encased in a neat wainscoting. The problems associated with climbing to the upper levels of a tall tower doubtless prompted a bequest at Pulham St Mary in 1504 (which was never realised), when money was left to make a vice in the steeple; and it can be seen that many masonry stairways to upper floors are later additions to towers.

Many churches have impressive west facades, reflecting the importance of the west doorway as the principal entrance. At Redenhall, for example, the west face of the tower is covered from top to bottom with intricate flushwork panelling, the west doorway has decorated spandrels and is flanked by stooled niches, and there is a fine large west window of four lights to the ringing gallery. There are impressive facades at Brisley and Ditchingham, South Repps has a six-light west window of exceptional size; and many smaller towers such as Great Cressingham and South Acre have west fronts of the highest quality. The west doorway is often chosen for a display of heraldry, doubtless reflecting the generosity of those who had subscribed to building work. Recognisable carvings of arms remain at Broome and Bressingham, while other towers have blank shields on which blazons might formerly have been painted. At New Buckenham the finely moulded arch is supported by shafted jambs, arms are carved in the spandrels as well as in a frieze above the doorway, and there is flushwork panelling on either side. The west facade at Swanton Morley is one of the finest, where the architect has brought the nave aisles forward to enclose the tower; the three windows have matching traceries, and a deep base course emphasises the unity of the composition.

The best interior view of many Norfolk churches is that looking west from the chancel step. Many later towers have very large arches through to the nave, allowing light from a large west window to fill the area where the font usually stands; and bequests at Topcroft in 1434 suggest that the lighting of the font was much in mind when the new west window was inserted in the tower. One has only to compare the naves at Diss and

Bressingham to see how a blank west wall detracts from the general appearance of the former church. The problem at Diss (as also at Riddlesworth) was that the tower stood at the edge of the highway; and any procession round the church would have to leave consecrated ground unless there was a passage through the tower. A different solution to the problem of providing a processional path resulted in the unusual arrangements at Norwich St Peter Mancroft and Metton. The ground stage of each tower has arched openings on three sides, with the west door opening directly into the nave through the east wall of the tower. Both towers have large west windows, and tall tower arches: the gallery at Metton is open to the church, but that at St Peter Mancroft has recently been filled by the church organ. At Norwich St John Maddermarket (and formerly at St Swithun's church) similar galleries allowed a public lane to run under the tower.

Ringers' galleries were probably provided because it was inconvenient for the bellringers to be immediately behind any west doorway that was used a a ceremonial entrance; a point which is made clear in the will of Geoffrey Elyngham of Fersfield. He leaves money for the construction of such a gallery in 1493: '*Item volo quod executores mei fieri faciant unum solarium in campanili dicte ecclesie obsimile et instar solarii in campanili ecclesie de Estherlyng ut processio festivis diebus subter pulsantes procedat.*' Ringing on various festivals is noted in early churchwardens' accounts at East Dereham, and it is very likely that processions would have passed through the main doorway of the church while ringing was in progress. Early ringers' galleries survive in towers such as Bunwell, Mattishall, Redenhall, Tibenham, Trunch and Wheatacre; and many towers have which have lost their galleries retain contemporary doorways which led to them from the tower stairways. The tower at Norwich St Gregory has a limestone ringers' gallery supported by a vault, with a second vault supporting the first floor: both vaults are delicately carved, with neat bell-holes. At Great Ellingham a modern ringers gallery has a much older staging in front of it, probably provided in the 18th century for the musicians who would have accompanied church services.

Inscriptions which remain on two pre-Reformation ringers' galleries show that they were erected at the expense of parish gilds. The tower gallery at Cawston, where building work was under way in 1421 and probably continued through to c.1480, has the following inscription carved on the face of the westernmost floor joist: 'God spede the plow and send us ale corn enow our purpose for to make at crow of cok of the plow lete of Sygate: to be marry and glede wat good ale this work mad.' At Worstead we read: 'This work was made in the yer of god MCCCCCI at the propur cost of the catell of the chyrch of Worsted callyd the bachellers lyte that god preserve wt all the benefactors of the same now and ever amen. Then wer husbonds Cristofuer Rant and Jeffery Deyn.' The implied connection between parish guilds and tower galleries suggests that there

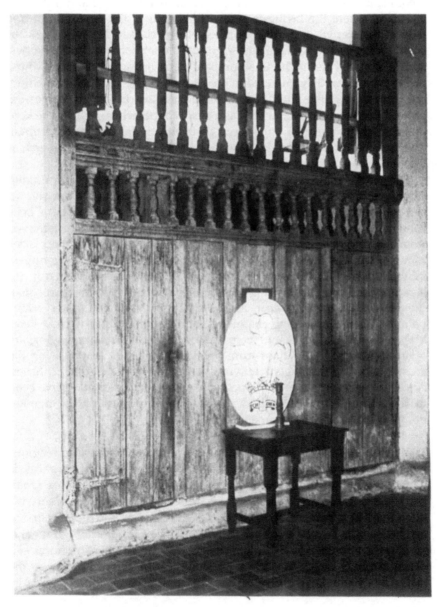

Wilby, ringers' gallery, dated 1637.
Photograph by the author.

might have been a small chapel, for the use of a guild priest, either on or below the gallery: holes in the gallery rail at Cawston are said to have served to hold the lights which were kept before the Plough Rood there.

Bequests leave no doubt that there was a chapel in the tower of St Andrew's church, Norwich, and images of saints in church towers are recorded at Hassingham, where there was also a light, and at Burgh, near Aylsham, where the bequests reads: 'I bequeth to the peyntyng of our lady at the stepyll vj d.' In a number of churches in Norfolk there are small niches in the walls of tower ground-floor chambers and galleries, and at Bunwell the niche is accompanied by a bracket. Some of these niches were obviously intended to hold lamps to give light in the evening, but there seems little doubt that in some cases the ringers' gallery, or the ground floor of the tower, served as a small chapel where lights were kept burning and where gild priests said their prayers for departed brethren. The curious squints through the walls on either side of the tower arch at Bramerton also suggest the former site of minor altars.

The general removal of ringers from open galleries to first-floor ringing chambers probably dates from the rise of changeringing: when shorter bell-ropes gave very much better control over the movements of bells rung in full-circles. At Deopham, for example, a low ceiling was removed from the first-floor chamber in 1678 (the date impressed in the plaster filling of the joist-holes); and it is very likely that this is when the ringers moved upstairs. In the early years of the 19th century the Mancroft ringers operated from a loft which was somewhat higher in the tower than the present ringing chamber, as illustrated in Ninham's water colour painting.[7] Upstairs ringing chambers, such as those at Norwich St Peter Mancroft and St Giles, where there was a great deal of change ringing, are often approached by a door from outside the church, emphasising the secular nature of the ringers' activities during the 17th and 18th centuries. Another reason for removing ringers from open galleries may have been to allow church orchestras and choirs to operate there, in the manner described so vividly by Thomas Hardy.[8]

Many churches which in the Middle Ages were appropriated to religious houses had no vicar, being served only by stipendiary priests; and it is equally likely that an absentee rector might install a chaplain to carry out parochial duties. Parish chaplains appointed by the monks at Norwich often lived in a 'camera' attached to the church when the proper parsonage house was farmed out with the rectory estate; and although there is no specific reference to living quarters inside the church, structural evidence strongly suggests such a possibility at Wicklewood, where the tower has rooms at the level of the first and second floors with large

[7]   See frontispiece.
[8]   Thomas Hardy, *Under the greenwood tree: or the Mellstock choir.*

fireplaces. The churches at Scoulton and Blo Norton have tower chambers with fireplaces, that at Blo Norton being particularly well-lighted and fitted with cupboards. At Great Witchingham there is in one corner of the tower chamber a fireplace with a fine brick flue and hood, while a neat latrine occupies another corner: Great Snoring tower, too, shows signs of domestic use. The Borough Assembly at Great Yarmouth[9] decided in 1540 that 'Richard Hampton beyng a servante or undersexton in the churche of Yarmouth shall have the chamber over the church porche frely to his owne use for his chamber to lodge in so longe as theassent of the comon assemble or counsell of the said towne shall perceve it mete and convenyent.' A sacristan might live over the porch of one church, in the tower of another, or even in a gallery at the west end of the nave.

If the first-floor chamber in a tower was occupied by a chaplain or by a sacristan, it is quite likely that he would be responsible for the safekeeping of church property, and that his duties would have included sleeping in the tower by night. There are several instances of tower chambers, such as at Forncett St Mary, where the doors are secured from within by a sliding bar, rather than by a lock which could be worked from either side of the door; and the churchwardens' accounts at East Dereham make frequent references to the repair of the treasury (probably the chamber above the south transept), as well as regular payments at certain times of the year to those who watched in the church by night. An opening through to the church would have been useful; and windows like that at Ashwellthorpe which looks from a strong-room above the porch towards the high altar are not uncommon. Many towers have small openings looking through to the nave from an upper chamber, which would have enabled a watch to be kept on the contents of the church. The windows on the tower stairs at Briningham and Hardingham, which admit very little light, could have had no other purpose.

An early 15th century will which provides for the purchase of a new chest with three locks to contain the church valuables at Hedenham, directs that the chest should be kept securely in the tower; and there is structural evidence for the use of many tower chambers as strong rooms. Doors to tower stairways are often very heavily framed and constructed, and one often finds a recess or cupboard built into the masonry immediately behind them. Even now it is not uncommon to find the cross and candlesticks, removed from the altar on Sunday, languishing on the tower stairs during the week. There are also numerous instances such as Little Ellingham and Hardingham, where heavily constructed safes are built into the walls of upstairs chambers. At Yaxham the round tower has a first-floor chamber in which there is an iron-bound cupboard with a lock: the chamber is approached from a limestone vice, constructed inside the

round tower, which has three iron-bound doors, one at the foot of the
stairs and two at the top. Between the ceiling of the ringing chamber and
the floor of the bell-chamber at Rushford there is a windowless room,
ideal for the storage of valuables, whose existence would not be sus-
pected. The first-floor chamber at Deopham was also well suited for
storing valuables, having the security of stout doors at the top and bottom
of the vice, and a framed and locked cupboard for smaller items.

In the old ringing chamber at Deopham there is a window almost at
floor level, whose opening just below the pitch of the nave roof is closed
by a wooden shutter. Cautley describes this opening as a 'sanctus bell
window', and states that its purpose was to allow a ringer in the tower to
ring the appropriate bell at a critical moment during the celebration of the
Mass. The gymnastics necessary to do this at Deopham and at other
places would be considerable; and there seems to be no reason for ringing
the Sanctus bell from the first floor when the rope could more easily have
been pulled from the gallery below. Despite Cautley's identification of
many 'sanctus-bell windows', it is worth noting that they are often above
the level of a former ringers' gallery; and in some cases there is also a
bell-cote on the gable between the nave and chancel, where a sanctus bell
could be conveniently rung from a position close to the altar. It seems
much more likely that openings like the one at Deopham have been
converted from their original use, which was to give access between the
steeply-pitched outer roof of a nave and a plastered ceiling, as many still
do. Some (like that at Worstead) are clearly associated with the weather-
ing of a lower roof which shows inside the west end of a newer and loftier
nave with an open timber roof; while others have been left high and dry,
opening outside the tower onto the leaded covering of a newer roof with
lower pitch, such as that at Norwich St Andrew.

One of the perquisites of the Chamberlain of Norwich Cathedral priory
towards the end of the 14th century was the income from the church of St
Nicholas, which stood outside the city walls in Bracondale. Among the
receipts from the church are sums raised by selling pigeons which lived in
the tower.[10] The dovecote at St Nicholas has long gone, but the inside of
the tower at Buckenham Ferry still retains the nesting holes for pigeons.

A peculiarity of Norfolk churches is the so-called 'sound-hole': which
is a traceried opening, sometimes very large, at the level of the first-floor
chamber. The original purpose was to ventilate the tower by allowing
drying air to circulate up through the timbers of the bell-frame and out
through the sound-windows, thus preventing decay. These openings,
which have often been glazed when the upper room has been converted
to a ringing chamber, are better described as ventilators, since they only
serve as sound-windows when bells have been hung behind them in an
incomplete tower, or have been brought down from a higher bell-

---

[10] NRO DCN Chamberlain's rolls.

chamber. There is a great variety in the design of these windows, some of which are very intricately traceried; and they have been the subject of an interesting and unpublished study by Mr Tom Roast. Fashion can be the only explanation for this unusual treatment of ventilators, louvred or fretted window openings of the usual kind being found in towers in most other parts of the country.[11]

Because the documentary evidence has survived in quantity it is tempting to assume that bequests were the main source of funds for church fabric and ornaments, but it is clear that a wide variety of other resources were tapped. Very few records of individual giving have survived, although this was greatly encouraged in pre-Reformation times; but a parchment roll of donors among the muniments at Wymondham is of exceptional interest.[12] It was important in pre-Reformation times to have one's name regularly remembered in prayer at the altar after death, and an entry in the Bede roll would ensure this. Many interesting entries are recorded in the Wymondham roll which is headed: 'This wrightyng made the xxviij[th] day of Marche in the yer of our Lord God the Mlcccccxxiiij makyth and berith minde and recorde of the names of such persons as hathe been benefactors onto the parisshe church of Wymondham Whoose actes to the pleasure of God in the seid church be remaynyng for the Which actes Ihu reward ther sowlys in eternall blisse And for that ye shall pray.' Among the entries is a prayer 'for the soule of John Clifton, Knight that gave xx[ti] li. to the buyldyng of the stepyll' also for the soul of Robert Chapman who gave the 'forebell' before his death in 1500. Other instances where individuals found the money required to build a tower, or to provide bells are recorded more permanently. A number of bells have their donors' names inscribed on them; and it is not unusual to find carved inscriptions on towers (and, indeed, other parts of churches such as the porch at Garboldisham) recording gifts towards building work. The base course of the tower at West Tofts has the inscription: 'Alle the begyners of the werke Andro Hewke, John Rolffe, John Olyver and Amy hys wyf, Wylyam Olyver, Wylyam Rolff, John Roff, John Hewke, Robert Rolff Syr John Wyse Parson.' At North Lopham stones bearing the initials of sponsors were built into the tower walls as the work progressed.

In later mediaeval times responsibility for church fabric west of the chancel arch rested firmly with the parishioners, the Rector being involved only with the chancel. In spite of this firm division there were doubtless many instances where clergy, and the patrons who appointed them, showed an interest in the fabric of other parts of the church. The

11 T. R. Roast, B.A. Thesis 1975, North East Essex Technical College, *Sound Holes, a feature of Norfolk church towers*.
12 Examined in the Muniment Room at Wymondham Abbey by kind permission of Mr Wright, the Abbey Archivist.

North Lopham, stones in tower wall carved with benefactors' initials.
Photograph by the author.

Abbot of Westminster gave money towards a new bell-frame at Swaffham, where he was patron; and Norwich Cathedral Priory, as impropriate
Rector, subscribed to towers at Barford and Norwich St Peter Parmentergate, as well as to bells at St Etheldreda and St John Sepulchre in the city.
In most local instances, such donors were careful to put on record the fact
that theirs were gifts of goodwill rather than obligations. A much more
likely benefit to be derived by a parish church from association with
influential laity through patronage, or with an important monastic house
as impropriate rector, was in the possibility of being put in touch with
highly competent masons and designers. There is little doubt, for
example, that the parishioners of Hardley used the same designer and
masons for the reconstruction of the nave of their church at about the
same time as St Giles Hospital fulfilled its rectorial obligation to rebuild
the chancel.

The interest which parish gilds took in the church fabric can be readily
understood, because their main purpose concerned parishioners rather
than clergy. Gilds provided galleries in the towers at Worstead and

Cawston, and an inscription on a bell shows that it was provided by the Corpus Christi Gild at Oxborough for their parish church. The fund-raising activities of both the Plough Gild and the Gild of St Peter were directed towards the tower and bells at Swaffham; and we find the Gild of Our Lady contributing towards the purchase of a heavy bell to be added to the ring at Walsingham in 1539.

Excellent organisation of resources during a long building campaign is recorded in the *Black Book of Swaffham*, made by the order of John Botwright in his 19th year as Rector. The *Black Book*, begins with an account of the financial position of the church in 1454, prior to a major building campaign; and incorporates a bede-roll, to be read annually on Whitsunday at a requiem mass for departed benefactors. Early entries in the bede-roll refer to those who had given sums of money or materials to work on the 'old' church and steeple and later entries show that work on the 'new' church and steeple was well advanced by the 1480s. Prayers are bidden for Robert Payn (whose will was proved on 25 September 1487) 'which gaff a cope of whyth damask and did pathe the mid aley of the old chirche with marbyll and did also make a part of the old chirche with all the chargis from the nether crose alley to the stepil and the rode awtyr and the chapell of the trynyte and gaff xx tune of frestone to the stepull and also in money to the edyfyeng of the stepyll xx marcas'. The suggestion that the new work was prompted by the partial collapse of the old church is contained in a prayer 'for the sowles of Symond Blake, gentylman and Jane his wyffe which did expend in pathyng with marbyll of the crosse alley before the chaunsell dore in reparation of the Organs broken with the Falling of the Chirche with glasyng of a window in the clarestory and in findyng of a fremason to the makyng of the church by the space of a yere and in money geven to the makyng of the newe stepyll xl li'. During the last twenty years of the 15th century large sums of money were given towards building the new steeple, and gifts of free-stone and lime suggest that the work was proceeding.

The East Dereham churchwardens' accounts, too, give a valuable insight into fund-raising for building work. Parish rates were levied, and there were collections for the building fund at Sunday services. Almost all wills written before 1550 contained bequests to the church fabric fund, and the accounts show that individual bequests were often realised over a period of years. Gifts in money must have been more welcome to the churchwardens than other bequests which occur, when it was not uncommon for a testator to leave to the churchwardens the income from such debts as were owed to him at the time of his death; bequests of 'parish cows' (milking-cows to be hired out to parishioners for fixed rents) must have presented problems. In addition to direct gifts of money and materials, bequests, and a levy for burial inside the church; rent was drawn from farmland, sheepwalks, and houses surrounding the churchyard.

In the larger parishes there were many ways in which funds could be raised, but some of the smaller villages found things more difficult. At Horsford monies bequeathed to the tower are first recorded in 1447, but in 1493 the churchwardens obtained a licence from the Bishop to collect alms throughout the Diocese for a whole year to help pay for rebuilding the church and tower. Later accounts at Dereham show an interesting trend towards church ales as a source of income, and the instructions given in a Bressingham will of 1530 show clearly how this method of fund-raising worked worked in smaller places:

> I bequeath to the churche of Brissingham v combe of Whete and nyne combe of malt being paied by myn executors after this forme folowynge. That is to saye at Wyssondaye next folowynge after my buryall a combe of whete and seven bushelles of malte for to make a churche ale and the moneye that comethe thereof to go to the profighte of the churche to be at the Disposition of the towneshippe whereto it thynke most necessarye and so forthe every Wissondaie next folowinge after a combe of whete and seven busshells of malte till the five combe whete and the nyne combe malte be paied.

Similar activities were organised by the parish gilds, and some idea of the festivities may be gained from a will in which the Rector bequeaths to his parishioners at Wheatacre 'for them to occupie when they have nede att Plowalys (Church Ales organised by the Ploughmen's Gild) and other busynesse my Greate speite and that done to be kepyd in the churche until they have nede'. It is almost as difficult for us to imagine the church-ales and ox-roasts organised for church fabric funds – and probably taking place in the church and churchyard – in the 15th and 16th centuries as it would be for a Tudor churchwarden to forsee the flower festivals, sponsored cycle rides and coffee mornings of the late 20th century.

No complete building account is known to survive for a pre-Reformation church tower in Norfolk, but the earliest fabric records[13] at Norwich Cathedral give a few years' expenditure on the construction of the great detached tower which stood south-west of the Cathedral church. During the year ending at Michaelmas 1300 Northamptonshire limestone was purchased at Barnack and French limestone at Caen, 'sea coal' was bought, and a large sum spent on the work of digging foundations. By 1304 building was in progress, with more deliveries of limestone, and local flints called 'calyon'. Four great beams were carried from Yarmouth for the work. Hay was provided for the oxen which drew carts up from the staithe carrying building materials such as lime, and water for mixing mortar. A team of rough-masons handled the structural work, while specialists fashioned ten buttresses each 14 ft. tall; and French stone bought

---

13 NRO DCN Sacrist's Rolls.

in 1305 included ready-cut mouldings. The complicated ornamental carving of the eight round windows was done by John de Ramsey, the freemason who seems to have been responsible for the design and building of the tower. Construction took about 12 years, and a great bell named after Prior Henry de Lakenham was cast in 1311 to mark the completion of the work. The maximum annual expenditure recorded in the incomplete series of rolls was about £65, for a very massive square tower whose foundations were revealed by excavation in 1881. The much smaller tower of the Great Hospital, which still stands in Bishopgate, was built towards the end of the 14th century, when costs amounted to about £25 per year.

Many parallels for other towers may be drawn from the churchwardens' accounts at Swaffham, which record 'the payments which wher payed by the hands of John Oxburgh and John Newell church revys of Swaffham market to the workmen that went aboute the stepull', beginning in 1506. It is clear that the masonry of the lower part of the tower was completed at about the same time as the body of the church; and that the bell-stage of the tower was not built above the level of the church roof until some years later. The incomplete tower had a temporary roof of thatch, and the bells were hung in a thatched bell-house in the churchyard so that ringing could continue while the new tower was under construction. A similar bell-house remains in the churchyard at Wood Rising, where the bells were hung after the collapse of the tower, probably towards the end of the 16th century. The construction and roofing of the upper part of the Swaffham tower occupied five seasons of building; and when one considers the size of the tower, this compares well with the estimated time of ten years given in a contract of 1487/1488 for the construction of the 60 ft high tower at Helmingham. As at Helmingham, the Swaffham churchwardens had provided a timber-framed and thatched lodge in the churchyard for the masons' use, as well as the necessary materials and building equipment for the work.

Equipment bought at the beginning of the work included baskets, shovels and smaller tools; and hurdles for scaffolding were secured to alder poles using 'bast' rope made from the fibres of lime bark. The lifting gear provided at Swaffham probably resembled the early windlass which remains in the tower at Deopham, where it was left after building work was completed. This windlass consists of a cylindrical roller mounted at one end in the tower wall, and at the other end in a stout vertical post; the cable would have passed over a pulley wheel high in the centre of the tower. The mechanical advantage of the machine would be about 1:10, allowing considerable weights to be lifted through the central traps in the tower floors. The Deopham lifting gear has much in common with the mediaeval windlasses in the towers at Salisbury Cathedral, Peterborough Cathedral and Tewkesbury Abbey; and the arrangement of the mortises for the spokes of the hand-wheel is said to indicate a date before the 16th century, from which early period very few examples survive. There is a hand-wheel at Louth, Lincolnshire which probably dates from the 16th century, and a small one has recently been removed from the tower at Poringland.

Limestone for facing Swaffham tower was brought to Brandon by river, unloaded there and carted by road to Swaffham; and each season's building work was concluded by thatching the new masonry. A contract was made for the timber framing of the tower roof in 1508, and finishing touches are suggested by the purchase of a pattern for a weathercock from a carver. The building season ending in Advent 1510 was the most costly of all, when large quantities of lead were purchased at Brandon, and moulds were made for casting the sheets to cover the roof. The top of the steeple was crowned with a leaded lantern, the timber structure of which was brought to Swaffham from Shipdham; and the payment for the lead-work of the lantern, made on the feast of St Peter-ad-Vincula (1 August) 1511, marks the completion of the structural work. The Helmingham contract stipulates that bells should not be hung until four years after building work was complete, and similar caution prevailed at Swaffham where no bells were hung until the tower had been allowed to settle for at least six years. Timber for the new bell-frame was collected in the spring of 1514, and the contract for making it was completed in August 1516. The bells had been removed from their temporary accommodation by 1517, when John Owold paid the sum of 16d. for the 'old bellehowse and the frame', and the 'steeple window' (doubtless the great west window) was glazed in the same year: the tower works must have been considered virtually complete in 1519 when the sum of 5s. 9d. was 'Receyvyd of Petur Gannock for the masonys loge that stode in the churchyard and for odther olde tymber'. A new bell weighing 28 cwt 12 lb was bought from Thomas Church of Bury St Edmunds, bringing the total number to five, and the accounts record the hallowing of the bells in the new tower between 1519 and 1521. The tower had been left unfinished in 1511, and it was not until twenty years later that a freemason was employed to complete the design by building a parapet from materials provided locally.

The Swaffham accounts allow the progress of the work to be followed in detail, and the wage bill – totalling £1. 04s. 00½d. – for a typical week during building works is of some interest:

Gyles the freemason and his apprentice	4s	
Antell the freemason and his servant	5s	
Simon Coo's wife for boarding the freemasons	3s	4d
Nicholas the mason	2s	3d
Nicholas Mason for his servant's work	1s	8d
Robert Meke, labourer 4½ days	1s	3½d
Richard Newell, labourer 4½ days	1s	3½d
Robert Honyngham, labourer 4 days	1s	2d

Richard Newman, labourer 4½ days	1s 3½d
Jaffery Bryan for 4½ days	1s 1½d
John Smyth, labourer 4½ days	1s 1½d
John Bryan, clerke, 2 days	6d

Gyles the Freemason, who was paid 12d. 'for hys costys and hys reward whan he cam to see the warke' and a further 10d. 'for his labour rydyng to Norwich to speke to a nodther mason', seems to have been in charge of the work on site; but Antell was receiving higher wages, probably for specialist work on window traceries and other limestone refinements. Nicholas was probably a rough mason in charge of the flintwork. In contrast to the commonly presented image of scores of masons swarming over the scaffolding (and almost certainly getting in each other's way), the Swaffham accounts suggest that the work-force varied little from the total of three masons with their servants, six labourers and a clerk of the works.

In many Norfolk towers there is structural and documentary evidence for building campaigns which extended over long periods. Lack of money must have been the most common cause of delay, and a Hackford testator in 1523 sounds resigned to the fact that work had probably been going on intermittently throughout his lifetime when he leaves 'to the reparation of the steple off the sam church iij s. iiij d. to be payd when hit shall fortune to have workmen there upon to Edifye it': the earliest bequest to the work was made in 1470. The great tower at Redenhall, which is comparable in size to the Swaffham tower, was called 'new' in wills of 1469, and was still under construction in 1498. A new tenor bell was cast in 1514, and the parapet is dated c.1518 by the rebus of the then Rector. A small tower at Carleton St Peter was described as 'new' in wills of 1503 and seems to have been built to the level of the nave roof when the church was hallowed in 1517; a distinct change in materials and details, as well as bequests through to 1537, show that a second campaign was needed to complete it.

The more recent building accounts for the brick tower at Denton give some idea of the time taken when building went on in consecutive years. The ground was cleared in 1702, and the foundations laid in the following year: six seasons of building are recorded in the extant accounts, and the tower was complete by 1714. It would appear that if funds and materials were available a typical village church tower, say 50 feet high and 10 feet square, could be completed in eight to ten years; while the building of a small additional stage to an existing tower might be accomplished in one or two seasons.

Similarity of design suggests a common source of inspiration for many groups of late 14th-century and 15th-century towers in Norfolk. In some cases this is due to direct imitation of existing examples or copying of

details, as directed in the contracts for both Walberswick and Helmingham towers in Suffolk. So few early building accounts survive for Norfolk
churches that it is impossible to give any account of the work of individual masons and designers; but it is important to question the commonly-
held assumption that much of the splendid building work seen in our
churches was accomplished by simple and unlettered craftsmen, building
solely by inspiration. There are many hints of well-established schools of
masons at Norwich and Lynn,[14] led by distinguished and widely-
travelled master craftsmen of high social standing.

John de Ramsey, who was in charge of building the clocher at Norwich
Cathedral Priory, was one of a family who worked at Ely and Lichfield
cathedrals, as well as at St Stephen's Chapel, Westminster and St Paul's
Cathedral in London. We find references in the Norwich Cathedral ac-
counts to parchment designs for window traceries being brought from
London; and one William de Ramsey was chief surveyor of the King's
Works by 1336. Another distinguished Westminster mason whose name
appears in Norwich documents is Robert Wodehirst, to whom the design
of the eastern clerestory at Norwich Cathedral is attributed, as well as the
fine churches at Swanton Morley and Norwich St Gregory. John and
James Woderove, brothers and freemasons, seem to have come first to
Norwich in 1415–16 (when they were admitted as freemen of the city) and
to have worked on the cloisters at the Cathedral Priory for a number of
years: at Michaelmas 1421 they each received a robe from the communar,
and their contract for vaulting three bays of the west cloister was completed in 1422. In 1428 James Woderove is named as 'Master of the Works
of the Great Cloister', and his salary of 4s. per week is the same as his
brother's: the fact that their recorded work for the Priory occupied only 12
weeks of that year suggests that they were also well-employed in other
places. James Woderove was probably employed by the Priory on a fairly
continuous basis, although he almost certainly did a great deal of other
work in his own right, and the accounts suggest that he was paid a
retaining fee as a consultant when there was no major work in progress.
Less is known about John Woderove than about his brother, almost certainly because the patrons for whom he worked have not left documents
in the quantities which survive among the Cathedral muniments. From
his will, written in 1442 and proved in 1443, we learn that he had 'land,
pastures, messuages, dove-houses and rents' in Bracondale, Trowse and
Carrow; and that he elected to buried in the parish church of St James,
Carrow. In his will he left sums of money 'to the repair and emendation'
of Norwich, St Peter Mancroft (13s. 4d.), Norwich, St John Maddermarket
(10s.) and Brisley (20s.), and it is possible that he worked at these three
apparently unrelated churches. The Priory accounts show that the Wo-
deroves not only supplied quantities of stone for building works at the

<hr>

[14] J. Harvey, *English Mediaeval Architects*, Gloucester, 1984, *passim*.

Cathedral, and for dependent churches such as Wighton, but also had a stock of masons' equipment independent of the works at the Priory, to which James Woderove gave a stone-saw in 1444. James Woderove was a mason of sufficient distinction to be summoned, with John Jakes, to Eton College in 1449, where King Henry VI's Master Mason seems to have required their specialist advice; and the offerings made to the Cathedral on behalf of his brother's soul show that James Woderove was a wealthy and successful man by the time of his death in 1453. It is very probable that most masons and designers had extensive practices, supplying designs as well as prefabricated details for a wide variety of churches and other buildings.

At a later date we find further evidence of the existence of a well-organised network of craftsmen in Norfolk and beyond. Although the name of Gyles, the mason mentioned at the start of the work at Swaffham in 1507, has not been found elsewhere, at least two of the freemasons mentioned in the accounts have been tentatively identified in other places. Robert Antell's name appears in the fabric accounts for various departments at Norwich Cathedral Priory, as well as at King's College Cambridge in 1508, and there is mention of a Robert Cobb in various accounts at Cambridge from 1508 through to 1537. Other contacts with masons and designers from further afield would have been inevitable when Norwich masons were impressed for official building projects, such as those who 'accordyng to the kyngs comyssion were taken up to my lorde Cardynalls works at York place at Westminster' in 1528.[15] Comparison of the design of the fine church at New Buckenham with the contemporary north aisle at Wymondham Abbey suggests common inspiration; with very similar window traceries and mouldings. It is interesting to find confirmation of this association in a Wymondham building account which shows that, during the course of building work limestone was sent to New Buckenham, presumably for the attention of a specialist carver at work on the church there.[16] Much research on this fascinating theme is needed, but sufficient information has been recovered to establish that the well-defined characteristics of pre-Reformation Norfolk churches and their towers stem from the involvement of highly competent and well-travelled architects, bringing in ideas from other parts of the country, and interpreting them in the context of locally available building materials.

It is worth remarking on the scarcity of post-Reformation church towers in Norfolk, as well as on those whose pre-Reformation designs were never finished. A few towers such as Toftrees, which were begun in fine style during the 16th century, remain incomplete; as do towers at Stratton

[15] NRO NCR Case 16a, Mayor's Court Book 1510–1532.
[16] Accounts of the Gild of Our Lady's Light, Wymondham, in the Abbey Muniment Room.

Strawless and Salhouse, which were started during the first half of the
15th century. At Stalham a massive tower was begun c.1498, when there
was a bequest to the parishioners who were about to begin the work of
the steeple; despite further bequests through to 1533, the tower barely
rises above the pitch of the nave roof. The lowest stages of the towers at
Kimberley, Wood Norton and Morley St Peter date from the 1530s, but the
bell-chambers are much later and in a different idiom. Scarning tower was
probably finished in the 1550s, but the contemporary tower at Felmingham lacks its parapet. Perhaps the last Perpendicular tower to be built in
Norfolk was that at Norwich St Stephen, referred to as 'new' in the 1540s
and receiving its finishing touches c.1600.

A number of brick towers were built in the 17th and 18th centuries to
replace earlier towers which had fallen; and one of the most interesting
cases of post-Reformation tower-building is at Denton.[17] A large part of
the round tower had collapsed before an Archdeacon's visitation in 1692,
and a Faculty petition was filed in 1698 as follows:

> The humble petition of the Inhabitants of Denton in the County
> of Norfolk Sheweth unto your Lordship that the church of the
> said parish being greatly out of Repair the churchwardens of the
> same parish (of Denton) have lately ratified the same to be re-
> paired in a decent and convenient manner the charge whereof
> amounteth to about forty pounds and that the steeple belonging
> to the said parish church wherein three bells did hang many years
> since fell down and the Inhabitants of the said parish have not bin
> able to rebuild the same wherefore the said bells have laid use-
> lesse in the said parish church ever since. That your petitioners
> are very desirous to erect a Shudd in the Churchyard to hang one
> bell therein for the conveniency of the parishioners of the said
> parish; but your petitioners and the rest of the inhabitants of the
> said parish are not in a condition able to pay the charge hereof
> and of the repairs [manuscript illegible] said church. Wherefore
> your petitioners crave that your Lordship will be pleased to grant
> unto the Inhabitants of the said parish your Lordships licence to
> erect a Shudd or building in the Churchyard of the said parish
> church fit and convenient to hang the largest bell for the conveni-
> ency of the Inhabitants of the said parish And to make sale of the
> other twoe bells and to dispose of the moneys for and towards
> the repaire of the said parish church and erecting the said shudd
> and hanging the said bell.

The Bishop set up a Commission whose shrewd Articles of Enquiry reveal
his Lordship's suspicion that the inhabitants were not as poor as the
Petition suggested: 'Are not the parishioners of Denton or the greater part
of them landowners . . . and of what yearly values are the same', 'Is not

---

[17] NRO FCP/1, now fragile and not produced for inspection.

Norwich, St Stephen, post-Reformation tower completed c.1601.
Lithograph by J. Sillett, c.1820.

Denton lookt upon to be a rich town and well able to pay and keep in good repair the Parish Church and Steeple without any extraordinary help.' In the depositions taken at Denton on 25 October, 1698 we learn that 'the Inhabitants say that they are of a middle sort and as other towns near, As to the Farmers they say the same thing of them viz. that they are of the Middle sort'. Mr Rogerson, the Rector of Denton, thought differently: 'both his Owners and Farmers in Denton are very substantial persons above the Common rank of his Neighbours parishes.' In a letter of 14 November, 1698 the Rector suggested to the Bishop that the inhabitants' reported valuations fell far short of the truth, and submits revised figures, as well as his perception of their unwillingness to pay up: 'All of them [the petitioners] save 3 families are dissenters and wholly of the Barne congregation, which their meeting Barne house thay have ordered and seated in or about the middle of the parish which design undoubtedly to take the people off from church: To the manner of which their Barne and speakers thereat and their provision for them they are rich enough needlessly and without Law [*manuscript defective*] to be about £50 charge per annum: as it is said and believed; but very poor presently when they are to pay anything to the maintenance of the church to which, by law obliged, they being universally rather willing to see it laid flat to the ground than be at any charge for repairs thereof.' The Dissenters were eventually persuaded to pay their rates, and the tower was repaired in a most economical way by building a rectangular brick extension onto the remaining semi-circular part of the tower. The Bishop had ordered that the rebuilt tower should rise above the ridge of the church roof, and Ladbroke's lithograph shows that it was built no higher than it need be; it was, however, good enough to contain the three fine bells which remain.

Other towers (mainly of brick), which were cheaply built to hold a small number of bells, are found at Hoveton St Peter (1623), Carleton Forehoe (1712), Hempstead by Holt (1744) and Great Moulton (1762). The vernacular design of these towers sets tham apart from more distinguished work at North Runcton (c.1703–1713), and St George's, Yarmouth (1714–1716); and is in distinct contrast to the efforts of 15th- and early 16th-century builders.

None of the above towers is very suitable for bells to be hung for changeringing; and only a handful of post-Reformation towers can be identified which were rebuilt or drastically adapted specifically for that purpose.[18] The work of 1608–1609 at Ketteringham is well-documented, when the collapse of the old tower was an excuse for rebuilding, and increasing the bells from three to five; and it would appear that Aldeby tower was rebuilt in 1633 to contain a ring of four bells. There is no doubt

18 See A. Woodger, 'Post-Reformation Mixed Gothic in Huntingdonshire church towers and its campanalogical associations', *Archaeological Journal*, Vol. 141, 1984. pp. 269–308. Mr Woodger suggests that over half of the church towers in Huntingdonshire show evidence of drastic modification in response to the rising interest in changeringing, which 'stimulated many more parish authorities into redesigning and rebuilding their old church towers than has been generally recognised.' He uses 'Mixed Gothic' features (such as Decorated style or 'Y' window traceries found together with more obviously Perpendicular designs) to identify many of the suggested post-Reformation towers. Reviewing the article in *Norfolk Archaeological Research Group News*, No. 45, 1986. Mr Edwin Rose states that Mr Woodger's findings 'are equally applicable to Norfolk': a surprising statement which is adequately disposed of by Dr Simon Cotton in his article 'Mixed up Gothic?', *Norfolk Archaeological Research Group News*, No. 53, 1988. The present writer can only confirm from his inspections of about half Norfolk's church towers that there is evidence to support post-Reformation reconstruction in only a handful of towers; and no strong trend towards building towers specially for changeringing. We are fortunate to have so much documentary evidence in Norfolk for pre-Reformation tower building, which, since Mr Woodger does not advance it, presumably does not exist for Huntingdonshire churches.

Thurgarton, temporary belfry constructed above the porch in 1671.
Etching by J. S. Cotman, 1817.

that the tower at Litcham (1669) was designed for a ring of five bells; and the excellent tower at Yelverton (c.1672), like St Augustine's Norwich (c.1683), has a contemporary five-bell frame which still contains only three bells. Perhaps the most obvious example of a tower which was designed for a heavy ring of bells is at St Peter's church, Thetford, where the ruinous old tower gave way to a fine new one in 1789.

There are very few completely 19th-century churches in Norfolk; and apart from Booton and Framingham Pigot, no Victorian towers which are distinguished by the originality of their designs. At Brettenham, Holkham and East Raynham there are good towers built in the local architectural tradition; but those at Brockdish, Norwich, Holy Trinity Heigham and Thorpe Episcopi, although large, are unexciting. Unlike so many modern church towers, Norfolk's most recent, at Wighton (1974), was designed to carry a changeringing six of reasonable weight.

Chapter Three

BELL-FRAMES AND BELL FITTINGS

The counties of Norfolk and Suffolk are particularly rich in carpentry and joinery dating from the years between 1300 and 1500. Norwich, it should be remembered, was one of the wealthiest towns in England during the Middle Ages, and wills written by inhabitants of many of the smaller towns and villages show that they too shared in the general prosperity. A proportion of the wealth derived from trade, particularly in wool and its products, was spent on building and adorning the parish churches; and it is now hard to imagine the earlier importance of weaving towns such as Lavenham, Kersey and Long Melford in Suffolk, or Cawston, Pulham and Worstead in Norfolk, which are now off the beaten track but whose large churches are out of all proportion to their 20th-century status. There are no longer important fairs or markets at small towns like Hingham, Foulsham, Docking and New Buckenham, where impressive churches dominate empty 'plains' and 'fairlands', which were once full of traders.

It is no coincidence that Norfolk and Suffolk feature so prominently in books concerned with mediaeval woodwork in churches;[1] and a Norfolk carpenter made the splendid choirstalls at Winchester cathedral around 1310.[2] There are still many ancient rood-screens, font covers and benches in local parish churches; and roofs such as Knapton, Trunch and Cawston, whose timbers were meant to be seen from inside the churches, have

The chapter deals with bell-frames and fittings in Norfolk and makes no attempt to put them into a wider context. So little has been published that it is hard to make comparisons. As in chapter 2, full references to most of the text of this chapter will be found in my thesis, London 1985 (abbreviated to: Thesis); dates for church towers, and by inference contemporary frames, have been published in P. Cattermole and S. Cotton, 'Mediaeval parish church building in Norfolk', *Norfolk Archaeology*, 1983 (abbreviated to: C&C). Particular thanks are recorded to Mr C. J. N. Dalton, Dr J. C. Eisel and Mr G. P. Elphick for reading the draft of this chapter and making many helpful suggestions.

[1] R. Brandon and J. A. Brandon, *Open timber roofs of the Middle Ages*, 1849. F. Bond, *Gothic architecture in England*, 1905. F. Bond, *Screens and galleries in English churches*, 1908. F. E. Howard and F. H. Crossley, *English church woodwork*, 1933.
[2] S. Jervis, *Woodwork of Winchester Cathedral*, Winchester, 1976, p. 19.

carved decoration of the highest quality, matching the sophistication of their engineering. Much of this early woodwork remains because it was well-made by talented craftsmen at a time when the prosperity of East Anglia was matched by the natural resources of the oak woods; and it has survived because the region was comparatively poor after the middle of the 18th century. Whilst a relatively large number of early timber bell-frames remains in Norfolk church towers, they have not attracted a great deal of study, largely because they are so difficult to get at. Excellent qualities of design and craftsmanship are seen in bell-frames such as those at South Creake and Wolferton; while long years of patching and minor repair have preserved frames such as those at Fritton and Tibenham, where bells are still rung in full circles. Bell-gear, being relatively fragile and subjected to constant wear and tear, has not survived in great quantity from the same period; but a few examples remain to give some idea of the fittings and furnishings of bell-chambers during the Middle Ages. The way in which bell-frames and bell-gear evolved during the 15th century reflects the developing style of bell-ringing;[3] and suggests the period when bells in Norfolk churches were first rung in full-circles.

[3] See J. C. Eisel, 'Developments in bellhanging', *Change ringing, the history of an English art*, 1987 for a brief account of the wider context. Dr Eisel considers that some characteristics of early bell-frames are peculiarly East Anglian developments; but the writer wonders whether it might not simply be the case that older frames in other regions have not survived in such quantity as they have in East Anglia. The only important study of frames in a particular locality so far published is G. P. Elphick, 'Sussex bell-frames', *Sussex Archaeological Collections*, Vol 84, 1945: later writers have relied to a large extent on this, and on Elphick's chapter in *Sussex Bells and belfries*, 1970. The present writer has been interested to compare the development of frames in Sussex and Norfolk, but disagrees with Mr Elphick's proposition that 'carpenters thought that a curved brace would direct a horizontal force into a vertical direction' (*op. cit.* 1945, p. 47), preferring to suggest that curved braces were used to get better joints with the king-posts and bottom cills. Simple bell-frames such as those illustrated at Lynchmere and Newhaven in Sussex may be compared with frames at Bixley and East Carleton in Norfolk, types which occur at all dates. King-post frames seem to have been made much later as a general rule in Sussex than in Norfolk, where examples later than c.1600 are the exception. The frame at Westfield in Sussex (*op. cit.* 1945, pl. XII), which has curved braces to king-posts, would have been old-fashioned in Norfolk by 1617; but the foundation timbers, jointed at a single level, would have been up-to-date. Angled braces were used in Norfolk for trusses and end frames long before those at Botolphs (*op. cit.* 1945, pl. XIX); but the important absentee from the Sussex frames is the 'scissors-braced' truss, seen in Norfolk from the late 14th century onwards. It is easy to see how this design developed by omitting the 'scissors' below the main braces, eventually producing trusses of types 'V' and 'W' (*op. cit.* 1945, p. 54), which were eminently suitable for bells rung in full circles. Trusses of this type with straight braces seem to have become the general rule in Norfolk around

It would be fascinating to discover how bell-ringing developed from its earliest days through to the beginnings of scientific changeringing in the 17th century, especially if this could be done by relating contemporary documents to what can be seen in church towers. J. C. Cox's book *Church-wardens' Accounts* (London, 1913) lists about 100 churches where documents survive in greater or lesser degree from the years before 1550; and the accounts for East Dereham, dating from 1402 but sadly incomplete, are the earliest surviving local records which give some idea of the basic equipment of a mediaeval bell-chamber. Accounts from a few other churches,[4] especially those at Swaffham and Shipdham which begin early

---

the beginning of the 17th century, perhaps 80 years earlier than in Sussex (*op. cit.* 1945, p. 47). Another important difference is the popularity of 'hollow-square' frames in Norfolk in the 15th century, as against the single 18th-century example in Sussex (*op. cit.* 1970, p. 235). The methods of dating by tree-ring analysis used by Mr Elphick are probably more accurate than the writer's use of documentary evidence for tower-building; but it does seem that developments in Norfolk were ahead of those in Sussex.

4   The few early sets of Norfolk churchwardens' accounts known to the writer are:

DENTON, (1505–1539): NRO PD 136/56.

EAST DEREHAM, (1402–1471): NRO Phillips MS 40,973, Box 5; and (1478–1498). NRO P 182 D.

NORTH ELMHAM, (1539–1577): Published: A. G. Legge, *The ancient church-wardens' accounts of the parish of North Elmham from A.D. 1539 to A.D. 1577 with descriptive notes and a glossary*, Norwich, 1891.

EAST HARLING, (from 1450): NRO Frere MS, Giltcross Hundred, East Harling Bundle. The entry in the Frere Mss is as follows: 'East Harling Church. A Manuscript in the hands of Thomas Tanner D. D. Chaunceller of Norwich 1721 begins with the Churchwardens accounts of the year 1450. Bells new in the year 1465. Gathering through the town on Plough Monday 1510 gathered 4 sol. The book ends 1638. 1450 steeple finished.' A notice by Extraneus (1863) on Church Ales quotes from the 1452 acounts and states that these were copies from Tanner's Mss. See 'Church Ales and Interludes', *The East Anglian*, Lowestoft, 1863, vol. 1, 383. Correspondence with the Bodleian Library, and the British Library has failed to discover the whereabouts of the documents.

SHIPDHAM, (1511–1566): NRO PD 337/85.

SNETTISHAM, (1468–1684): NRO PD 24/1.

SWAFFHAM, (1505–1595): NRO PD 52/71.

TILNEY ALL SAINTS, (1443–1589). Published: A. D. Stallard, *The transcript of the churchwardens' accounts of the parish of Tilney All Saints, Norfolk, 1443–1589*, London, 1922.

GREAT WITCHINGHAM, (1528–1637): NRO BOL 93.

GREAT YARMOUTH, (15th century), a very few extracts are transcribed in Chancellor Tanner's Index to the Institution Books of the Bishops of Norwich. NRO Norwich Diocesan Records, REG/30–31. Further short extracts appear in ms. *Notitia Ecclesiastica* ff. 213, 214, 218, 219. NRO DCN 226A.

in the 16th century, add something to the picture; but there is no large documentary resource for this early period in Norfolk. One finds in churchwardens' accounts of most periods a constant succession of minor repairs to the bell-gear – which includes wheels, ironwork and clappers; while more significant items, such as recasting broken bells and rehanging them, are often recorded in detail.[5] We need to look among these

---

The Sacrist's rolls of Norwich Cathedral Priory (at NRO and indexed by date) contain a very large number of references to the regular maintenance of the bells in both towers there. New clappers seem to have been very expensive: in 1403–1404 it cost 22s. 6d. for a clapper for 'Stockton' and 29s. 10½d. for one for 'Lakenham'. A new 'soller' made in the central tower between 1405 and 1407 is interesting because the mortises in the stonework for its joists remain; and it was clearly the floor on which the 18th century ringers of the cathedral bells stood. As originally conceived, the first floor of the central tower was immediately below the bells, leaving an open lantern to flood the crossing with light. The bells must have been rung using very long ropes, and therefore not swung so high as to be difficult to control. It is interesting to surmise whether the new floor was installed to make a more vigorous style of ringing possible. When the bells were trussed in 1421–1422 a smith was paid for 'Wyndding bondes and nayle', suggesting that nailed straps were used to secure the bells to their headstocks; but a more advanced method of bell-hanging is suggested a few years later, when the accounts for 1439–1440 record major work in both towers. This work begins with the sale of *'antiquo meremio videlicet confractis bellestokkes.'* The account provides an early reference to bell-wheels, and it is clear that cast bronze bolsters were used to support the cannons of the bells. Gudgeons are mentioned among the ironwork, and the 'keyes' are presumably to secure slotted bolts: *'Item Stephano carpenter' pro nove suspensione stokkyng et Whelyng campanarum in le clocher, et campanili in choro, in grosso ad proprios sumptus preter vesturam vj li. xiij s. iiij d. In bolstris ereis noviter fusis pro eisdem campanis xxj s. iij d. In novis ferramentis pro eisdem campanis videlicet Keyes boltes goiones et clavis cviij s. viij d.'*

[5]   Thomas Wryght, who was frequently employed to work on the Dereham bells, seems to have taken a bell down, and rehung it when it returned in 1488, after new casting by John Baly at the Norwich foundry owned by Richard Brasyer: *'Et solutis Thome Wryght pro depositione tertie campane vj d. Et solutis in potationibus diversarum personarum apud iuvans iij d. Et solutis Roberto Boleyn emisso usque Norwic' ad loquendum cum Richardo Brasyer et suis expensis et labore viij d. Et solutis pro expensis Richardi Brasyer apud Derham una cum regardo dato servienti ipsius Richardi Brasyer xv d. Et solutis Johanni Baly de Norwico pro effusione dicte campane iij li. vj s. viij d. Et solutis in expensis et regardis datis ibidem tribus temporibus ij s. iiij d. Et solutis pro labore dictorum prepositorum existentium eodem tempore ij s. Et solutis Roberto Deye pro cariagio et recariagio dicte campane v s. Et solutis Thome Wryghte pro le stockyng et le wyndyngup eiusdem iij s. iiij d. Et solutis Richardo Newman pro factione unius le coler ad le stok ac reparatione de lez boltes et Feder lockez cum clavibus emptis ad idem opus xxj d. Et solutis Willelmo Jeckys et Richardo Style emissis versus Norwicum ad interloquendum cum prefato Richardo*

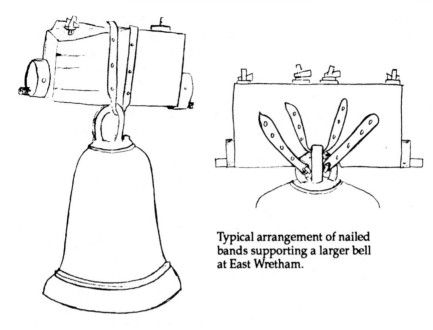

Typical arrangement of nailed
bands supporting a larger bell
at East Wretham.

Small 13th-century bell at Snettisham,
secured by nailed bands through
cannons.

references for some indication of how bells were furnished and rung; and
it would be foolish to expect a uniform approach in a county where there
were – and are – churches in so many parishes of widely differing importance and wealth. Although the written evidence relating to early bell-
frames and bell-hanging has to be gleaned from very few sources, making
it difficult to be absolutely certain what was going on, there are strong
indications that in some towers the bells were being rung in full circles by
the end of the 15th century.

Almost every bell cast before the end of the 19th century had specially
designed loops (called 'cannons') cast onto its head, through which iron
hooks were passed to secure it to a timber headstock. One early method of
fixing the ironwork to the timber was to beat the ends into flat straps,
which were then nailed to the sides of the headstock, and a few bells

*Brasyer et Johanne Baly xvj d. Et solutis in expensis tribus temporibus vj d. Et solutis
Johanne Pylche pro scriptione unius obligationis et unius indenture concernentium
dicte campane iij d.'*

secured solely by nailed straps are still found in Norfolk churches (Snettisham sanctus bell and the 15th-century bell at East Wretham, for example). Seasonal shrinkage and expansion of the timber made it impossible to keep bells tight on their headstocks, and when bells were swung vigorously there was a real danger of loose ironwork giving way. The very first item in the 1402 churchwardens' accounts at East Dereham is 'payd for the trussyng of the lytyl belle xvj d.'; and the accounts for 1462 show that when Thomas Bradlee charged 5s. 4d. for hanging a new bell at Dereham, the irons costing 10d. were called *ligatura ferrea*, suggesting straps or bindings rather than bolts. The regular 'trussing' of the bells, which always required a large number of nails for securing the ironwork, usually cost between 2d. and 10d. each time.

A rather different method of fixing is suggested a few years later when Thomas Bradlee was paid a relatively large sum for about one week's work at Dereham: '*Item pro farsatura campanarum solutis Thome Bradlee ac etiam pro faccione de le kevelys – v s. Item in comensali ipsius Thome et suis servientis solutis Richardo Westhaghe – ij s. j d.*' According to Latham[6] '*farsatura*' means 'bolstering'; and the *Oxford English Dictionary* gives 'bolsters' as horizontal straps or pads for giving support, 'kevelys' are defined as pins or hasps for fastening, while a 'forelock' is a wedge thrust through a hole in the end of a bolt in order to keep it in place. Forelocks duly appeared in 1468 when bells were tightened up on their headstocks: '*Item paid for trussyng and mendyng of the ij lesse bell in the clocher for nayle and forlockys to the same – viij d.*' These entries in the East Dereham accounts appear to record the use of slotted bolts secured by small wedges (forelocks or kevels) to fasten the cannons.

Similar arrangements are recorded when the Swaffham tenor was quarter-turned in 1542. The hanging-irons are clearly defined: '*Item paid for xxiij pownde of yerne and the warkmanschypp therof that ys for to seye ij clampys ij payre of scherys with bowlsters and forlokkys belongyng therto – vij s. iiij d.*' It appears that the bolsters were iron bars through the double cannons, the clamps were iron bridging pieces placed across the headstock, and the assembly was connected by two pairs of metal straps at an angle (*O.E.D.* 'shears'), secured by wedges through slots at their top ends. They were also using bolts with forelocks at Snettisham after c.1470, and at Shipdham after c.1513.

A common 17th-century method of hanging a bell was to provide the main support by using wedged shear bolts which were attached to bolsters through the double cannons as decribed above; while additional support came from nailed bands through the single cannons. Ironwork of this type was often re-used or copied when bells were rehung in Norfolk towers, and there are good examples at Tittleshall and Swainsthorpe. One 17th-century bell at Topcroft has sophisticated wedged ironwork with no

[6] R. E. Latham, *Revised mediaeval Latin word list*, 1965.

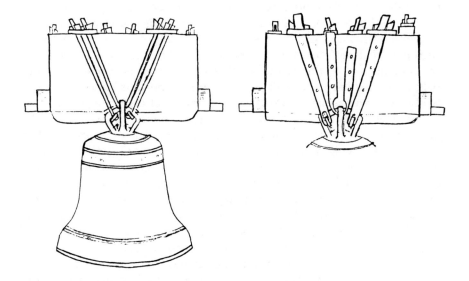

Bell-irons at Topcroft, showing (left) seventeenth-century cannon straps secured by wedged bolts at their heads; another set of irons (right) has been converted from older nailed bands.

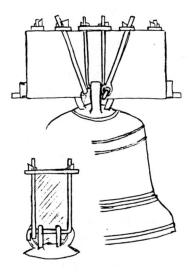

Seventeenth-century interlocking ironwork supporting a bell at South Acre.

nailed bands, while another set of similar irons has been converted from older nailed bands. A rather curious form of wedged ironwork is found on pre-Reformation bells at South Acre and West Newton, where one of each pair of shear bolts is bent to pass under the headstock and through the cannons, connecting with the other bolt by a hook. Almost all early bells examined have a 'U' bolt passing through the argent and secured by wedges driven against a plate or washers on top of the headstock. As late as 1668 Duckworth[7] found it necessary to recommend that bells should be fastened with 'Keys at the top of the Stock, and not with plates nailed to the sides', showing that bell-hanging was still a very primitive science, and that East Anglian advances were by no means universal. It is clear from entries such as that at Swaffham in 1587 that a great deal of prepara-tion was needed before any special ringing: 'Item paid to John Brewer for iij days worke abought the bells at the coronatyon with ij d. in nayles – iij s.' It was not until the advent of threaded bolts and nuts at about the beginning of the 18th century that steeplekeeping became less of a full-time job.[8] Entries for 'trussing' and 'bolstering' bells in churchwardens' accounts suggest that many bells were supported solely by nailed bands, others by wedged bolts, and some by a mixture of the two, right through to the 19th century.

The axles fitted to the headstock which enable the bell to be swung are usually referred to in old accounts – and at the present time – as 'gud-geons'. On smaller bells these were sometimes driven into holes drilled in the end-grain of the headstock, but on larger bells the gudgeons were more often recessed into the bottom surface of the headstock, and secured there by tail-bolts. The new 'coler ad le stok' supplied at East Dereham in 1488 was probably an iron hoop which was heated and shrunk over the end of the stock to secure the gudgeon pin and prevent the end-grain of the headstock from splitting: a similar arrangement is suggested at Swaff-ham in 1575 when 6s. 8d. was paid 'for vij li. of yearne for weggs and rynges for the great bell'. Gudgeons were known to work loose, and the 'hyrne wegghys' bought at Snettisham in 1486 may likewise have been used to prevent the gudgeons from moving in the headstocks, as they were at North Elmham in 1565. The gudgeons rotated in heavy 'brasses',

[7]   *Tintinnalogia, or the art of ringing*, 1668, reprinted 1970, p. 136.
[8]   Thomas Newman used wedged bolts for hanging the bells at Ashwellthorpe in 1707, but screwed bolts with nuts to clasp the wheels. The earliest dated use of screwed and nutted bolts for heavier duties so far discovered by the writer is at Field Dalling, where Thomas Gardiner hung a new five in 1750: and the black-smith left behind a large spanner for the square nuts. The churchwardens at Stratton St Mary paid the blacksmith 1s. 6d. for '2 staples and skrew for the bells' in 1794 (NRO PD 122/33). Wedged bolts were used at Winfarthing in 1684 when the sum of 2s. 6d. was spent on '10 small bolts to clasp the wheels together with shears and collars' (NRO PD 78/47) while larger 'Bolts and sheres' cost 19s. for the bells at Dickleburgh in 1740 (Accounts at the church).

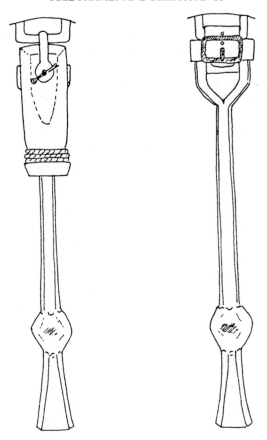

Busk-boarded clapper *c.*1600 at Illington (left); and
earlier form with buckled leather baldrick.

the name commonly given to the bearings which were sunk into the top
members of the bell-frame; and there are frequent references to oil and
grease for lubrication.

Until recently bell clappers were almost invariably made from wrought
iron of the best quality, as the churchwardens at St Gregory's church,
Norwich found in 1609 when they paid 24s. 'to Dollman for a Clapper for
the greet bell contaynyng Fifftie pounds and a half of Spanish Iron besides
the oulde clapper chaunging'. This seems expensive when compared with
the sum of 59s. paid a few years earlier for recasting a bell weighing 6 cwt
at St Margaret's church, just across the road.[9] Clappers come in a variety
of shapes, ranging from those with very long flights as found in many

9   Norwich St Gregory: NRO PD 59/54. Norwich St Margaret: NRO PD 153/42.

pre-Reformation and 17th-century bells, to those which consist of little more than a heavy collar shrunk onto the end of the shaft. Constant striking wears the clapper more quickly than the bell, and there are many references to 'quartering' the clapper shafts, thus bringing an unworn part of the clapper-ball into contact with the bell.

An iron staple, which was carefully positioned in the bell-mould before the molten metal was poured, originally projected down inside the crown of an old bell to provide a fixing point for the clapper. Early references[10] suggest that clappers were fixed to the crownstaple by leather thongs, which would have been adequate when bells were either swung through a small arc, or sounded by pulling the clapper against the soundbow. A more sophisticated method of suspension, mentioned at East Dereham from 1420 onwards, was by means of a thick leather strap with a buckle, connecting the crown-staple to a stirrup at the top of the clapper. The Snettisham churchwardens bought 'halfe one horse skynn' in 1476, and there are frequent payments for the leather needed to make and mend these 'bawdricks' for the clappers. In many churches a sadler would have a regular contract for maintaining the baldricks, and there is a certain resignation in the relevant entry at Dereham: 'Et solutis pro Whyt leder pro reparatione lez Bauderykes erga natura eodem Anno una cum factura eorundem v d.' Buckled leather straps were used well into the 17th century in some churches, and a hardwood spacer would reduce wear on the leather and provide a less sloppy pivot for the clapper. At Loddon in 1600 we find the sum of 4s. 'paid to Alexander for mending the bell claper and makynge of a buckell for the bell'. Tallow was used to keep the leather baldricks supple at Swaffham in 1583: 'Item for ij bawdryks makyng with tallow for the bawdryks – v d.'

There is no doubt that a better suspension was needed for the clapper when bells were rung in full circles, and it was probably during the 16th century that 'busk-boarded' clappers first appeared. The leather strap was replaced by an iron linkage, and the whole assembly stiffened by lashing it to a short wooden shaft, hence the payment of 1d. 'to the collar maker for a thonge to the bawdryke' at Swaffham on 1575. A further refinement was to form a 'T' at the top of the clapper in place of the older stirrup, and to provide two carefully shaped pieces of elm to clasp the clapper shaft and form a split bush (sometimes reinforced with an iron band) which fitted round the crown-staple. On the service bell at Happisburgh, and at

---

[10] William le Alblaster and others were said to have caused a fire in the house of John de Belaya on 10 June 1264. They had stolen the clappers of the bells at St Peter Parmentergate (and cut the bell-ropes at St Vedast and St Cuthbert's churches) to prevent people from coming to put the fire out. This suggests that the clappers were easy to remove. W. Hudson and J. C. Tingey, *The records of the city of Norwich*, 1906, pp. 206, 207.

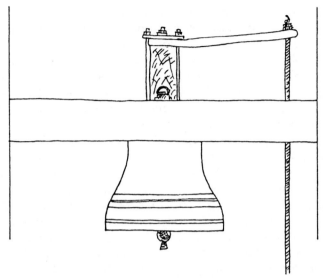

Bell hung between parallel beams with a chiming
lever, as at Bixley.

Caister St Edmund there are excellent examples of old clappers of this
improved 'bottle-boarded' type, so called from the shape of the elm baldrick.

The apparatus for swinging a bell is almost invariably referred to as a
'wheel' in old accounts, even when attached to a small sanctus bell; and
the writer has so far come across no payments for making or repairing
levers. It appears that any sector of circle could be called a wheel, regard-
less of whether or not its circumference was complete. Although early
half-wheels can still still be seen on bells at Little Melton and Tacolnestone, and examples are preserved as curiosities in the churches at Eccles
and Salhouse, there are no convenient references to 'half-wheels' in contemporary churchwardens' accounts. With half-wheels it is possible to
swing bells through at least a half-circle, the clappers striking when the
mouths of the bells are facing horizonally. The sound produced is bright
and resonant, bringing out the full tone; and in many towers where the
bells are raised and lowered 'in peal', present-day ringers believe that the
most impressive sound is when the bells are half-way up. It is difficult to
swing bells much higher with half-wheels, largely because the path taken
by the rope makes it impossible to exert sufficient force when the bell is
above the half-way mark. Although an additional strut, with a notch in
the end to catch the rope, can improve the performance of a half-wheel, it
must have been very difficult to control the swing of the bell. An obvious
development of this additional strut is to treat is as another spoke, and

extend the circumference of the wheel to three-quarters of a circle, thus
giving the ringer very much better control over his rope and allowing him
to swing the bell backwards and forwards to positions near the point of
balance on either side. Before pulleys were placed under the bell-wheels,
a ringer could only pull when the bell was swinging in one direction,
leaving it to return under its own momentum. This system, known as
'dead-rope' ringing, would not allow the order in which the bells
sounded to be altered very easily or precisely.

Ringers[11] eventually found that if they tied a 'Fillet, or little Cord' to the
rim of the bell-wheel, and fitted a roller below, the rope changed direction
and slowed down at the 'Forestroke', where it could be controlled just as
easily as it was at 'Backstroke'. It seems that the 'dancing of the Rope'
which allowed the ringer to catch at the forestroke was referred to as the
'Sally'; and that ringing 'Under Sally' was a style where both strokes were
properly controlled, a great advance on 'dead-rope' ringing. Speaking of
'the *Properties* wherewith a *Young Ringer* ought to be qualified . . . before
he is entered into a *Company*', Duckworth suggests that 'he is able to *Set a
Bell Fore-stroke and Backstroke*, as the terms are'; and that he should 'Know
how to *Ring Round*, or *Under Sally*'. Ringers today recognise the above as a
sound statement of policy in teaching beginners; and the only difference
in terminology is that the word 'sally' no longer describes the movement
of the rope, but has come to refer to the coloured woollen handgrip which
allows the ringer to identify the exact place where he should catch the
rope in order to steady it before pulling at the forestroke.

The Martham[12] churchwardens' accounts record a payment for a three-
quarter wheel in 1674, a few years after the bells at Horham, Suffolk were
made up to eight. Two three-quarter wheels still survive at Horham,
where the bells were still capable of being rung at the beginning of the
20th century, thus confirming that scientific changeringing was perfectly
possible before the almost universal adoption of 'whole-wheels'. The
single bell at Toftrees has an old three-quarter wheel; and an interesting

---

[11] Duckworth, *op. cit. passim.*
[12] See the churchwardens' accounts, kept at Martham church. Information from
     Mr R. W. M. Clouston confirms the three-quarter wheels at Horham; and the
     fact that the bells could be rung 'up' is clear from the fact that two full peals on
     the Horham bells are recorded in the reports of the Norwich Diocesan Associ-
     ation of Ringers. It is surprising how opinions can differ over the period when
     three-quarter wheels were common, and when they were generally replaced by
     whole wheels. J. C. Eisel (*op. cit.*, pp. 26, 57) comments on the bell installation at
     Ludlow, where three-quarter wheels were introduced in 1624–25 and stays in
     1655, that the tower 'seems to have been in the forefront of developments in
     bellhanging, more than would have been perhaps expected.' A. G. G. Thurlow,
     Church bells and ringers of Norwich, p. 14: 'Conservative Ludlow was apparently
     still using three-quarter wheels in 1624–25.'

early whole-wheel at Great Dunham has been made by extending a much older half-wheel.

Bell-wheels are apt to become warped, especially when new, by the constant succession of damp airs and drying winds which blow through the sound-windows of even a well protected bell-chamber. This is the reason for the payments at Snettisham for 'settyng' the wheels at frequent intervals after about 1470; and for regular small repairs recorded elsewhere. The Swaffham accounts record payments of 8d. 'for a bar and ij laths for the bell whele' with 3d. 'to tack nayles for the same work' in 1582; while more sophisticated iron struts are suggested when the Toft Monks[13] churchwardens paid 'to Chapelyn for the trimminge of the bell wheel with a Iron – 7d'. in 1628. The process of restoring the true profile of a warped wheel is implied by a variety of expressions, and the churchwardens at Norwich St Gregory bought 'two irons to stay the whele' of their Sance bell in 1606. When Duckworth in 1668 suggests nailing 'Stays from the Stock to each Spoke, to keep it [the wheel] from warping', he is referring to a method which had been adopted long before. In Norfolk towers there are many bells with ancient wheels, each having several softwood 'stays' intended to keep them correctly aligned.

Three-quarter wheels would not have come into fashion unless ringers had wished to swing the bells well above the horizontal; and they would have discovered that it was quite possible to overturn a bell by pulling too hard at the wrong moment. The result would be inconvenient since the rope would go out of control, with a hign risk of damage to the bell-gear, as well as to the ringer. Snettisham churchwardens paid 6d. in 1514 for 'checkys for the great bell': which could be apparatus to check its progress and prevent overbalancing, possibly in the form of a fixed bar. George Elphick discovered such a 'fixed' bar at Singleton,[14] Sussex; and the writer noticed a similar bar at Guist where the bell was rehung using very old ironwork in a frame which is clearly a 19th-century copy of a much older one. It seems most likely that fixed bars were intended to stop the bell from overbalancing at the forestroke during 'dead-rope' ringing. It would not have taken long to discover that such a device was easily damaged, and that a considerable strain would be placed on the cannons and hanging irons when a bell was abruptly checked. The next development was probably a fixed bar attached to the headstock which engaged in a movable catch attached to the bell-frame; this had the advantage of allowing the bell to be rung just past the balance point, and of preventing its overturning, unless the rope was pulled hard enough to break the mechanism. A further benefit was that the device could be used to rest, or 'set', the bell with its mouth upwards, allowing the ringer to release the rope

---

[13] *The East Anglian, Notes and Queries,* Vol III, new series, p. 23.
[14] G. P. Elphick, *op. cit.* (1970), p. 241; 'fixed' rather than 'sliding'.

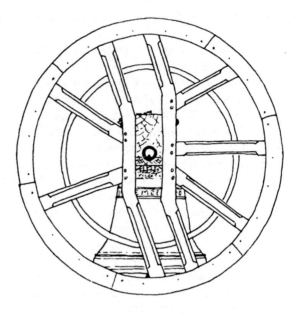

Half-wheel, later converted to a whole wheel, at Great Dunham.

Three-quarter wheel from Whissonsett, now at Tacolnestone.

from his grasp. It would then no longer be necessary to leave the bell with its mouth downwards[15] between 'peals'.

At this point it is worth reflecting on what one would expect early scribes to call the device used to stop a bell from overbalancing; and the *Oxford English Dictionary* gives one early usage of 'stay' as 'the action of stopping or bringing to a stand or rest', and as 'an appliance for stopping'. This seems to fit the context of 'stays' recorded at Dereham around 1486 rather well; and there are other plausible examples. Peter Northeast recognises such a stay in 1536 at Boxford;[16] and it is likely that the 'two ashin poles for latches for the bells' which cost 4d. at Mildenhall[17] in 1554 were for the same purpose. One of the problems in interpreting early references to 'stays' in churchwardens' accounts is the confusion caused by using the same word in two distinct contexts: either as a device against which to rest a bell with its mouth upwards, or as a strut to prevent the bell wheel from warping. This difficulty should not, however, prevent us from looking carefully at the various references and judging from their contexts what type of stay was intended.

When the third bell of the ring of five at East Dereham was rehung in 1491 we find payments for 'a waynscot boord bowt of Alan Goldsmyth which was occupyd to the iij[d] bell whele – iiij d. Item for nayle to the same – ij d. ob. Item for makyng of the whele and hangyng of the same bell – iij s. j d'. It is not clear what type of wheel was being repaired, but payments for supplying stays at about the same time suggest strongly that the bells were rung in full circles. The earliest reference to a stay, in 1486, reads: 'Et solutis Thome Wryght pro faccione unius steye pro tercie campane – j d.'. When another 'steye' was required a year later the bellwright was again paid 1d., this time 'pro posicione unius le steye ultra campanam', making it clear that the stay was placed in a suitable position to prevent the bell from being overturned.[18] In 1513 the Shipdham churchwardens paid

---

[15] E. Morris, *History and art of changeringing,* 1974 edition, p. 15. Morris concludes from the fact that the time occupied in many early peal performances included raising and lowering the bells, that it was not until well into the 18th century that stays and sliders were fitted. On p. 15 Morris implies that when a bell was 'set' the ringer held it just over the balance, taking its weight without resting it against a stay; and he goes on to contradict this usage on pp. 16, 17.

[16] P. Northeast, 'Boxford churchwardens' Accounts', *Suffolk Records Society,* Vol XXIII, 1982.

[17] *The East Anglian, Notes and Queries,* Vol I, p. 186.

[18] It should be noted that Dr J. C. Eisel (*op. cit.,* p. 57) dismisses the Dereham stays as probably wheel struts; and he suggests that the reference to fitting a stay above the bell [*ultra campanam*] should be interpreted in this way. Much hinges on the present writer's translation of '*ultra*'; for which Latham (*op. cit.,* p. 499) gives 'above (of place) c.1266, c.1450'. This usage is confirmed in the same Dereham account when the finial above the porch and the roofs above various chapels were repaired. Correspondence on the matter was published in the

4d. 'to John Huntman for makyn of on stay for the gret bell and for a bolt of iron'. Nails would have surely have been a more convenient way of fixing a lightweight strut to the bell-wheel than an iron bolt, which seems much more likely to have been used for securing the heavier piece of timber needed to prevent the bell from overturning. Another new piece of timber 'for the stay of the grett bell' at Shipdham cost 2d. in the following year; and in 1518 William Barne was paid 10d. 'for makyng of the steys of the belles'. Although the wheels fitted at Dereham and elsewhere were probably sufficient for the bells to be rung in full circles, many churches continued to use half-wheels which enabled their bells to be swung through a smaller arc in a less controlled way. Duckworth's observation that 'the trussing or taking up of a great Bell into the Stock by a notch, makes the Bell go easier, and lie lighter at the hand (that is) when it is set' makes perfect sense for a bell with a stay; which would feel lighter when pulled off from handstroke, where it is usually 'set'. Norfolk ringers still talk about 'setting' their bells against the stays at the end of a touch; some bells are 'deep-set' while others are 'fleet' or 'light-set'.

In the contract[19] dated 1488 for the new tower at Helmingham, Suffolk, there is a clause requiring that no bells should be hung until four years after the building work was finished. This precaution allowed the fabric to settle before imposing on it the stresses caused when bells are rung. There is rarely any disturbance of the tower masonry where the foundation timbers of an old bell-frame enter the walls, showing that these were usually put in place during building. The trusses of the frame could be assembled later, when the tower was ready for the bells. In some towers it can be seen, by comparing the widths of bell-pits and the clearances in the floor traps, that large bells must have been hauled up the tower and through the floors before the bell-frame was completely assembled. Early-

---

Ringing World, 1987, pp 680, 745, and 889; with an article by Dr Eisel on p. 1016. It seems to the present writer that a competent carpenter would hardly need to be told which of the several struts restraining a wheel was defective, even less would the scribe need to record in his accounts precisely which one was mended. The pieces of timber used when minor repairs were made to doors, windows and other carpentry were commonly described in terms such as 'splents', 'stulpes', 'bordes' and 'planks'; but the use of the word 'steye' suggests something special. The supposition that the East Dereham bells were rung 'up' remains strong in the writer's mind; and it should be pointed out that only odd years of the Churchwardens' accounts survive, so the regular replacement of stays which would be expected over a continuous period is not recorded. The Shipdham accounts beginning in 1511 are at NRO PD 337/85.

[19] L. F. Salzman, *Building in England down to 1540*, 1953, pp. 547–549.

16th-century accounts for building a bell-frame survive at Swaffham,[20] where it appears that the contract was signed with Edmund Aleyn during the first week of March, 1515; and the next three months were spent choosing and felling trees in various places, including Bradenham, Shipdham and Saham Toney. The bell-hanger's expert knowledge was employed in selecting suitable timber; and he seems to have assembled the frame in the tower by July 1516, when the brass bearings in which the bells were to swing are first mentioned. The considerable sum of 34s. 4d. for gudgeons (or axles) shows that the headstocks were also in preparation. It would seem that the bells had been removed from a temporary bell-house[21] to the tower by the time the bell-hanger's contract was completed in August 1516. Further entries in the accounts show that Edmund Aleyn was employed on a regular contract to maintain the bells for a sum of 3s. 4d. per year, with his board and lodgings; and there are payments for transporting his tackle between Swaffham and other places. Contemporary accounts at Tilney and North Elmham show that Edmund Aleyn had similar contracts at those churches; and we find that 'Edmund the bellhanger from Elsing' was paid for work on the bells at St Giles Hospital, Norwich in 1489.

These specific examples may well give a general indication that although minor repairs and routine maintenance were entrusted to local people, the expertise required to construct a bell-frame and hang new bells was not readily available everywhere. The similar design and details seen in many pre-Reformation bell-frames suggests a consistency of thought on the principles of bell-hanging, which implies the involvement of professional workmen, rather than local craftsmen with individual ideas. The only two professional bell-hangers of this period whose names have been found by the writer are Edmund Aleyn of Elsing and Thomas Morker[22] of Beccles (who hung the bells in the new tower at Walberswick in 1466–1468).

---

[20] Swaffham churchwardens' accounts, NRO PD 52/71. The entries for this work do not appear as a continuous block, but have been extracted at intervals. The monies received towards the work appear as in the appendix on pp. 134–137:

[21] *Ibid.*, 'Item recd. of John Owold for the olde bellehowse and the frame – xvj s.'

[22] Thomas Morker, 1495, NRO NCC wills, Wolman 213. He held considerable lands in Gillingham, on the opposite side of the river from Beccles: see Gillingham Estate Papers for deeds in the period 1467 – 1486, NRO GIL/1. Edmund Aleyn appears at 'a certain carpenter from Elsing' in the Tilney accounts, also by name in the accounts at Swaffham and North Elmham. St Giles Hospital, Norwich, Accounts (NRO NCR Case 24a) record: *Et de xx d. solutis Edmundo Belhanger de Elsyng pro factura le loks pro fenestris in campanile per v vices per v dies per diem iiij d. Et de xx d. solutis pro campanis ex campanile ibidem ad humum deponendum et pro eisdem ad campanilem predictum sufficienter levandum. Et de 3s. solutis pro clavis, stapulis et pro forlokks emptis ad idem opus.* There were also the anonymous bell-hangers at Dereham in 1480: *Et solutis pro expensis duorum*

Excluding the the tree recorded at North Lopham c.1400, and the present arrangement at Witton by Crostwight where the bell is lashed to a beam by means of a stout chain, the simplest type of bell-frame is found at Bixley, where the single bell hangs in one of two pits formed by parallel beams which span the tower. This arrangement is adequate for small bells hung for chiming, but when larger bells are rung 'up' the horizontal forces would cause a 'battering-ram' effect at the points where the beams enter the tower walls, thus damaging the masonry. A further disadvantage is that the downward force is exerted at the unsupported centres of the beams. Bixley tower was never finished,[23] and it appears that the existing frame was temporarily installed to await the completion of a taller tower with a proper bell-chamber. A slightly more sophisticated bell-frame at East Carleton has a pair of additional struts to the tower walls.

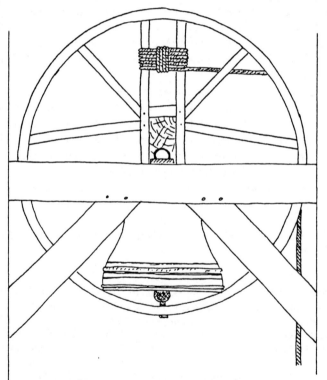

Bell hung between braced parallel beams, as at East Carleton.

___

carpentarium venientium de Bokenham et Bradenham pro le frame campanarum infra le clocher supervidendo et cum eis colloquendo pro facture unius nove frame dicto anno xij d.
[23] See the two very late bequests (1526 and 1535) to the tower (C&C).

In order to divert the vertical forces away from the centres of the supporting beams, the bearings of a bell are mounted on trusses whose lower members are jointed to substantial wall-plates which spread the forces. An analysis of early bell-frames in Norfolk suggests that although there were numerous variations in minor detail, only two basically different designs were used for the trusses. Both attempt to prevent the sagging of the beam which houses the bearings of the bell, and to counteract the 'battering-ram' effect of the large horizontal forces, with rapidly alternating directions. These two designs are radically different from the almost standard trusses adopted in frames from about 1600 onwards.

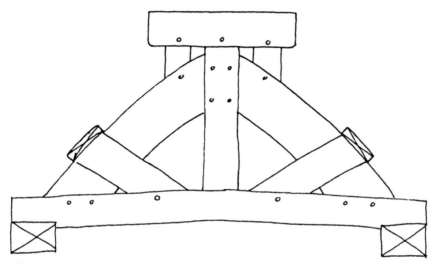

King-post truss, with short frame-head and head-struts, as formerly at Forncett St Mary.

The most common truss found in early bell-frames consists of a vertical king-post mounted on a cambered tie-beam. This is usually supported by a pair of braces to counteract the horizontal forces which would cause unsupported king-posts to rock from side to side during ringing. Straight braces between the king-posts and foundations would meet both timbers at an acute angle, where it would be difficult to make a good mortise and tenon joint; and it appears that most carpenters preferred curved or angled braces to improve this aspect. The main advantage of this design is its strength and simplicity, since it requires only six mortise and tenon joints. The chief disadvantage is that, because of the rigidity of the triangular shapes, the effect of the horizontal forces at the axles of the bell is to put the joints at the feet of the braces alternately in tension and compression: the inevitable wear at these points will eventually allow a slight rocking of the king-post under ringing stresses, affecting the stability of the frame and increasing the physical effort needed to ring the bell.

The gudgeons are usually mounted in brass bearings set into mortises in the timber of the bell-frame. Evidence from elsewhere[24] shows that brasses were sometimes sunk into the end-grain of a king-post; but this practice is unsatisfactory because the large horizontal forces during ringing are likely to split the timber. The usual practice is to mount a horizontal frame-head at the top of the king-post, using a mortise and tenon joint, and to recess the bearings into the upper surface.

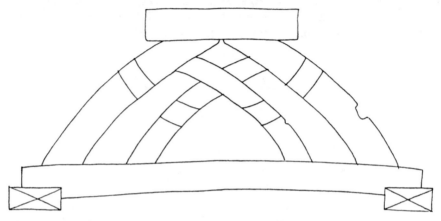

Scissors-braced truss, with short frame-head, as at Westfield and Ridlington.

Although rather less common than king-post trusses, the scissors-braced truss is a very much more satisfactory design. In this type of truss the frame-heads are supported by pairs of inclined braces, which may be curved, angled or straight. The main braces are then additionally supported from beneath by means of a pair of smaller braces, crossed like scissors. The absence of a king-post removes the vertical components of force from the centre of the truss to points near the outer ends, and the supporting braces add rigidity to the structure, as well as tending to prevent the horizontal forces from causing the frame-head to drift backwards and forwards during ringing. There is also much less tendency for the truss to rock during ringing since there is no vertical post to act as a pivot: the joints are, therefore, subjected to much less strain. A disadvantage of this type of truss is that it requires more timber than a king-post truss: there are also more joints (eight mortise and tenon and a halved joint at the centre of the scissors).

Although a correctly-hung bell produces little sideways force along the line of the gudgeons, it is usual to have struts between the trusses; and it is common for a short-headed frame to have a horizontal transom just below the level at which the bell clappers swing. Transoms are usually

[24] G. P. Elphick, op. cit. (1945), p. 41 and (1970), p. 227.

fixed by oak dowels into notches in the braces of the trusses. Short frame-heads set on either king-post or scissors-braced trusses are very likely to work loose under the stresses of bell-ringing, which increase as the bells are swung higher; and a bell-frame was commonly arranged with rectangular bell pits having long frame-heads connected by a transverse rail across their ends. This rail, by acting as a horizontal spacer between the trusses, made the older transom obselete. Short-headed frames are now rare; and while it is difficult to see the surviving scissors-braced trusses still in use at Westfield and Ridlington, an excellent example is preserved beside the modern frame at West Bradenham. The three bells, dating from the last quarter of the 14th century, at Great Walsingham are now hung 'dead' in the contemporary short-headed king-post frame.[25] The tendency for the frame-heads to rock during ringing is usually counteracted by short vertical 'head-struts' on either side of the king-post, supported from the upper surfaces of the braces and mortised both into them and the frame-heads. When a short-headed frame has been modernised by introducing long frame-heads and transverse rails, the notches for an earlier transom at a lower level can usually be found. Although many frames were originally built with long frame-heads, there are other examples where it can be clearly seen that these are a later addition.

Alterations at Forncett St Mary[26] show clearly how a 15th-century king-post frame for three bells was provided with long frame-heads and corner posts at a later date. The bottoms of the trusses have lap-dovetail joints to the foundation beams, which are built into the tower walls and rest on off-sets; and the present long frame-heads are supported by vertical king-posts with curved braces. Each truss has vacant mortises designed to receive members, including short head-struts, which were not needed when long frame-heads were introduced. Other mortises suggest that originally there rose from the foundations other struts which enclosed the curved braces, and had tenons at the top ends entering mortises in a horizontal transom. A new transom, provided at a later date, was secured in place by iron spikes instead of the more usual oak dowels.

The scissors-braced frame at Tibenham[27] probably dates from c.1437, when money was left for making the new bells. Originally constructed as a short-headed frame for a ring of four bells with a tenor of 25 cwt, the long frame-heads were probably added when the frame was adapted to take a ring of five bells c.1519. All the trusses have recesses for spacers which became redundant once the long frame-heads were installed, and the north-east corner of the frame still retains a superfluous pair of crossed struts. One of the short frame-heads remains, serving as a packing

---

[25] Great Walsingham: frame dated by inference from that of the bells, cast by William Silisden 1376 – 1409.

[26] Forncett St Mary: see p. 106.

[27] Tibenham: see p. 107.

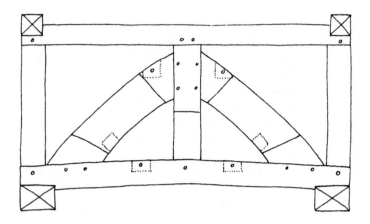

Long frame-heads added to an older bell-frame at Forncett St Mary.

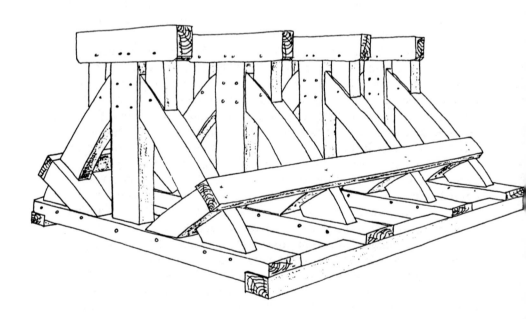

Original design of the bell-frame at Forncett St Mary.

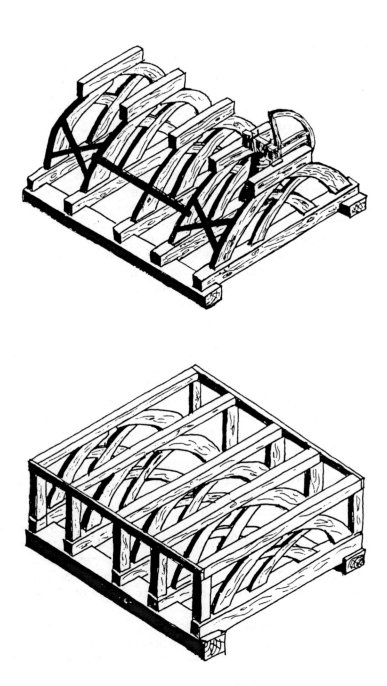

Four-bell frame at Tibenham: (top) as constructed c.1437; and
(bottom) as adapted early in the sixteenth century.

between the bottom cill of one of the trusses and the floor. The long frame-heads, which certainly pre-date the 1787 restoration of the bells and their increase to a ring of six, may well date from the 16th century. The entire frame, which retains much of its original timber, is a remarkable survival; and it is noteworthy that the six bells, which were last rehung in 1868, are still able to be rung in full circles – although with difficulty, and only during the winter when the timber is damp and the frame joints are fairly tight.

It is worth noting that long-headed frames built before the middle of the 16th century rarely have the jowled vertical posts seen in the bays of contemporary timber-framed houses. Although jowled posts were used in the 17th-century reconstruction of the frame at Tittleshall, contemporary bell-hangers generally preferred to strengthen their frames by inserting curved 'knees' at joints where there was stress. The repairs of 1736 at Little Melton show jowled verticals supporting long frame-heads, both in the newly constructed outer trusses of the frame, and added to the 14th-century trusses which remain in the middle bell-pit. Similar posts appear in the apparently late frames at Heckingham and Ormesby St Margaret.[28]

Although there are only two basically different types of truss, there are many variations in detail. Some of the oldest king-post frames, such as those in early 14th-century towers at West Newton and Whinburgh, have very shallow trusses with sharply curved feet; and another early three-bell frame, at South Creake, was extended to take five bells before 1552. Others like them are found at East Bradenham, Saham Toney (c.1465–1505) and Brandon Parva, with a particularly fine example at Gooderstone.[29] Most king-post frames are rather taller, some having braces with a continuous slight curve like those at Forncett St Mary (c.1432), Great Dunham and West Winch; while others have angled braces like those at Wacton. Paired braces supporting both king-posts and frame-heads appear in later frames such as Fritton,[30] Gimingham (c.1470–1504), Stalham (c.1498–1533) and Great Fransham (c.1487–1500). One of the finest frames with paired braces, at Swannington,[31] can be dated by an entry in the 1552 Inventory of church goods: 'William Alen, Edmund Tympe churchwardens do present that we have sold one chales of the weyght of xiij once at

[28] A new ring of four, cast for Tittleshall in 1623, fits the frame perfectly. Parts of the Little Melton frame are contemporary with the tower; and the repairs are dated by a carved inscription. The frames at Heckingham and Ormesby are clearly later than the towers.

[29] The towers at South Creake, Gooderstone and East Bradenham appear to be 14th-century. Brandon Parva tower (c.1508), probably dates from the completion of the church, see C&C.

[30] Fritton bells may date from the reign of Edward VI, as may the top part of the tower (Thesis).

[31] HBW.

Bellframe dated 1726

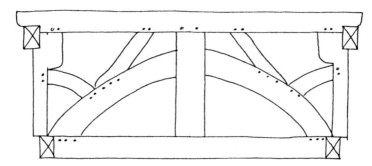

Trusses of central pit

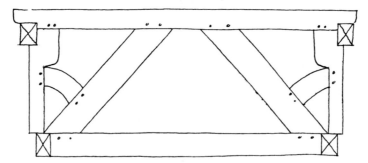

Extreme trusses of outer pits

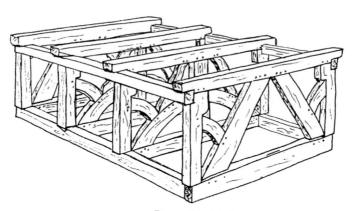

Perspective sketch

Sketches of the Little Melton bell-frame. Largely rebuilt in 1726, the central king-posts and braces of the original frame remain.

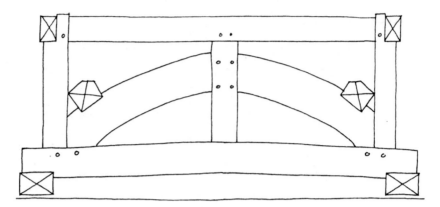

King-post frame with wide trusses at Whinburgh.

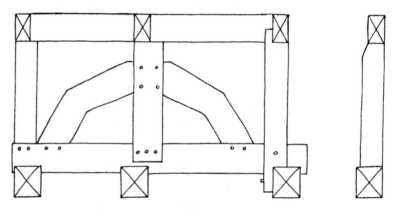

Section of king-post frame, with angled braces at Wacton.

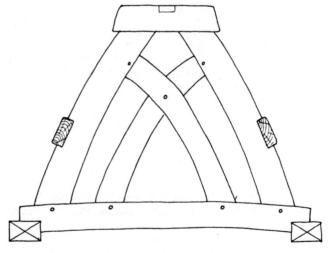

Tall scissors-braced truss formerly at Briningham.

iiij s. lij s. the whyche we have bestowyd upon a belleframe And so noth-
inge remayneth in oure handes'. Another excellent frame is found at
Shotesham St Mary (c.1535), where there are doubled braces to the middle
pit and single braces to the outer pits of a three-bell frame.

The two trusses of a tall scissors-braced frame remain in the 14th-cen-
tury tower at Briningham,[32] and a similar frame was rebuilt lower down
when the tower at Helhoughton (c.1473) was shortened; there is another
frame of the same type at Bintree (c.1384). Some of these tall frames must
have rocked alarmingly when the bells were rung, and a splendid 19th-
century copy of a scissors-braced frame at Larling has stout wedges between the top cills and the tower walls. A more compact design appears at
Tibenham (c.1447), and a sectional drawing[33] of Norwich cathedral tower
in 1784 shows a similar frame which must date from c.1470. While good
scissors-braced frames remain at Norwich St Peter Parmentergate
(c.1434), Postwick (c.1437) and Stanfield; one of the most accessible is at
Castle Acre (c.1396). The finest surviving scissors-braced frame is probably that at Wolferton, which was apparently put into the tower after a
major fire c.1486.[34] The only five-bell frame of this type discovered by the
writer, at Thompson, has never received its full complement of bells.[35]

Most bell-frames have massive foundations which absorb the constantly
varying forces transmitted as the bells are rung, thus minimising the
movement of the bell-frame as a whole. It is quite common for the foundations of an early frame to be arranged on two or three distinct levels,
using shallow dove-tail joints at the ends of timbers, and recesses where
members cross. To counteract the 'battering-ram' effect produced by horizontal forces the lowest members of the trusses are almost always jointed
to heavy timbers running at right angles to the direction in which the bells
swing. These timbers spread the horizontal forces along the length of the
bell-chamber walls; and the vertical forces are contained by resting the
foundation members on wide off-sets. It is often noticed that the tower
buttresses finish at, or just above, the level of the bell-frame foundations,
this being the level where the forces are communicated to the fabric of the
tower. The massive buttresses at both East and West Bradenham show
how two rather slender towers were strengthened to take quite heavy
rings of three bells; and new buttresses added to Alburgh tower c.1504
reach to the level of the bell-frame.

[32] Briningham tower is stylistically dated to the early years of the 14th century.
[33] A. G. G. Thurlow, *Church bells and ringers of Norwich*,1948, plate VII. The tower
was gutted by the fire of 1463, and work on the bells was completed by c. 1469.
NRO DCN Sacrist's Rolls.
[34] NRO Diocesan Records, Bishop Goldwell's Register, Bishop's licence to collect
alms throughout the diocese to rebuild the church, consumed to the foundations by a fire.
[35] The Thompson frame seems to be later than the 14th-century tower.

Sketches of the Thompson bell-frame.

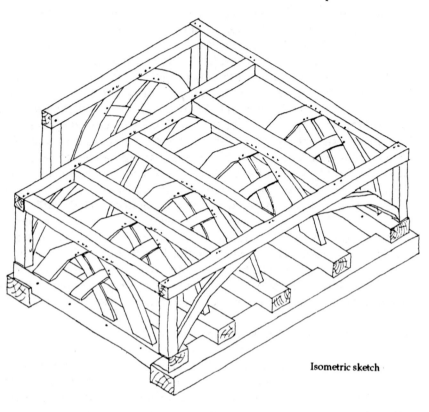

Isometric sketch

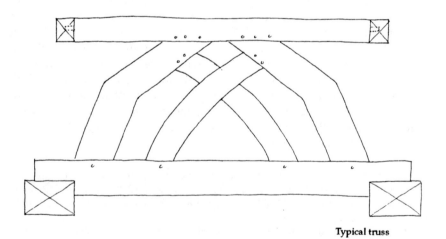

Typical truss

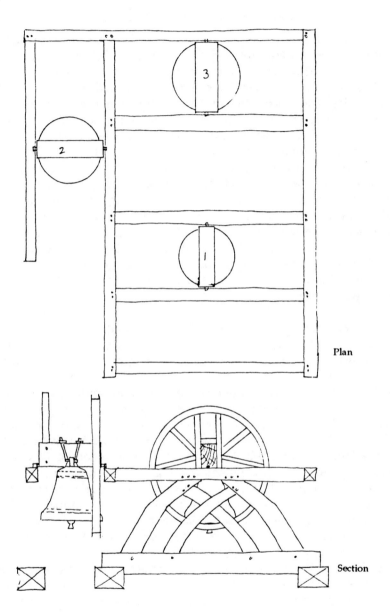

Plan

Section

A few inches below the foundations of old bell-frames there is usually a stout floor with a central trap big enough to allow bells to be removed for repair. The purpose of the floor is to give easy access for repairing the bell fittings, as well as to restrain a bell-clapper if a baldrick should break during ringing. The space below the frame foundation ensures free circulation of air around important timbers, and allows the inevitable accumulation of rubbish from masonry and birds to be easily removed.

Since the structure of a bell-frame is relatively uncomplicated, only the simplest joints are used. Foundation timbers commonly have recessed dovetail joints at their ends, and there is usually a simple recessed joint where members cross. Plain mortise and tenon joints are ubiquitous, and shouldered tenons are sometimes found. Paired tenons at right-angles are used to secure the frame-heads, and a 'dog-leg' assembly, using tenon joints, is often employed at the feet of corner-posts and end-posts. Because there is so little variety in the joints used, and small scope for innovation, it has not been possible to use them for dating bell-frames in the same way as other timber-framed structures.[36]

A bell swinging through a full circle needs a pit about three times as long as it is wide; and for an old bell weighing 10 cwt (which would be rather longer than a modern bell of the same weight) the bell-pit would need to be about 3 ft 4 inches wide by about 10 ft long. The plan adopted for a bell-frame depends on the size and shape of the bell-chamber, and on the number and weight of the bells to be hung there. Although a few churches in Norfolk had as many as 5 bells in 1552, the most common number was three. In a square tower it is possible and convenient to arrange a frame for three bells to swing side by side in parallel pits, with the largest bell in the middle pit and the smaller bells on either side. The bells usually swing east to west because the buttressing effect of the church building makes the tower fabric much stiffer and stronger in that direction. By placing the heaviest bell in the central pit there is less twisting effect on the fabric when the bells are rung. It would require a bell-frame measuring about 11 ft square to accommodate a typical ring of three bells with a tenor of about 10 cwt. A ring of four bells in parallel pits would probably need a frame measuring about 11 ft wide by 14 ft long; and it is much more usual for the frame to have one bell swinging at right-angles to the other three. The four-bell frames at Wheatacre (c.1506–1522) and Trunch[37] are good early examples of the latter type.

A much more common plan for a four-bell frame is to arrange the bell-pits around a vacant central space with two bells swinging each way. Compared with the plan of the frames at Trunch and Wheatacre, the

[36] C. A. Hewitt, *English historic carpentry*, 1980, and *Church carpentry, a study based on Essex examples*, 1982.
[37] Trunch dated by style of tower, which suggests 14th-century work.

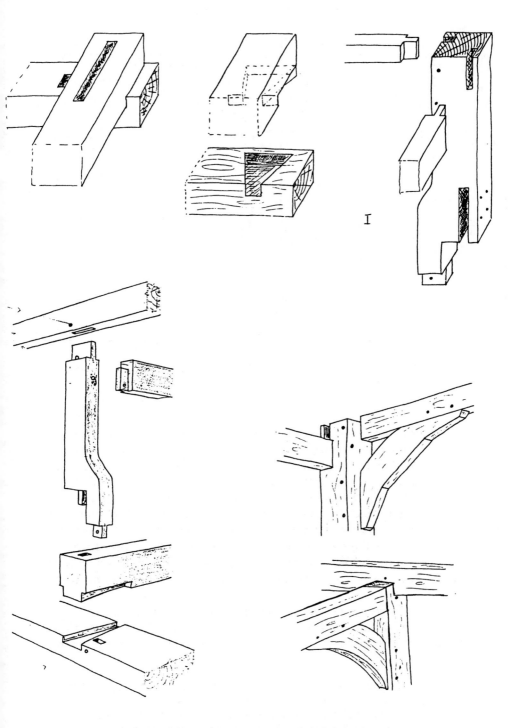

I

Sketches of joints and assemblies commonly found in bell-frames.

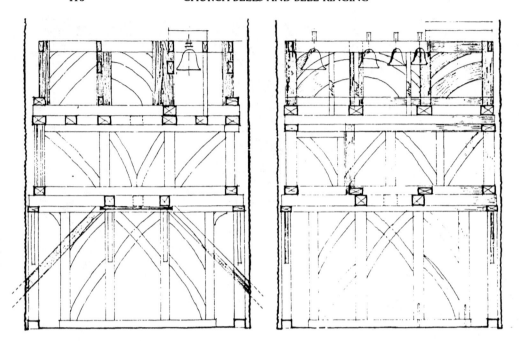

The fourteenth-century bell-frame and supporting structure at
Snettisham. *Sketch by Peter Field-Phillips.*

'hollow-square' plan offers little reduction in over-all size, but has the
advantage of transmitting the ringing forces in two perpendicular directions.[38] At Bressingham, for example, the two heavier bells swing east-
west, the stronger way of the tower, while the lighter pair of bells swing
north-south. Many 'hollow-square' frames pre-date the beginnings of
changeringing, and the fact that the bell-ropes did not fall in numerical
order was not seen as a problem. In small towers the outer ends of the
bell-pits are often left open, thus allowing the bells to swing outside the
area of the frame. The trusses of 'hollow-square' frames usually have
braced king-posts, and there is little doubt that the design is immensely
strong.

The 'hollow-square' frame at Snettisham[39] is one of the most impressive in Norfolk. Here a massive structure designed to hold four very
large bells is supported on a huge sub-frame, which in turn rests on a

[38] Correspondence with Dr J. C. Eisel and Mr C. J. N. Dalton suggests that this
design was not commonly found outside East Anglia.
[39] Snettisham frame almost certainly dates from before the churchwardens' accounts begin in 1468; and the 1552 Inventory confirms that there was a ring of
four with a tenor of 16 cwt.

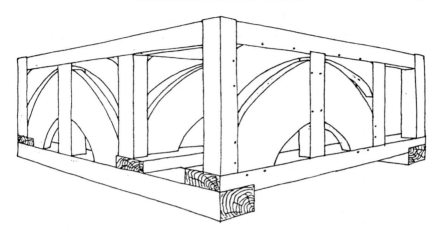

The fifteenth-century bell-frame at Shimpling.

complicated series of struts and braces designed to bring the stresses as low as possible. Another huge frame which still supports bells rung in full circles was probably placed diagonally in the earlier tower at Attleborough c.1523; and the frame at Cawston (c.1421) retains a great deal of its original timber, having also a pre-Reformation extension to take a fifth bell. Smaller frames of the same type are found in the octagonal belfries at Bedingham (c.1513–1520), Swainsthorpe (c.1509) and Shimpling (c.1466), and in the round towers at Seething and Wacton (c.1400). Several 'hollow-square' frames have had an additional bell-pit formed in the central space when a ring was increased to five bells, Bressingham (c.1431) and Elsing being good examples.[40] The writer remembers the awkward 'rope-circles' at both Attleborough and Shelfanger where before recent rehanging bells used to hang in central pits. At Shelfanger there was one rope in each corner of the ringing chamber with the treble rope in the middle, making ropesight very difficult. The frame at Wendling, where the tower is too small for the bells to fit on one level, has very tall trusses which enable them to hang in two tiers.[41] The frame at Topcroft is another interesting variation with open-ended pits and 'X' braced trusses, which may well date from Brend's work on the bells in 1640.

The design of the foundations of 'hollow-square' frames is interesting, and there are a number of variations. Some frames have relatively simple foundations based on beams which span the full width of the tower, while others are based on a set of four interlocking timbers, each too short to span the tower. Good examples of 'hollow-square' frames with simple

[40] Elsing church and tower seem to be a complete entity c.1350.
[41] The Wendling frame may date from the removal of bells to the parish church when Wendling Abbey was suppressed in 1528.

Typical 'Hollow Square' frame for four bells.
Sketches of the fifteenth-century bell-frame at Bressingham.

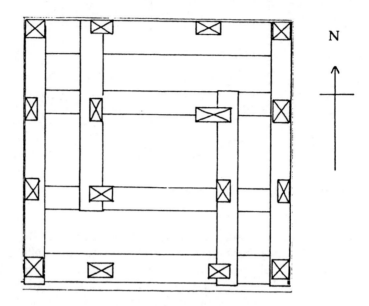

N

↑

Plan of foundation timbers of the bell frame.

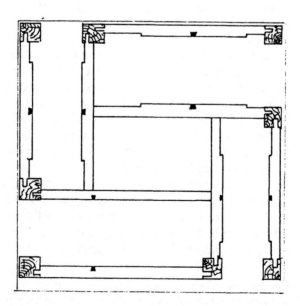

Plan of frame-heads of the four-bell frame.

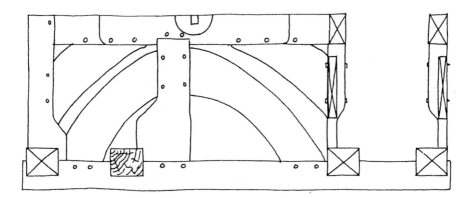

Section through bell-frame showing truss design.

Elevation of beams supporting
the treble bell.

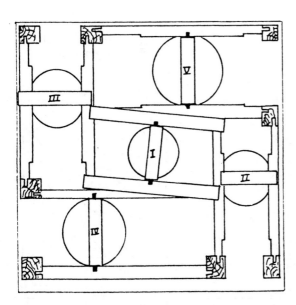

Plan of the bell-frame as extended for five bells. Note the
treble bell in the central space; and the difficulty of
producing a rope circle.

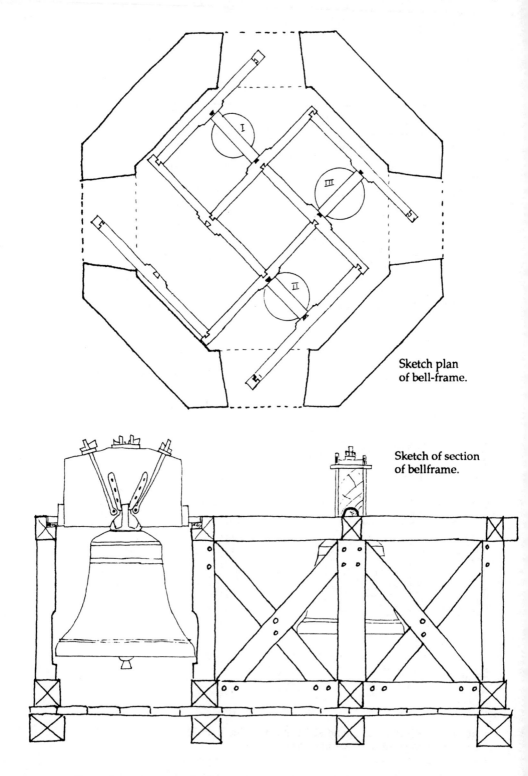

Sketch plan
of bell-frame.

Sketch of section
of bellframe.

Typical arrangement of a four-bell frame in the octagonal bell-chamber at
Topcroft. The cross-braced trusses are unusual.

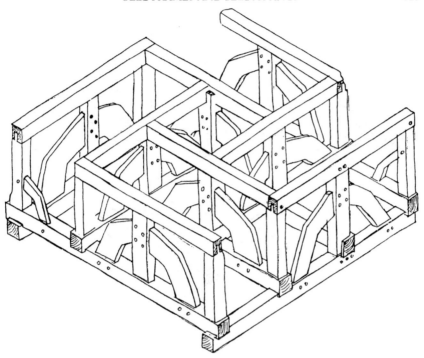

The fourteenth-century bell-frame at Wacton.

foundations beams are found at Shimpling, Bedingham and Wacton; and frames with interlocking foundations can be seen at Carbrooke, Felmingham (c.1522–1546), South Repps, Great Witchingham and Weston Longville (above the modern frame for six bells), while the Hevingham frame preserves a large part of such a design.[42] 'Hollow-square' frames at Stockton and Tuttington are apparently 17th-century, and the same design continued in use through to the end of the 19th century.[43]

[42] See Carbrooke churchwardens' accounts 1627, NRO PD 124/30. 'We have payd and layd out in chardges for the sayd town towarde the building of the bell-frames and other Chardges alowed by the Inhabitants the sum of xv li. xviiij s. vj d.' The 1629 Inventory (*ibid.*) mentions five bolts taken off the old bell-frame. Weston appears in 'A certificate of ruined and decayed churches, 1602', *The East Anglian*, Vol II, 233): 'The Steple latelie fallen down through the Negligence of the Inhabitaunts there . . . '. The bell-frame cannot be earlier than 1602. The South Repps frame seems to have been built for a ring of five bells dated 1641. No positive evidence at Great Witchingham or Hevingham.

[43] Day's four-bell frame at Raveningham (1885) is of this type, with a pit for a fifth bell above.

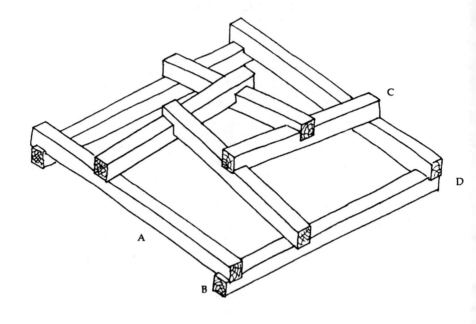

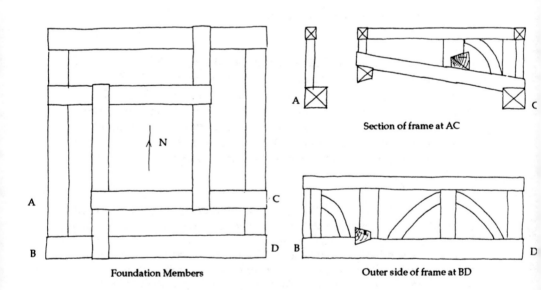

A

B

C

D

N

Foundation Members

Section of frame at AC

Outer side of frame at BD

Bell-frame with foundations of the 'interlocking' type, as at Carbrooke, Felmingham, Great Witchingham, etc.

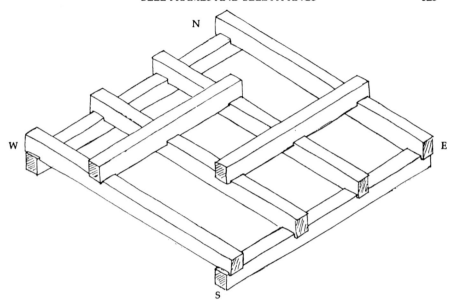

Foundations of the 'normal' type, as at Shimpling, Harpley, etc.

In most square towers the bell-frame is fitted with its outer members parallel to the walls of the bell-chamber and close to them; and the pegs which secure the joints in the outer members of the frame are driven from inside, leaving the tapered ends to protrude unsawn into the inaccessible space between the timbers and the wall. This indicates that the bell-frame was assembled on its foundations after the fabric of the bell-chamber was completed, and not during building. A few bell-frames are arranged diagonally in square bell-chambers, with their corners resting in the reveals of the sound-windows, an arrangement which would not increase the available area for hanging the bells unless the tower walls were very thick. Although it would have been easy to get at the corners of the frame during construction, this advantage would be outweighed by the fact that the corner-posts, with their many vulnerable joints, are placed where they are most exposed to the weather. A possible reason for placing a bell-frame diagonally is because this is often the strongest direction of a square tower.

Fitting a square bell-frame into a round tower is almost proverbially difficult, and it would require an internal diameter of over 14 ft (with an outside diameter of about 20 ft) to circumscribe a 10 ft square bell-frame. In some cases the problem is overcome by excavating recesses to accommodate the corners of the frame, to the considerable detriment of the masonry. The round tower at Tuttington has been so deeply excavated that the upper stage has been secured by numerous iron tie-bars. An alternative way to arrange a three-bell frame is for the largest bell to

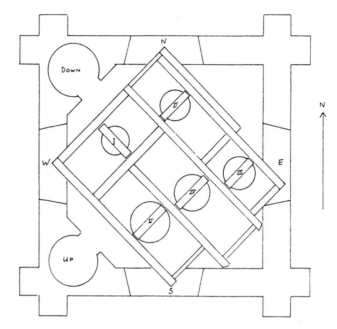

Frame fitted diagonally in the square tower at Deopham.

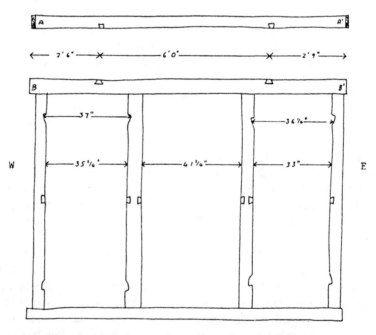

Plan of typical 17th-century five-bell frame, at Norwich St Stephen. Note that the pit for the largest bell is in the centre of the frame.

swing into a pair of opposite window reveals, and to shorten the outer trusses of the bell-frame, thus accommodating the smaller bells in the reduced space on either side of the middle pit, as at Eccles and Wramplingham.

By placing the corners of the frame in the window reveals and opening the splays, it would be possible to get a 10 ft square frame into a tower whose outside diameter was about 16 ft 6 inches; and a 'hollow-square' frame with open-ended bell-pits can be arranged with the bells swinging close to the windows. Even so, the outer timbers of the frame would still be clear of the curved walls of a round tower, and a good method of making maximum use of the available space was to construct an octagonal wall to contain the bell-frame. It is probably significant that the smaller round towers are those which most often have octagonal bell-chambers.

The usual 17th-century plan for a five-bell frame had the three heaviest bells swinging side-by-side in parallel pits, with the two lightest bells at right-angles swinging mouth-to-mouth. In most cases the tenor bell was placed in the centre of the frame, the most satisfactory place for distributing the forces as the bells are rung, but a difficult arrangement of bells from which to draw the ropes into a proper 'circle'. This practice seems to have fallen from favour in later bell-frames, where the position of bells is usually dictated, at least in part, by the need for the ropes to fall to the ringing-chamber in a 'circle' with good enough 'ropesight' for change-ringing to take place with ease.

The considerable interest in changeringing which developed during the 17th century was responsible for significant changes in the character of many rings of bells. Modifications in the structure of a bell-frame were necessary when a lighter ring of five or six bells displaced an older and heavier ring of three or four bells; and many old frames show that they have been altered and adapted to accommodate remodelled rings of bells. The Ashwellthorpe frame, which has held five bells since 1707, was extended and partly rebuilt from a structure designed for three bells c.1400.[44] The oldest trusses had king-posts supported by curved braces with short head-struts, and it appears that when a new tenor bell was added c.1504 a wider pit with a massive new king-post truss was formed at the west end. The two remaining pits of the old frame were shortened when a new pit was formed for a bell to swing east-west, the new trusses being similar to that along the west wall, but slighter in section. When the bells were again augmented in 1707 the wide tenor pit of 1504 was narrowed to accommodate the two trebles, and result is a very make-shift frame for five bells. This can never have been very satisfactory, and there

[44] Ashwellthorpe: see pp. 126, 127.

Sketches showing the development of the bell-frame at Ashwellthorpe.

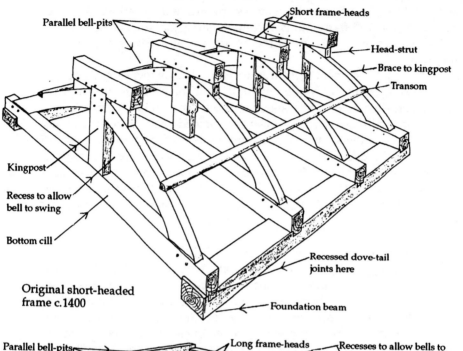

Parallel bell-pits
Short frame-heads
Head-strut
Brace to kingpost
Transom
Kingpost
Recess to allow bell to swing
Bottom cill
Recessed dove-tail joints here
Original short-headed frame c.1400
Foundation beam

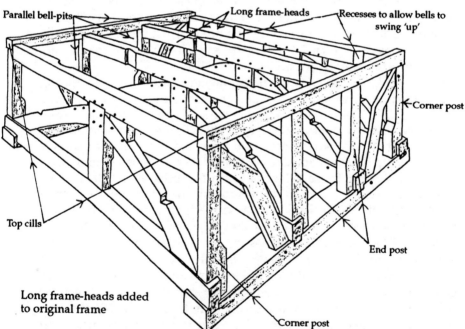

Parallel bell-pits
Long frame-heads
Recesses to allow bells to swing 'up'
Corner post
Top cills
End post
Long frame-heads added to original frame
Corner post

A short-headed frame for three bells was first converted to a long-headed frame, retaining the original head-struts.

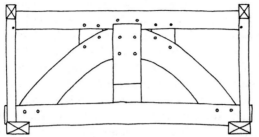

Original truss c.1400, long frame-heads added.

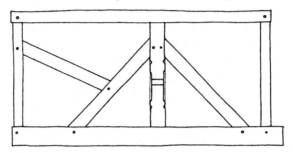

Truss c.1500

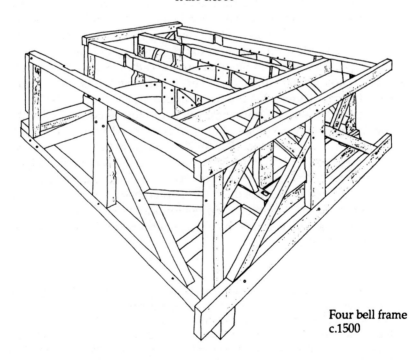

Four bell frame
c.1500

An extra pit was formed c.1500, and the trusses of that date are crudely formed
from straight timbers.

is an interesting note in the churchwardens' accounts;[45] 'Anno 1706 This Year our Bells were Cast, Churchwardens thought not fitt, In Book to place their account, They were asham'd of itt.' Much of the existing bell-gear dates from 1738, when a carpenter was paid £7. 4s. 6d., presumably to rectify faults in the work of 1707. The introduction of generally lighter bells allowed a reduction in the size of timber used in construction, and the design of the trusses was altered to reflect the different requirements. The interesting additions and alterations to the frame at Carleton St Peter show that, when the plan was extended to accommodate a proposed ring of five bells, the older design of king-post trusses was abandoned in favour of a much simpler arrangement where the trusses consisted of a pair of straight braces inclined at an angle of about 60°, between the frame-heads and the foundations.

A fine bell-frame designed for a ring of five bells to be rung in full-circles remains at St Stephen's church, Norwich,[46] where the standard of carpentry is excellent. The plan of the frame has the three largest bells swinging north-south (the stronger way of the tower in this case) in parallel pits, with the two smallest bells at right-angles in a long, open-ended pit; and the tenor bell, which would have weighed about 11 cwt, was hung in the centre of the bell-frame. There are no king-posts, and the trusses supporting the three heaviest bells each have a pair of straight braces meeting below the bearings; while the pit containing the two lightest bells is less heavily braced. The foundations of the frame are jointed together on a single level and are supported by a stout boarded floor.

The importance of the St Stephen's frame is that its construction can be securely dated to 1605–1606, and that it was installed by a named carpenter. Thomas Dymee (as his name appears at St Stephen's) seems to have worked in several churches, often in close conjunction with the Norwich bell-founder, William Brend, who supplied almost all those bells cast between about 1590 and 1630 for Norfolk churches. The two men are mentioned at Norwich St Peter Mancroft[47] in 1603: 'Item paid to Dymond the Carpenter for workmanship done by him about the hanging of the bells and for Timber besides the XX of September As apperith by his bill xxx s. Item paid unto Willm. Brand bellfounder the XXI of April 1603 for the making of a new bell now hanging in a frame in the steple as appearith by his bill xvij li.'

---

[45] Churchwardens accounts: *penes* Mr H. Bothway, Fundenhall Grange, to whom the writer is grateful for permission to quote from them.
[46] Norwich St Stephen's churchwardens' accounts (kept at the church) show that the frame was built at about the time the tower (which used to have the date '1606' in the flintwork above the north doorway) was finished. The bells were hung two years later.
[47] The Mancroft accounts have been dealt with by Mr D. Cubitt in an article in the *Ringing World*, April 1977.

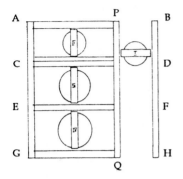

Present plan of frame

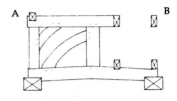

Frame truss A B

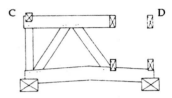

Frame truss C D

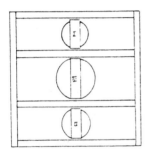

Original plan of frame

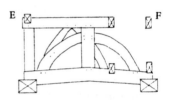

Frame truss E F

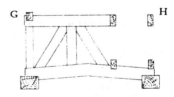

Frame truss G H

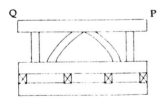

Frame truss Q P

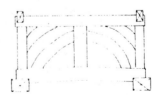

Frame truss, original form

Sketches showing the development of the sixteenth-century bell-frame
at Carleton St Peter, and the seventeenth-century modifications
designed to accommodate a ring of five bells.

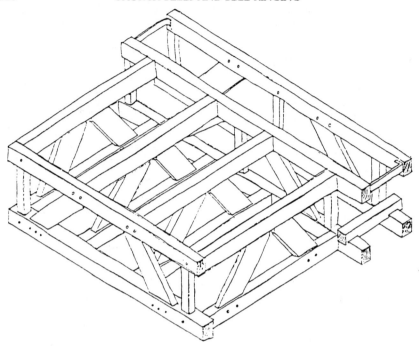

Typical seventeenth-century 'changeringing' five-bell frame at Aslacton.

At Loddon,[48] where a bell was recast by Brend in 1618, we find: 'Laid out to Dymond for hanging the bell 5s.' He was probably the carpenter who came from Norwich in 1616 to make a complete frame for the new ring of five:

Chardge at Norwich for the Carpenter 3s. 4d.
For his supper and bed at Loddon 6d.
To Miller for the carryinge the timber for the frames 7s. 0d.
For the hewing thereof 5s. 0d.
For the sawinge pitt makinge 4d.
To old Grene for the Sawinge 7s. 6d.
To the Carpenter for his work £6 13s. 4d.
To him for one new wheele [amount missing]
Halfe inch bord for the mending of the other wheles [amount missing]
For woode for the fange [amount missing]
Wood for the stay of the Great bell [amount missing]
For leather for the five baldericks [amount missing]
For makeinge them 2s. 0d.
To the Bellefounder for the bell waighinge six hundred and two

---

[48] Loddon, NRO PD 595/19.

and fifty pounds at five pounds the hundred £32 6s. 5d.

For the shotinge of the brasses weighinge nyne and fifty pounde at vj d. the pound 29s. 6d.

To Goslinge for the fetching of them 16d.

For bread and beare at the takinge up, and the carters for bringinge home of the bell 18d.

to Grene bord wages for the drawing up of the bell 12d.

For a stocke to that bell 3s. 0d.

To the carpenter when he hunge the bell and made the carries for the clocke A dayes board and wages [illegible]

For the collers and gudginges for the bell bought at Norwich 3s.

At Norwich St Gregory,[49] where a great deal of early ringing is recorded on the light ring of five, there is a constant succession of payments to 'Dymond the Carpenter' for new wheels, and for rehanging various bells. It is clear that the carpenter was as important as the bell-founder in providing and maintaining suitable bells for changeringing. Frames with simple trusses like those at St Stephen's church are found associated with early-17th-century rings of bells at Aslacton and Broome; and the trusses of these frames are similar to those installed in the 1670s at Yelverton. Norwich St Augustine's, Caston and Heydon have contemporary five-bell frames of the same type, and a fine three-bell frame was put in the new tower at Denton in about 1710.[50] There are many other examples of a design which continued to enjoy almost universal popularity through to the 20th century.

Despite its obvious weakness for bells which were to be rung 'up', the king-post truss did not fall completely from favour.[51] Trusses added at Hanworth in the 17th century were of this type; and the frame at Shelton (1683) is of king-post construction, although unlike pre-Reformation frames in almost every other detail. Other frames of what had become an archaic design appear at Ormesby St Michael (probably 1616), Brancaster (dated 1754) and Metton (dated 1793); while modern copies of king-post frames are found at Filby (1877) and Burlingham St Andrew (1923).

There are other differences – apart from the design of the trusses – between older frames and those constructed during the 17th century and later, the most significant being in the design of the foundations. In older frames the foundation members are usually jointed together with mini-

49 Norwich St Gregory, NRO PD 59/54.
50 Norwich, St Augustine tower fell in 1677 and was rebuilt in 1683 (CBN p. 172). The five-bell frame at Caston predates the increase to six in 1756, being designed for much larger bells: the Heydon frame is very similar. The rebuilding of Denton tower was completed in about 1712: NRO PD 136/58.
51 Shelton frame can be dated from entries in the churchwardens' accounts (NRO PD 358/83). The frames at Brancaster, Filby and Metton have dates carved on them, and two digits of the date are carved on the Ormesby frame. The work at Burlingham is recorded on a mural plate in the church.

mum loss of timber, to form a structure on two or three distinct levels, which relies for its rigidity on the strength of massive timbers, which were often cambered to give them the necessary stiffness to span the tower effectively. From the 17th century onwards, however, bell-frames were usually supported by a heavily framed floor which spread the forces generated during ringing. Much smaller timbers could be used for the foundations of the frame, which were jointed together at a single level using simple mortises and tenons; and the support given by the floor along the entire length of the foundation beams compensated for the weakening effect of the many joints. The heavy weight of many of these frames was usually sufficient to prevent movement relative to the floor, without any need for clamping or jointing to the floor beams.

A preliminary survey suggests that about 75 churches – one-tenth of Norfolk's total – have substantial remains of old and interesting bell-frames; and although some are quite good enough to hold bells which are merely chimed, many are in very poor condition, and quite unsuitable for bells to be rung in full circles. In recent years old frames have been preserved when bells have been rehung, either hauled up to a higher level as at Saham Toney; or they have been left in the old bell-chamber when a new frame has been placed lower in the tower, as at Beetley, Norwich St George Colegate and South Repps. It is sometimes a problem to reconcile the conservation of an ancient and interesting bell-frame with parishio-ners' wishes to restore their often equally ancient and interesting bells to traditional use; and it was sad but inevitable that the old timber frame at Little Walsingham had to be taken out of the tower to make way for a new metal frame when the bells were recently rehung.

Some of the most interesting bell-frames are those where alterations to the original design reveal something of the history of the ring of bells which they contain. Few frames have been more drastically altered when extra bells were introduced than that at Norwich St Lawrence,[52] where a four-bell frame was adapted first for five bells and later for six. At Field Dalling it can be seen how the wide pits of a three-bell frame were nar-rowed and converted when the old bells were replaced by a lighter ring of five in 1752; and at Martham a 14th-century four-bell frame has dated additions of 1682 and 1717. The bell-installation at Tittleshall is of great interest, apparently dating from the casting of a new ring of four in 1623. The frame here appears to have been rebuilt from an older 'king-post' version, and the bells are still secured to their headstocks using shear-bands through the single cannons and wedged bolts through the double cannons. At Hanworth the three-bell frame (c.1483–1490) was extended to take five bells by 1635, and the problem of getting a good rope 'circle' was solved by hanging one bell on a higher level than the others. The Wood-

[52] Thurlow, *op. cit.* p. 3, fig. 1.

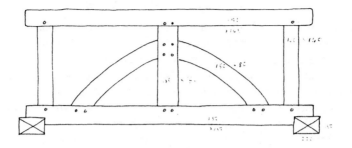

Frame truss.

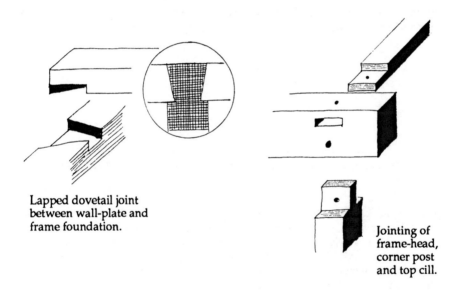

Lapped dovetail joint
between wall-plate and
frame foundation.

Jointing of
frame-head,
corner post
and top cill.

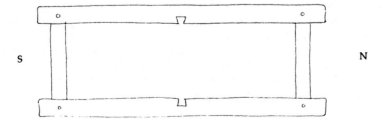

S

N

Archaic frame made in 1683 for a single bell at Shelton.

ton bells were an early ring of six (1641), and the complicated two-tier framework for them remains above the modern installation.

There are one or two very unusual frames, such as that at Ickburgh, where the three bells hang diagonally across a tower which would be too small for them to hang in line. The cross-braced trusses have no king-posts, like those in the early frame at Alderford. The three-bell frame at Riddlesworth has one pair of trusses with crossed braces, and another with sharply angled braces. A very interesting frame in the tower at Hockwold[53] has been dated to the early years of the 14th century: the three pits here have curved braces, and the king-posts extend upwards to form a gallows arrangement above the frame-heads. Perhaps the most curious frame of all is at Norwich St Andrew,[54] where a two-tier frame was designed to take a ring of eight bells in 1705. Six bells hang in an octagonal lower tier with the two trebles on a bridge above: augmentation to ten bells in 1825 added a further tier to the frame, and produced one of the oddest sequences of ropes in any ringing chamber.

APPENDIX

Early 16th-century accounts for building a bell frame.
Extracts from Swaffham churchwardens' accounts, NRO PD 52/71.

Thes be the Receytys Receyvyd be the hands of us Aubery Gryggs, Watyr Payn and John Newell Church revys of the Church of petur and pawle of Swafham market sythens the last cownte made the iiij[te] sondaye of Advente the yere of owre lord God mccccxiiij[te] (et anno regni regis Henrici VIII sexti).
Rec. of the plowmony to the reparation of the Stepull xxxvj s. viij d.
Receyvyd be the hands of Sir Robert Boson of the good wille and mynde of Margaret Sergeaunt to the edifyeng of the belle frames xiijs. iiijd.
Receyvyd be the good wille of the Abbot of Westmynster toward the reparation of the belle frame be the hands of Thomas Leman Vyker xx s.
Rec. of the goodwylle of the brethren and systern of saynt peturrys gylde be the hands of Tebald Bryell to the hangyng up of the bellys vj s. viij d.
Rec. of the plowemony to the reparation of the bellys as it apperith in the plowe booke anno regni regis henrici octavi septimo xix s. v d. ob.
Rec. be the hands of John Newell for the profer of Thomas Leman, clerke, in full payment of his profer for the hangyng up of the bellys x s.

[53] Mr G. Elphick has dated the Hockwold frame by tree-ring analysis to the early years of the 14th century. Thanks to Mr R. W. M. Clouston for this information.
[54] Thurlow, *op. cit.* pp. 10,11, figs 4, 5.

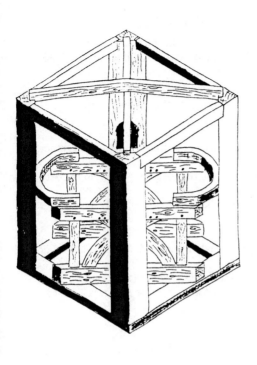

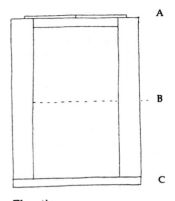

Elevation

A

B

C

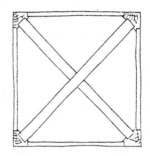

Plan at A

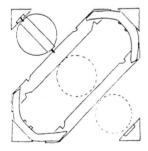

Plan at B

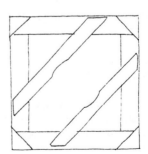

Plan at C

Unusual 'high-sided' diagonal bell-frame at Ickburgh.

The payments for work on the bell-frame and on the purchase of materials, recorded at intervals during the period between Advent 1514 and Advent 1516, are here extracted:

Payd to the belwrygth for his expences and hys arnest mony xij d.

Payd in mete and drynke and wages whan the tymber was sett home from Mr Awdeleys xxij d.

Payd for carynge of his takull viij d.

Payd in Expences that same tyme the Wrygth whas her to sorte owte the tymber vij d.

Payd to Edmunde Aleyn in arnest whan we made the bargeny with hym in party of payment of xj li. vj s. viij d.

Payd to Edmunde Aleyn in Arnest whan we made the bargeny in the weke after Wynwall xij s.

Payd for a tre at Est bradenham x d.

Payd for mete and drynke and other expences when they did swarre the tymber owte a towne xx d.

Payd in expences for mete and drynke whan the sollers wher made cleyn iiij d.

Payd to Edmund Aleyn Wrygth in the weke befor passyon sondaye last past in party of payment of his bargeny xviij s.

Payd for a tre at Est bradenham viij d.

Payd for caryage of a tre xij d.

Payd to Edmund Aleyn the yonger in palmesonday weke in party of payment of hys bargeny iij s. iiij d.

Payd to John Tennant of Schypdam for iij trees x s. iiij d.

Payd for a lode of woode carynge from Schypdam xiiij d.

Payd in expences whan the tymbyr whas set from thens vj d.

Payd for a lode of tymbyr caryng from Sametony xij d.

Payd in expences that same tyme the tymbyr cam from Sametony iij d.

Payd for a lode of tymbyr xv d.

Payd for woode fellyng iij s. iiij d.

Payd Richard Belys for burdyng the wrygts xij d.

Payd John brown baly for x peces of tymber xiij s. iiij d.

Payd Edmund Aleyn wrygth in party of payment of hys bargeny the mondaye after Trynyte sondaye iij s. iiij d.

Payd to Edmunde Aleyn wrygth a dayes werke whan he wente to chose the tymbyr and for other men for ther expences xvj d.

Payd to John Symonds of Stoberd for iij dayes werke hewyng and swaryng of tymbyr iij d.

Payd to Men of Bradenham for a dayes werke helpyn to lode the cartes and owther besydes iij d.

Payd in Expenses and in mete and drynke to the carters when they caryed tymbyr from Sametony Wytness Wylham Langham and Gilberd Fecket ix d.

Payd Edmund Aleyn the Sondaye next after mydsomer in party of payment of his bargeny x s.

Payd for viij loode caryyng from Same parke gate xiiij s. ij d.

Payd that same time in expences iij d.

Payd to Edmund Aleyn upon marymawdelyn evyn in party of payment of hys bargeny xx s.

Payd in mete and drynke for caryyng of the grette tymber to the stepull dore vj d.

Payd to Edmund Aleyn the weke that saynt Bartylmew whas yn in party of payment of his bargeny iij s. iiij d.

Payd to Edmund Aleyn upon saynt Edward's daye last in party of payment of his bargeny xx s.

Payd to Edmund Aleyn the wrygth be the hands of Awbry Gryggs in party of payment of his bargeny vj s. viij d.

Payd to Mr Griggs be the hands of John Newell that he schuld paye to Mr Bullen for ix okes xviij s.

Payd to Edmund Aleyn belwrygth in party of payment of hys bargeny iij s. iiij d.

Payd to Robert Taylor for to go seke the bellewrygth xij d.

Payd to Edmund Aleyn upon Saynt Barnebees evyn the Apostoll in party of payment of his bargeny xxxiijs. iiij d.

Payd to Edmund Aleyn upon Saynt Jamys day in party of payment of hys bargeny xl s.

Payd for iiij^{xx} li. schetyn for the brassers xiij s. iiij d.

Payd for v^{li} of new brasyng xx d.

Payd to Pratt of derham for xiiij^{te} ston of yerne werke for Gogynnys in full payment xxxiiij s. iiij d.

Payd to Harry Man for mendyng of yren that went to the bellys x d.

Payd to Edmund Aleyn bellwrygth the sondaye nexst after bartylmewdaye in full payment of his bargeny of xj li. xl s.'

Chapter Four

NORFOLK BELL-FOUNDERS AND THEIR BELLS

Although most bells cast during the second half of 16th century and later have dates inscribed on them, this is rarely the case with older bells; and it is very difficult to ascribe early bells to named founders with any precision. Walters gives a complete list of bells which bear dates between 1296 and 1559, and only three of the 40 entries in his list relate to bells in Norfolk churches: Salhouse (1481), Islington (1556) and Reepham (1559). He also lists early founders whose names appear on bells; including four from Norwich: Richard Baxter, Richard Brasyer, William de Norwyco and Thomas Potter; four from King's Lynn: John Godyng, Edmund de Lenne, Thomas de Lenne, John de Lenne; and three whose place of origin is not known: Walter Blower, William Silisden and Thomas Derby.[1]

There is no doubt that a great deal of travelling was necessary to obtain the metal required for casting bells; and contact between founders working in Norfolk and those working in other places would have been inevitable. The Sacrist's accounts at Ely for 1345/1346 show that John of

Since this chapter is heavily annotated, the reader is reminded of the abbreviations used to identify sources.

ANF   Wills proved in the Norfolk Archdeaconry Court (Norfolk Record Office).
CBC   J. J. Raven, *The church bells of Cambridgeshire*, 1881.
CBE   C. H. Deedes and H. B. Walters, *The church bells of Essex*, 1909.
CBN   J. L'Estrange, *The church bells of Norfolk*, 1874.
CBS   J. J. Raven, *The church bells of Suffolk*, 1890.
DCN   Manuscripts belonging to the Dean and Chapter of Norwich (Norfolk Record Office).
NCC   Wills proved in the Norwich Consistory Court (Norfolk Record Office).
NCR   Records belonging to the City of Norwich (Norfolk Record Office).
NED   Deeds enrolled in the Norwich City Court; among the records of the City of Norwich (Norfolk Record Office).
NRO   Norfolk Record Office.
OFB   Old Free Book of the City of Norwich, NRO NCR Case 17b.
PRO   Public Record Office, Chancery Lane, London.

[1]   H. B. Walters, *Church Bells in England*, 1912, pp. 317, 318. Mr R. W. M. Clouston reminds the writer that Walters did not know of the bell dated 1254 at Lissett, Humberside.

Gloucester, the bell-founder employed to cast four very large bells for the Cathedral, went himself to Lynn, and sent his apprentices to Northampton in search of bell-metal: he also went as far as Lynn to find suitable clay for making his bell-moulds.[2] After the great belfry had been completed c.1310 at Norwich Cathedral Priory, the Master of the Cellar sent to London for suitable metal from which to cast a large new bell at the expense of Prior Lakenham; and the metal was brought to Norwich for the bell to be cast by local founders.[3]

It is hardly surprising that bells produced by contemporary founders working from different centres are similar in some respects, and there are a number of characteristics which may help in dating them. The proportions of a bell (especially the ratio of height to diameter) appear to give a good general indication of the approximate date; and it is generally accepted that older bells are taller. The inside of a bell is formed by baking a clay mould (the core); and a model of the bell is laid onto the core, using soft loam, with ridges (moulding wires) on the outside, produced by rotating a moulding template (strickle). Hard clay is then laid over the loam model and baked to form the outer matrix (cope) in which the bell is cast. Bells made from the same pattern would have identical moulding wires; and it is likely that a founder would have a set of similar strickles for bells of different sizes. The moulding wires appear as half-rounds, bevels and flat bands, whose pattern depends more on fashion than necessity. While half-rounds and bevels in various combinations are commonly found, flat bands are more common on bells cast before c.1520.

Most bells have neatly-formed inscriptions placed in a band below the shoulder at the time of casting; and until comparatively recently the letters were formed from wax impressions made in a set of pottery moulds. The wax letters, attached to the soft clay model of the bell, melted when the cope was baked, leaving indentations into which the molten metal ran at the time of casting. Most pre-Reformation bells have inscriptions in Latin, the universal language of mediaeval scholarship and, of course, the church. Various forms of the Salutation are found, ranging from the simple '*AVE MARIA*', at Caistor by Norwich to fuller versions; and other invocations of Our Lady, such as '*Maria Stella Maris Succurre Piisima Nobis*' are common. Rhyming couplets are found on early bells throughout the country, and stock inscriptions such as; '*Virginis Egregie : Vocor Campana*

---

[2]   D. J. Stewart, *On the Architectural History of Ely Cathedral*, London, 1868, p. 117.
[3]   NRO DCN 1/1/22 (1310–1311).
In metallo ad campanam apud London' xx li.
In cariacione eiusdem metalli xj s.
In liberatione Nalli apud London' per manus Bauchun v s.
In liberatione Thome de Celar' et Crop versus London iiij s.
In factura campane et in expensis sic patet per billam
xij li. ix s. ij d.
[The names which appear are those of monastic carters and servants.]

Marie', *'Sum Rosa Pulsata Mundi : Maria Vocata'* and *'In Multis Annis : Resonet Campana Johannis'* are common. References to the Annunciation were popular, such as: *'Missus De Celis : Habeo Nomen Gabrielis'* and *'Hac In Conclave : Gabriel Nunc Pange Suave'*. A number of tenors have a reference to the baptism of bells, linking this, perhaps, with a dedication to St John Baptist: *'Munere Baptiste : Benedictus Sit Chorus Iste'*. A few local saints appear in inscriptions such as: *'Meritis Edmundi : Simus a Crimine Mundi'* at Denton, and an invocation of St Etheldreda at Morley St Botolph.

Since early bells do not themselves yield a great deal of firm evidence about their founders various documents have been examined: including wills, deeds and churchwardens' accounts.[4] These show that bell-foundries were well-established in both Norwich and King's Lynn as early as the 13th century; and it seems likely that there was another foundry in north-east Norfolk during first half of the 15th century. L'Estrange's researches into the history of local bell-foundries, published in 1874, form an excellent starting point for the history of bell-founding in Norfolk; but more recent examination of documents suggests that a substantial revision of names and dates is needed.[5] The assumption that founders working from different centres were necessarily in competition may have been true in some cases; but it would appear from documents that there was more cooperation between them than has been generally supposed. It is also quite clear from Norwich bell-founders' wills that the foundry was organised as an atelier where a number of independent craftsmen worked. Some were definitely bell-founders; while others produced related metal artefacts, such as pots, pans, mortars, and brass bearings. It has also been suggested that monumental brasses were made by bell-founders during the early years of the 16th century.[6]

Many of the earliest bell-founders were itinerant, setting up their furnaces and foundries where work was required, and conveying the necessary metal and tools to the site where a bell was to be cast. An excavation has revealed a 12th-century bell-casting pit inside the walls of the destroyed church of St Michael at Thetford; and another has been found at the 11th century chapel, recently excavated within the earthworks of

---

4   Mostly at the Norfolk Record Office.
5   J. L'Estrange, *The church bells of Norfolk*, 1874.
    L'Estrange's account of the Norwich bell-founders appears to be defective in a number of ways; and it is clear from surviving documents that bell-founders were active in Norwich at least from the early years of the 13th century. The assumption that Robert Brasyer was not involved in bell-founding, and that his son Richard I was the first bell-founder of that family, appears to be untenable; and it is certain that bell-founding flourished in Norwich between 1513 and 1530.
6   R. Greenwood and M. Norris, *The brasses of Norfolk churches*, 1976, p. 32.

Rising Castle.[7] A number of apparently 14th-century bells have also been ascribed to itinerants; but this was before it was known that founders were operating from Norwich as early as the 13th century. It seems much more likely that these wide-spread, but very similarly designed bells are survivors of a group centred on Norwich. The names of founders such as William Eldhouse, Walter Blowere and Robert Plummer have been found on bells in mid-Norfolk, but have not so far appeared in Norwich documents. There were, of course, itinerant founders as late as the 18th century: but they seem to have been a minority. It is also quite difficult to separate genuine itinerants, such as Michael Darbie (c.1660) and Henry Yaxley (c.1670) from others such as the Newmans (around 1700) who operated from a small number of centres on a fairly regular basis.

NORWICH BELL-FOUNDERS

The distribution of pre-Reformation bells in Norfolk and Suffolk suggests that Norwich was an important bell-founding centre from at least the 13th century; and documents provide the names of a number of early bell-founders. The Norwich Domesday of 1378 gives the regulations for levies on goods shipped at the Common Staithe, among them a requirement for 'excessive loads such as bells' to be the subject of special negotiation.

There is also archaeological evidence[8] for bell-founding from various sites in Norwich, including two bell-casting pits discovered by Alan Carter and Jan Roberts in the 1970s. It has been suggested that the one found at Bacon's House, Colegate, was used for casting a small bell for the neighbouring church of St George, Colegate; and the second pit was hurriedly identified and recorded as archaeologists watched the development of a site in Ten Bell Lane. More evidence for bell-founding comes from a site in World's End Lane (to the north-east of the Cathedral, off Bishopgate) where the significance of a number of pits found in 1973 has recently been recognised by David Evans. They have been provisionally dated to the 12th or 13th century, on a site which had been heavily quarried for sand and gravel, as well as being used for dumping rubbish and silt dredged from the river bed. Mr Evans points out the destruction caused in the Cathedral Close by the 1272 riot, and suggests that some of the quarrying activity was associated with subsequent rebuilding. Both Cathedral towers were badly damaged by fire, and it is possible that the

---

7   See B. K. Davison and R. Mackay, *Mediaeval Archaeology XV*, 1971, pp. 130, 131. Also B. M. Morley, Department of the Environment, unpublished excavation at Castle Rising communicated to the writer in February 1981.

8   M. Atkins and D. H. Evans, 'Excavations in Norwich 1971–1978', *East Anglian Archaeology'*, forthcoming. Grateful thanks are recorded to Mr Evans for permission to refer to this ahead of publication. See also note 3, above.

bell made for Prior Lakenham c.1310 might have been cast on a convenient site of this kind. Certain trades were excluded from the built-up areas
of towns by the end of the Middle Ages; and there was pressure for
industries where there were nasty smells, or risks of accidental fire (such
as lime-burning, pottery making, blacksmithing and other metal working), to be located on waste ground away from densely populated areas.[9]
The World's End Lane site would have been very suitable for bell-founding; and had the added advantage that river transport was close at hand.
The area near the Castle was also thinly developed, and it is interesting to
find a number of 14th- and 15th-century bell-founders owning property
in and around the castle ditches.[10]

Godfrey le Belleyetere
Mentioned in a document c.1260, probably working c.1220

Ralph le Belleyetere
Mentioned in a document c.1260

There was without doubt a strong association between personal names
and the trades or crafts of their owners in mediaeval Norwich and Norfolk.[11] The lists of freemen, beginning in 1317, show this clearly, as do
early documents belonging to both the Cathedral and the Great Hospital.
As late as c.1480 we find the East Dereham churchwardens resorting to
Robert Themyll (thimble) for repairs to the vestments, to Edmund Wryght
for carpentry, and to William Thaxter (thatcher) for reeding the roofs of
the almshouses. The term 'bellyeter' appears in early Norwich documents; and the Oxford English Dictionary gives 'bell-yetter, literally bell-
pourer'. The term 'yetting' and variants were in use at late as 1590 when a
new bell was cast for Tibenham.

   The earliest evidence for Norwich bell-founders is contained in three
deeds belonging to the Dean and Chapter of Norwich. In a deed which

---

9   See C. Platt, *The English mediaeval town*, 1979, p. 57; also H. Harrod, *The castles
     and convents of Norfolk*, Norwich, 1857, pp. 136–138.
10   NCR Case 17b, Norwich Domesday, fo. 23d.
11   The term 'bellyeter' appears in Norwich documents from c.1260, and the *Ox-
     ford English Dictionary* definition (see under 'bell') is 'bell-yetter, literally bell-
     pourer'. The term 'yetting' and variants were in use at late as 1590 to describe
     the operation of casting a bell (see the Tibenham churchwardens' accounts at
     the Cambridge University Library among the Buxton Mss., case 34, bay 3, shelf
     2). W. Rye, *A short calendar of the deeds . . . enrolled . . . 1285–1306*, Norwich, 1903,
     p. xii, describes one John de Rudham, *'campanarius'*, as the earliest of the Nor-
     wich bell-founders. The rolls of the Cathedral Priory, however, suggest that he
     was a clerk whom they employed on a number of causes, and his description as
     'campanarius' is much more likely to imply that he was responsible for arrang-
     ing the ringing of the cathedral bells for various occasions.

can be dated to the period 1257–1266, one John le Peintur conveyed a tenement in the parish of St Peter in Conesford,[12] Norwich to the Prior and Convent of the Holy Trinity, for the health of his soul and those of his father and mother. The income from the tenement was to be at the disposal of the Refectorer. John le Peintur refers in the deed to his father, Godfrey le Belleyetere; and the abuttals of the property mention an adjacent tenement occupied by Ralph le Belleyetere.[13] Assuming a date c.1260 for the conveyance of the property from John le Peintur to the Prior and Convent, it would appear that Ralph le Belleyetere was alive at that time; and the fact that the donor was sufficiently well-established to make such a gift suggests that he was probably in his middle-age, and that his father, Godfrey le Belleyetere, might have been working from c.1220. It is possible that Ralph le Belleyetere was casting bells on the site, although this cannot be confirmed from the documents; but it is interesting to notice that the abuttals of the deeds refer to neighbouring bell-founders, glasswrights, and latoners, as well as the painter himself. Perhaps this particular area in the parish of St Peter Parmentergate might have been a centre where a number of ecclesiastical craftsmen were based.

Martin le Belleyetere
Mentioned in a document of 1290

Martin le Bellyetere was fined for harbouring a groom belonging to another tithing in the city in 1290; and although this is the only reference so far discovered, it may be significant that he belonged to a tithing in the same area of Norwich as the two bell-founders suggested above.[14]

---

12 The parish is that which is at present referred to as St Peter Parmentergate, as is clear from the returns of rent from the property which appear in the Refectorer's rolls (DCN 1/7): in a roll for 1450, for example the property is specifically defined as a tenement formerly owned by Ralph le Belleyetere in the parish of St Peter Parmentergate in Conesford.

13 Three deeds remain. DCN deed no. 206 is dated 3 May, 1331, and confirms rent from the tenement (referring to previous occupiers) due to the Castle fee. DCN deed no. 558 is undated but refers to Prior Roger, who can only be Roger de Skerning, 1257–1266, there being no other Prior with that Christian name: the deed is, in fact, a lease of the property to Walter de Marisco and gives the abuttals, mentioning a rent due to the Castle fee. DCN deed no. 105, undated, is the original deed of conveyance between John le Peintur and Prior Roger and has eight witnesses in common with deed no. 558, suggesting that it is almost contemporary. Neighbours include Robert le Glaswright (in DCN deed no. 206) and Thomas de Surlingham (in DCN deed 206) who appears in a deed of 1332 (NCR Roll 8, membrane 20.) as a latoner.

14 W. H. Hudson, 'Leet Jurisdiction in the city of Norwich during the XIII and XIV centuries', *Selden Society Publication*, London, 1892, p. 42.

Robert de Walpole
Mentioned in documents during years 1314–1322

Robert le Belleyetere and Letitia his wife appear in two enrolments relating to property purchased in the parish of St Michael-at-Plea in 1314 and 1316. A further reference to Robert de Walpole 'alias le Belleyetere', when an adjoining property was conveyed in 1322, probably refers to the same man.[15]

Alan le Belleyetere
Mentioned a document of 1316

In a deed of 1316 one Alan le Belleyetere, described as the son of Richard Poche of Preston, conveys property in the parish of St Martin-in-Balliva to Geoffrey de Wodenorton, chaplain.[16]

William de Norwyco
Probably active during the third quarter of the 14th century

The name of William de Norwyco, which has not been traced in the Old Free Book,[17] appears on a number of bells near Norwich. The single bell at Hellesdon is inscribed: 'IOHNES DE HEYLESDON ME FECIT FIERI IN HONORE MATRS CRESTI WILELLMVS DE NORWYCO ME FECIT'; and the words suggest that John de Hellesdon caused it to be made during his lifetime. The advowson of Hellesdon was conveyed to Walter de Berney, Richard de Hellesdon and his son John de Hellesdon in 1362/63, and on a brass recording the date of his death in 1384 John de Hellesdon is described as patron of the church.[18] This suggests that the bell was cast within the period 1362–1384. Other bells bearing his name are found at Barford and Bintree. As will appear later, a reference in a Norwich document to 'William le Belleyetere' in 1397 is much more likely to refer to another bell-founder; and the fact that this was a sufficient identification for him suggests that William de Norwyco had been dead, or away from Norwich, for some long time before that date.

[15] See NED Roll 7, membrane 3 (1314), Roll 8, membrane 5 d (1316); and Roll 10, membrane 2 (1322).
[16] NED Roll 7, membrane 15d.
[17] After 1317 admissions to the Freedom of Norwich are recorded in the Old Free Book (NCR Case 17b). Many 'braziers' are recorded from 1327 onwards, but only those who seem definitely to have been bell-founders are here recorded. John de Sutton is the first to be styled 'belleyetere', in 1403. The full list of freemen is found in J. L'Estrange, *Calendar of the freemen of Norwich 1317 to 1603*, 1888. The earliest Landgable Assessment is recorded in the Norwich Domesday, fo. 36 (NCR Case 17b).
[18] Blomefield X, pp. 426, 431.

Three bells from Forncett St Mary. Pre-Reformation tenor, second bell of 1603 by William Brend (showing crude repair by a local blacksmith), treble of 1707 by Thomas Newman. *Photograph by the author.*

Fourteenth-century king-post frame, with later frame-heads, at West Newton. *Photograph by Christopher Dalton.*

Fourteenth-century scissors-braced frame at Thompson. *Photograph by the author.*

Detail of the braces of the West Newton frame, showing the horizontal transom supported by short struts. *Photograph by Christopher Dalton.*

Detail of the frame at Bedingham, showing open-ended bell-pit with double-braced outer truss. *Photograph by the author.*

Seventeenth-century bell-house at Wood Rising, built to carry the bells after the collapse of the tower. *Photograph by the author.*

The Field Dalling bells in their eighteenth-century fittings, before rehanging. *Photograph by the author.*

Detail of the Field Dalling bell-frame. *Photograph by the author.*

Ground pulley, 1754 at Fundenhall. *Photograph by the author.*

Headstock of bell dated 1577, formerly at Illington, showing contemporary nailed bands and later screwed ironwork. *Photograph by the author.*

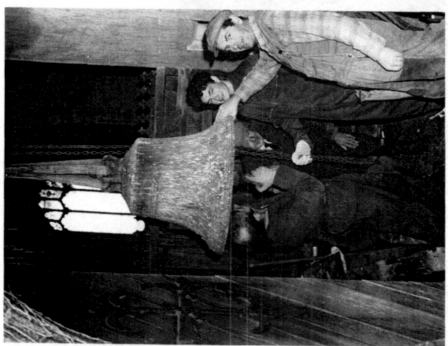

Pre-Reformation bells removed from disused churches at Illington (left) and Forncett St Mary (right). *Photographs by the author.*

Early fifteenth-century bell by Thomas Potter, at Boxford, Suffolk. The cannons have been removed, and the lip has been heavily chipped for tuning. *Photograph by Christopher Dalton.*

Disused bell probably cast by Richard Brasyer I, at Ufford, Suffolk. The
bell has fine cannons, but has lost the top part of its argent. *Photograph
by Christopher Dalton.*

Bell cast by Richard Brasyer II, at Tacolnestone (formerly at Norwich,
St Peter Parmentergate). *Photograph by the author.*

Wedged ironwork supporting the seventeenth-century treble bell at Wacton. *Photograph by the author.*

Bell cast by William Brend of Norwich, 1615, at Great Ellingham. *Photograph by the author.*

Bell cast 1721 by John Stephens, hung with its contemporary fittings at Seething. Note the high quality of casting. *Photograph by the author.*

Bell cast 1599 by Thomas Draper of Thetford, at Illington. *Photograph by the author.*

Bell cast 1671 by Edward Tooke for Norwich, St Peter Parmentergate (recast for Tacolnestone in 1982). Note the poor quality of the casting, when contrasted with bells by earlier founders. *Photograph by the author.*

Fifteenth-century bell cast by John de Guddinc (or Godyng), at Wendling. *Photograph by the author.*

Early fourteenth-century bell cast by Thomas de Lenne, at Long Stratton. The lip has been heavily clipped to sharpen the note. *Photograph by the author.*

Lettering and marks on a fourteenth-century bell at Long Stratton, probably cast by Thomas de Lenne. *Photograph by the author.*

Lettering and marks used by Thomas Derby of Lynn, from a bell at Ampton. *Photograph by the author.*

William de Sutton
John de Sutton

Both mentioned in a Yarmouth document of 1370; William made a freeman of Norwich c.1391, and last mentioned in a Norwich document of 1402; John made a freeman of Norwich in 1403/04.

Although not admitted to the freedom of Norwich until c.1391, William de Sutton was casting bells (with John de Sutton) long before. In a Yarmouth borough court roll[19] William and John de Sutton plead against Thomas Ledbetere for damages of £20. The two founders were melting metal in order to cast a bell for St Nicholas Church, probably in temporary inclosure nearby; when Thomas came armed with a knife and threw 19 lb of tin into the molten metal so that the bell was ruined. It is not clear whether Thomas was a business rival, but it seems certain that William and John were itinerants who had set up a temporary foundry to do a specific job in Yarmouth.

When William was admitted to the freedom of Norwich[20] in 15/16 Richard II he was described as a brazier; and in March 1392 one John Smith conveyed to William de Sutton, Emma his wife and Robert Brasyer a vacant piece of ground in the parish of All Saints. In 1394 'William de Sutton le Belletyetere' bought more land in 'Wastelgate' jointly with Robert Brasyer; and the two seem to have had close business connections. He is last mentioned in a deed of 1402, when property immediately to the west of the church of St John Berstrete (now called St John Timberhill) was conveyed to William de Sutton, John de Sutton and others.[21] John de Sutton, admitted to the freedom of Norwich in 5 Henry IV (1403/04), is the first to be described as 'Belleyetere' in the Old Free Book.

William de Notyngham
Admitted as a freeman of Norwich 1376, will proved in 1396

William de Notyngham was described as a brazier in his admission to the freedom of Norwich[22] in 1376, and a deed[23] dated 1419 conveys property which had been formerly occupied by 'William de Notyngham, bellfounder and citizen of Norwich'. In his will,[24] which was proved in 1396,

19 NRO Y/C4/84. The writer is grateful to Mr Paul Rutledge for drawing his attention to this document.
20 OFB fo. 38. John's admission to the freedom of Norwich: OFB fo. 40d.
21 NED Roll 15, membranes 7, 16 and 38d; also Roll 16, membrane 11d. In August 1989 the writer inspected a bell pit excavated by Ms. Jez Reeve ahead of the development of the Castle Mall. Due west of St John's church, the excavation site appears to be very close to the property conveyed in 1402.
22 OFB fo. 35d.
23 NED Roll 17, membrane 16.
24 NED Roll 15, membrane 29d.

the testator is called 'William de Notyngham, citizen of Norwich'; and an entry in the Landgable assesment for 1397 refers to property which formerly belonged to William le Belleyetere, in the relatively open area which surrounded the castle and its ditches. It seems probable that his foundry would have been near the castle; while his tenement in the Barley Market was more likely to have been either a dwelling house or an investment property. The fact that the property near the castle was not bequeathed suggests that a transaction with another founder might well have taken place shortly before his death.

L'Estrange notices the admission of William de Notyngham to the freedom of Norwich in 1376 and surmises that 'a few years residence in Norwich would have entitled him to call himself William de Norwyco'. J. J. Raven goes further in his description of a bell at Conington, Cambridgeshire, which he describes as 'the handiwork of William de Notyngham, afterwards known as William de Norwyco'. The distinction between the two Williams seems to be confirmed by documentary evidence, especially the will of 1396 which refers to William de Notyngham. If he had altered his name after a few years in Norwich, it is hardly likely that he would have reverted to his former name in his will; or that the deed of 1417 would have used an obselete name. While it could be argued that William was 'of Nottingham' while in the Norwich, and 'of Norwich' when away from home; it is worth recording that his family might well have been established in East Anglia for one or two earlier generations, since one Richard de Notyngham (parson of Homersfield) conveyed land in St Vedast parish in 1322.[25]

Robert Fuller, also called Robert Brasyer
Freeman of Norwich 1377, will proved 1435

Robert Fuller is described as a brazier from Stoke Ferry in his admission to the freedom of Norwich[26] in 1377; but numerous records of property transactions in the city court rolls and elsewhere show that he was commonly called Robert Brasyer by 1381. This is confirmed in 1393 when he presents a charter before the city court as 'Robertus le Brasyere', and is

[25] CBN p. 25; CBC p. 137; and see NCR Private Deeds, St Vedast parish.
[26] Admission: OFB fo. 35d.
There are many references among the enrolled deeds; see especially: 1380 (DCN deed N 54.) Robert Fuller, brazier, purchases a messuage in St Stephen's parish; 1381 (NED Roll 14, membrane 12) Robert Brasyer purchases a messuage in Wastelgate; 1383 (NED Roll 14, membrane 18) Robert Fuller is mentioned in abuttals of a messuage in St Stephen's parish; 1389 (NED Roll 14, membrane 32) 'Robert Fullere alias le Brasyer' purchases a vacant piece of ground bounded on all sides by the highway of Wastelgate. See also OFB fo. 46, where the entry refers to Robert, the father as a bell-founder and Richard, the son as a goldsmith.

Monumental brass to Robert and Christiana Brasyer, at Norwich,
St Stephen's church. Rubbing by kind permission of the vicar and
churchwardens. *Photograph by the author.*

cited in the same document as 'Robertus Fuller le Brasyer'. Among peti-
tions filed in the Court of Common Pleas are several relating to Robert
Brasyer of Norwich, who is particularly described as a bell-founder both
in 1390 and 1415. He is also referred to as a bell-founder when his son,
Richard Brasyer I, was admitted to the freedom of Norwich in 1424/25.

Robert Brasyer occupied a prominent place in Norwich:[27] as one of the
four bailiffs who governed the city in the years 1391, 1398 and 1403. When
the charter of 1404 empowered the citizens to elect a mayor and two

27 B. Cozens-Hardy and E. A. Kent, *The Mayors of Norwich 1405–1835*, 1938, p. 17.

sheriffs, he was elected sheriff: becoming mayor in 1410. He also represented Norwich as a burgess in the Parliaments of 1413 and 1417. Deeds show that he invested in a great deal of property in Norwich, usually in association with other wealthy citizens; and his business interests were wide-ranging. He acquired a tightly-packed group of properties in St Stephen's parish from 1380 onwards; and from his will we know of his dwelling house, with shops beneath and to the south (facing what is now Rampant Horse Street). There was a hall, pantry, buttery, kitchen and other domestic offices; and we read of domestic utensils which included jugs of silver and gilt. There were also rented properties facing Wastelgate (now called Red Lion Street), and a house with garden (facing the present Brigg Street). He owned most of the properties on a large island site, in the centre of which was 'Brasyer's Inn'. It was in 1385 that 'Robert Fullere alias le Brasyer' purchased a 'vacant piece of ground bounded on all sides by the highway of Wastelgate', which would have been suitable for bell-founding.[28] Kirkpatrick described this property in 1728 as follows: 'There is a triangular checker of buildings between the said Red Lion and the other two lanes mentioned above (Wastelgate and Over Wastelgate) which was the workhouse of Robert Brasyer and his descendants who were eminent Brasiers and Bellfounders. It is now a dwelling house and common brew house: near the west corner of it is the said Great Cockey.' Kirkpatrick[29] related the conveyance of 1385 to an entry in the Chamberlain's accounts for 1507/08, when 13d. was spent in repairing the 'common gutter called the cockey against the messuage of Master Brasier'. His notes recall '*regiam viam ex omne parte* – so must be Brown's brewing place, late Baldwins, N.B. Brasier's workhouse lately Mr Baldwin's brewhouse'. A later deed tells us that the triangular piece of ground certainly passed through the three generations of the Brasyer family to John Aleyn; but it appears that the main centre of bell-founding operations was on the opposite side of Wastelgate adjoining the property which became known as 'The Three Bells'.

Robert Brasyer's first wife, Katherine, is named in deeds[30] between 1380 and 1389; and it seems likely that his two sons whose wills[31] were proved in 1426 and 1428, were born of this first marriage. William Brasyer was Vicar of Reydon, and John Brasyer was Vicar of Debenham. Another son, Richard Brasyer I, in his will names Margery as his mother, giving us the name of Robert Brasyer's second wife; and a third wife, Christiana, is named in Robert Brasyer's own will.[32] Strong connections with the Church are suggested by the fact that a third son, John Brasyer is de-

---

[28] NED Roll 24, membrane 6.
[29] See W. H. Hudson, *The streets and lanes of the city of Norwich, a memoir by John Kirkpatrick*, 1889, p. 19; also Kirkpatrick Mss. Nos 41–45, NCR Case 21f, g.
[30] See DCN deed N54; and NED Roll 14, membrane 32, for example.
[31] NCC wills, Surflete 7.
[32] NCC wills, Surflete 177 and A Caston 122.

scribed as *'clericus'* in his father's will; while Robert Brasyer, a monk of Norwich Cathedral Priory whose funeral expenses are recorded in a Sacrist's roll[33] of 1472, may well have been another son.

Robert Brasyer was one of the wealthiest Norwich men when he wrote his will in 1434, 'having come to old age'. His wife inherited measures of cloth and pack horses; but the fact that the bell-foundry is not mentioned suggests that the ownership had passed to his son during the father's lifetime. Robert Brasyer was buried in the chapel of Blessed Mary on the north side of St Stephen's church, where he endowed a chantry for a period of five years following his death. His memorial brass was removed to the back of the nave when the church was re-ordered last century; and beneath male and female figures is the inscription: *'O vos omnes picturas intuentes devotas ad deum Fundite preces pro [animabus] Roberti Brasyer istius civitatis quondam Aldermanni et maioris et Christiane uxoris eius Quibus requiem eternam donet Deus Amen.'*

John de Lopham
Admitted to the freedom of Norwich 1379, mentioned in documents until 1398

John de Lopham was admitted to the freedom of Norwich[34] as a brazier; but the only connection which can be traced with bell-founding is his association with William de Notyngham, as executor of his will.

Peter Bonde
Admitted to the freedom of Norwich 1400, mentioned in documents until 1453

There is strong circumstantial evidence for identifying Peter Bonde as a bell-founder, not least the fact that he was an executor of Robert Brasyer's will. He was admitted to the freedom of Norwich in 1400 as a brazier, and a deed of 1418 shows that he was associated with Thomas Potter. Both men had an interest in a property in Wastelgate which can later be identified as the principal site of the Norwich bell-foundry. Appearing in a list of householders in Conesford in 1453, he was dead by 1457: when his widow calls herself Katherine Brasyer, and refers to her late husband as Peter Bonde in one place, and as Peter Brasyer in another. The only evidence of his work was found by L'Estrange, who found a reference to his supplying brass for a mill spindle at Hellesdon.[35]

---

[33] DCN 1/4/93.
[34] See OFB fo. 38; NED Roll 15, membranes 27 and 34.
[35] See OFB fo. 38; CBN p. 28; NCC wills, 177 Surflete.

Thomas Potter

Admitted to the freedom of Norwich 1403, alms given at his funeral in 1428

Thomas Potter was described as a brazier in his admission to the freedom of Norwich, and is confirmed as a bell-founder by the inscription of the tenor bell at Erpingham, formerly at Norwich. St John de Sepulchre, which reads: '+ Has Campanas Tu Formasti Pottere Thomas'. His name appears in a deed of 1418 as the joint purchaser, together with Peter Bonde and John Huberd, of a property in Wastlegate, in the Parish of St Stephen, which can be identified in later documents as the site of the principal bell-foundry in Norwich through to the 1570s. The surname Potter is of interest in the suggestion, confirmed by the will of Richard Brasyer I, that the Norwich bell-founders were also involved in the production of other metal artefacts, including cooking pots. Potter's trademark, which appears on the Erpingham bell, is a three-legged cooking pot of a type recently excavated from a site in Norwich, and on display at the Castle Museum. The account rolls of the Gild of St George of Norwich for the period April 1427 to April 1428 record the receipt of alms at the exequies of five members, including one Thomas Potter; suggesting a possible date for his death.[36]

Richard Baxter

Mentioned in documents during years 1416–1457

Although he describes himself in deed of 1423 among the parish records of Northwold as 'brazier and citizen of Norwich', Richard Baxter's name has not been found in the Old Free Book; nor does he seem to have enrolled deeds in the city court. His name, however, has been found on bells at Fundenhall, Ketteringham and Trimingham, all of them of the finest quality; and there are a few other similarly marked bells which could be attributed to him. L'Estrange notes that Richard Baxter supplied two bells to the College of The Blessed Virgin Mary at Mettingham in 1416/17; and a bequest in 1418 may suggest the date of work at Fundenhall. It is probable that Richard Baxter worked at the Norwich bell-foundry, as an associate founder rather than as a tenant or employee; and that he invested his income in property in the county rather than in the city. The latest reference to him has been traced in the will of Katherine Brasyer, written and proved in 1457: where he is bequeathed a sum of 40 shillings, and a further sum if he promised not to impede her executors.[37]

---

[36] See OFB fo. 40d; NED Roll 17, membrane 12; and NCR Case 8e, Roll 5 Henry VI – 6 Henry VI.

[37] See Northwold deed, NRO PD 373/191; CBN p. 27; NCC wills, Brosyard 58.

Richard Brasyer I
Admitted to the freedom of Norwich 1424, will proved in 1482

The elder Richard Brasyer was admitted to the freedom of Norwich as a goldsmith in 1424/25; an entry which might be surprising if it were not realised that a very adequate number of bell-founders was already practising in Norwich. Ten years later his father appears to have passed the ownership of the bell-foundry on to him; and his name appears in a list of braziers compiled in 1450/51. Thomas Potter died in 1428, Peter Bonde died just before 1457; and by the end of the 1450s Richard Baxter would have been getting old. It seems likely, therefore, that Richard Brasyer began to take a more prominent place in the work of the bell-foundry during the 1450s. The city records show that he filled a number of offices during his lifetime, being sheriff in 1436, and mayor in 1456 and 1463. He was a householder in a 1453 list for Conesford, and appears as alderman of the ward of Berstrete when the Muster Roll was made in 1457. His will of 1475 makes it clear that he owned a great deal of property in the city, including 'Brasyer's Inn' in the parish of St Stephen and a number of tenements in Wastlegate which he must have bought from executors after his father's death. Some of his wealth was invested in rural Norfolk, and his will mentions considerable lands in Wramplingham, Wymondham, Barnham Broom, Great Melton and Carleton Forehoe. The foundry was left unconditionally to his son, Richard Brasyer II, with a clause requiring the tenants of the property to give an account of themselves and of the terms of their leases. The suggestion is that, although Richard Brasyer I had retained full ownership of the foundry premises and of the instruments of the craft (which he bequeathed to his son), a number of other founders were working in the premises as craftsmen in their own right, and not simply as the employees of the master-founder. The mention of pot-metal and brass pots in the will shows that the output of the foundry was not limited to church bells. Brasyer's Inn was to be sold to pay various debts; and the income from the manor of Banyard's in Kimberley was to provide a chantry priest for five years. Richard Brasyers's will was proved in 1482, and he was buried in the Lady Chapel at St Stephen's church, Norwich. It was apparently not until his son died in 1513 that there was any permanent memorial to him in the church.[38]

---

[38] See OFB fo. 68; OFB fo. 106d; CBN p. 29; NCC wills, A Caston 122; B. Cozens-Hardy and E. A. Kent, *The Mayors of Norwich 1405–1835*, 1938, p. 27; W. H. Hudson and J. C. Tingey, *The records of the City of Norwich*, 1906, pp. 284, 408.

John Magges
Admitted to the freedom of Norwich 1437/40, mentioned in documents up to 1470

John Magges was admitted to the freedom of Norwich, as a brazier, in 16–18 Henry VI. He is mentioned in the accounts of the Gild of St George, Norwich at an assembly in 1452 where 'it was agreed that thes persones folwyng to be officers for the next day comyng: John Magges and William Elmham Lightberers. Thomas Lound Banerberer'. He received a small bequest in the will of Katherine Brasyer in 1457. His bell-founding activities are confirmed by entries in the churchwardens' accounts at Walberswick, for which church he cast three bells in the period 1466–1468. The wording of the accounts suggests that the 'fowndyr of the Bellis' had performed the complete contract for a ring of five bells which were placed in the newly-completed tower. The latest reference to him is in a deed of 1470, referring to property in the parish of St Michael Berstrete.[39]

John Baly
Admitted to the freedom of Norwich 1479, and mentioned in a document of 1488

John Baly was admitted to the freedom of Norwich in 1479, on the same day as Richard Brasyer II; and both were described as braziers. When John Baly cast a bell for East Dereham church during the period 1486–1488, it is clear from the accounts that he was working closely with Richard Brasyer.[40]

Richard Brasyer II
Admitted to the freedom of Norwich 1479, died 1513

The younger Richard Brasyer, who was admitted as a brazier to the freedom of Norwich in 1479, inherited his father's foundry in 1482. Like his father and grandfather, he was much involved in the civic life of Norwich, being sheriff in 1495 and mayor in 1510. The suggestion that he organised

---

[39] See OFB fo. 49; and M. Grace, 'Records of the Gild of St George of Norwich 1389–1547', *Norfolk Record Society*, 1937, p. 45. See also: R. W. M. Lewis, *Walberswick Churchwardens' Accounts*, 1947, pp. 73–75.
1466: 'Item payde to the fownder of the bell – iij li. Item payde to the fownder of the bells for a full payment of the iij bell – xij li. Item payde to the belle maker onward of party of payment for the newe belle – vj li. Item to the carter for bryngen hom of the bells – iij s. iiij d.' 1468: 'Item payd to jonne magys in party payment for a bell – xl s. Item for a denture makynge for the same bell – v d. Item to the fowndyr of the bellis for a full payment of the leste belle – viij li. Item for bryngyn hom of the belle xxxxij d. Item payd for the bellys halwyng – xxv s. viij d.' See also: NED Roll 19, rotulet D, membrane 1.
[40] See OFB fo. 106d, and NRO PD 182 D.

the bell-foundry in a similar manner to his father is borne out by entries in the East Dereham churchwardens' accounts for 1486–1488, where it appears that a bell was cast by John Baly; and that Richard Brasyer received the churchwardens, supplied them with wine, and dealt with the necessary agreements. 'Brasyer's Inn', owned by both Robert Brasyer and Richard Brasyer I at different times, had been sold by executors in 1482; but Richard Brasyer II had acquired a similar property, known as 'The White Hart' in St Stephen's parish, where he could provide accommodation and refreshment for those who had travelled to Norwich to do business with him.

When Richard Brasyer wrote his will in 1505 it appears that he had no heir to his considerable fortune. To his wife Katherine he left his dwelling house and adjoining rented property, also half of his household valuables and half the value of his properties in Newgate: his manor of Hillis was to be enjoyed by his wife during her lifetime and after her death it was to be sold for the benefit of their souls. He also made a number of bequests to civic projects in Norwich, which included the repair of the city walls and the banks of the common river. In the will Richard Brasyer also requires his executors to retain the bell-foundry, so that one of his apprentices could assume control and enable outstanding contracts to be completed: 'Item I will that oon of the conyngest men of my occupation that hath be my prentice have the occupation of my workhous xij moneths and a day under my executors to make my charge and my bargeyns that I have to make aftre that if it can be sold to a reasonable price with all the bell moldis and wheights and other stuff longing therto I will it be sold and if thei can not sell it I will it be letten with all the bell muldis and croks and all other instruments therto longing for x li a yere or xxᵗⁱ marcs as well as thei can lett it to the performance of this my last will'. Income was set aside to provide a chantry priest 'of good name and good fame to sing and pray for my faders soole, my moders soole, and Katerine my wiff soulle, Robert Brasiers solle, Cristian his wiffs ssolle, Andrew mans solle, and Collet his wiffs, and for the solles of Kateryn and Cristian, and for all the solles that I and my said fader and moder ar beholden to and for all good Cristen sollys in the chapell of our Ladi in the said churche of saint Stephen by the space of v yerys'. The directions for completing the Brasyer memorials are complicated; and would have been fulfilled by Katherine his wife and Thomas Gryme, priest, the executors who proved the will in 1513. A marble stone was to be bought, on which images of himself and his wife, with their arms, were to be laid; and a further stone for his father's grave was to have a picture, and the son's arms placed on it. Two images were to be set on his grandfather's grave (which apparently already had a stone) by the executors. Greenwood and Norris suggest that Richard Brasyer II might himself have been involved in making monumental brasses, listing 56 possible products which include the Brasyer brasses at St Stephen's church, Norwich.

The instructions for completing the memorials seem not to have been literally carried out: for Blomefield records an inscription (confirmed by Mackerell) as follows: 'Orate pro anima Ricardi Brasyer Senioris Norwici Civitatis olim Aldermanni ac etiam pro anima Ricardi Brasyer filii eius predicte Civitate quondam Aldermanni et Maioris qui ab hac luce mugravit v die mensis Septembris anno domini Mcccccxiii.' Perhaps Katherine remarried after her husband's death, and adjusted the arrangements for the memorials accordingly.[41]

John Aleyn
Admitted to the freedom of Norwich 1505, burial recorded in 1555

John Aleyn was admitted to the freedom of Norwich in 1505 as a hosier, an identification which may seem curious for a man who later appears as a bell-founder; but other examples are not unknown. It is incidentally clear from an entry in the Proceedings of the Municipal Assembly at Norwich in 1525 (when properties rented by John Aleyn in Tombland had burned down) that he had acquired the bell-foundry from Richard Brasyer's executors. The Assembly required that 'John Alen shall bynd his mese in the parishe of Saynt Stevyn late Richard Brasiers for the sure payment of rent' of 10s., due to the city on the Tombland property, now greatly reduced in value. His connection with the Norwich bell-foundry is also confirmed through a number of other documents, including the will of William Barker, a later bell-founder.

Richard Brasyer's will left the foundry in the hands of a former apprentice; and it is probable that John Aleyn's initial interest in the business was mainly financial rather than practical. In deeds of 1523, 1524 and 1528, however, he is described as a bell-founder; thus confirming that he became more closely involved with the craft, even if he did not relinquish his nominal interest in hosiery. We know of a bond for a new bell cast by John Aleyn for Hanworth church in 1521; and that he made a treble and a tenor bell for the church of Castle Rising in 22 Henry VIII (1530/31). Although William Barker occupied the bell-foundry for a few years before his death in 1538, it appears that John Aleyn continued his interest in metal-working: since he was entrusted with remodelling the pewter belonging to the Gild of St George in 1544. The parish register of St Martin at Palace church, Norwich, records in 1555 the burial of one John Aleyn, whose will gives little indication of any connection with church bells.[42]

[41] See OFB fo. 106d; B. Cozens-Hardy and E. A. Kent, *The Mayors of Norwich 1405–1835*, 1938, p. 40. See also: NRO PD 182 D. See also the three wills: NCC Surflete 177; NCC A Caston 122; and NCC Coppynger 81: and for the 'White Hart' see NED Roll 21, membrane 91. See also Mackerell's notes in the church chest at St Stephen's, Norwich for details of the Brasyer brasses.

[42] OFB fo. 123. Deedes and Walters give an example (CBE p. 233). In a deed of 1533, Roger Reve of Bury St Edmunds describes himself as a clothier and

William Barker
Admitted to the freedom of Norwich 1530, buried in 1539

When William Barker was admitted to the freedom of Norwich in 1530, he was described as a bell-founder; and he may well have worked for John Aleyn – possibly as a surviving apprentice from the days of Richard Brasyer II – before taking charge of the business. When he came before the Mayor's court in June 1535 to receive the sum of 40s. for 'the makyng and Workemanshippe of a new basse bell to the Township of Becles', it appears that the original contract had been made between the Beccles folk and John Aleyn. He had clearly attempted to purchase the bell-foundry and its appurtenances from John Aleyn, but seems to have experienced various difficulties in running the business. In December 1535, the wardens of metalworkers swore in the Mayor's Court that 'William Barker bellefounder hath insufficiently caste and made to his occupation of Braser iiij morteris in defaute of Workemanship puttyng therto white mettall'. There was also a controversy over the ownership of 'certen bell metall and Shroff': which was settled in 1537 when William Sandryngham, pewterer, was ordered to divide the metal, which had been lodged at the Gildhall, equally between William Barker and Thomas Nicholls. The previous year the Court had taken the unusual step of ensuring that 'John Wells promyseth and granteth to serve well and truly William Barker Bellefounder untill Christmas for ij s. vj d. the weke fyndyng hymself mete drynke chamber bedding and washinge and all other necessaryes, and the seyd William Barker to cherish the seid Wells as a servant and paye his wages trulye'. The final blow seems to have come in 1538, when John Aleyn and William Barker appeared for the Court 'to here the mater beyng in variance between them and to make an order and fynall ende theryn as shulde seme by ther discrecions'. The Court ordered William Barker to pay John Aleyn 40s. in four instalments 'in full satisfaction and

---

warrants a bell 'whiche the within bound Roger hath made' to continue sound for a year and a day. See also: NCR Case 16d. Proceedings of the Municipal Assembly, 1491–1553, fo. 142. See also NED Roll 21, membrane 53; and deeds quoted in E. A. Tillett, *St George Tombland, Past and Present*, Norwich, 1891, p.17. See also H. L. Bradfer-Lawrence, *Castle Rising – some notes on the church and castle*, Norwich, 1933, p. 53, who gives no reference for the statement. A search among the papers in the Bradfer-Lawrence Collections (NRO) has not revealed his sources, but it is unlikely that such a definite statement, detailing the bells cast, would be made without sufficient authority. The bells were removed from Castle Rising tower at the restoration of 1841 (*ibid.*) and the smaller went to Levens church, Cumbria: it was recast in 1846 and no record was made of the inscription (correspondence with the Levens Estate, 1980). See also NRO AYL 145 for the Hanworth deed; William Barker's will, NCC wills, Godsalve 283; M. Grace, 'Records of the Gild of St George in Norwich, 1389–1547, *Norfolk Record Society*, Norwich, 1937, p. 153, for the Gild pewter; and NRO PD 12/1.

contentacion of all the seid maters causes contraversies accounts and demaunds, excepted alweye reserved to the seid John Alen and to his executors and assignes all suche detts and demands as at this daye remain in writing obligatorye concernyng the sale of certen housez late sold by the seid John Alen to the seid William Barker'. William Barker appeared before the court again, just after Michaelmas, to report that John Aleyn would not accept the sum of 10s. which he had offered on several occasions, throwing it down on the ground. His rather trying career as a bell-founder ended with his death on 18th January 1539.

In his will, written in 1538, William Barker bequeathed his dwelling house called 'The Three Bells' to his wife, together with his 'working house', on condition that she paid off all monies for which the houses were mortgaged to John Aleyn. In a deed of 1554, Sir John Godsalve conveys to Thomas King, Grocer, a capital messuage with tenements, rents, shops, lofts, chambers, entries, lands, buildings and gardens, known as 'le Thre Belles' in St Stephens' parish, together with a triangular site opposite. The properties are described as having been acquired directly by Thomas Godsalve (father of Sir John) from William Barker, bell-founder, previously belonging to John Aleyn and formerly the property of Richard Brasyer. There is also a reference to a quitclaim, dated 1540, in which William Barker's wife and executors renounce their interest in the properties. The implication is that William Barker's wife, as his executor, had sold the properties to Godsalve, paying off various apparently heavy debts owed to John Aleyn.[43]

Thomas Lawrence
Admitted to the freedom of Norwich 1541, burial recorded in 1545

There is little doubt that the suppression of a large number of religious houses in the late 1530s would have had a very marked effect on the craft of bell-founding. Not only would a major market have been removed, but there would have been a considerable number of secondhand bells available for sale. Elphick notes the effect on the trade of London bell-founders at about this time, and the migration of many of them to the provinces. One of the migrants was Thomas Lawrence, whose activities in London have been traced as early as 1522 when, as an executor of the will, he bought the foundry and plant of William Culverden. Lawrence was admitted to the freedom of Norwich, described as a bell-founder, in 1541; and his burial is recorded in the register of St Stephen's church, Norwich in 1545. He is not named as an owner of the bell-foundry property in

---

[43] OFB fo. 117. See also: NCR Case 16a, Proceedings in the Mayor's Court 1534–1540, fos 6, 9, 22d, 29, 30d. See also notes on John Aleyn above. See NCC wills, Godsalve 283. His burial is recorded in the register of St Stephen's church, Norwich (kept at the church). See also NED Roll 24, membrane 6.

either the deed of 1554, or in the books of Landgable rents, where the foundry appears to be in the hands of the Godsalves, of whom he was probably a tenant.[44]

Since so many bells became available when the contents of monastic houses were sold off, it is not surprising to find a number of Norwich merchants dealing in secondhand bells, a trade which required a great deal less technical skill than bell-founding. The churchwardens at Norwich, St Lawrence bought four bells from the College of St Mary in the Fields; and the Wymondham parishioners bought the bells from the abbey steeple at the Dissolution. Certificates returned to Edward VI's Commissioners in 1549 show that Mr Braye of Norwich had bought bells from Seething, and that the Woodton churchwardens were able to sell a bell to Robert Barwick of Norwich. When the North Elmham churchwardens needed a new bell in 1542, they bought it from Mr Rugge, a Norwich merchant. A number of Norwich churches were closed in the 1550s; and the records of the Great Hospital, whose treasurer seems to have acted as Receiver for the Mayor and Aldermen, record the sale of bells from St Crowche, St Clement Conesford and All Saints Fybriggate.

Some local merchants who had bought bells may not have found it easy to dispose of them; and at least one Norwich speculator was in trouble in 1551 for sending bell-metal overseas. In a deposition made before the Mayor and Aldermen of Norwich one Leonard Meere of North Walsham remembered events which had taken place in 1546, when his master, William Gilbert of Norwich had trussed up in certain barrels a quantity of bell-metal which was then sold to Hans Vossart to be conveyed beyond the seas. A number of Yarmouth merchants had accumulated bell metal to the value of £57. 13s. 3d., which was sold by auction in 1548 towards the building of a new haven. John Bowle, William Bysshop and William Harebrown may not have been moved solely by charity in giving two tons of metal towards the work.[45]

Austen Bracker
Probably itinerant, but working mainly from Norwich in the 1550s

A small number of bells in Norfolk and Cambridgeshire churches can be ascribed to Austen Bracker, whose name appears on a bell at Shouldham and whose type appears on a bell dated 1556 at Islington. Identical lettering is used on bells at Long Stratton and Cratfield, in conjunction with Norwich bell-foundry crosses and founders' marks. The Long Stratton

---

44 CBC p. 45. See also OFB fo. 117; and Landgable at NCR Shelf 18d.
45 NCR Case 24a, Great Hospital Account Rolls. See also: W. Rye, *Depositions taken before the mayor and aldermen of Norwich 1549–1569*, 1905, p. 37. See also: Norfolk Record Society, Vol. XXXIX, 1979, p. 71.

bell was not mentioned in the 1552 Inventory for that church, but is unlikely to have been cast during Elizabeth's reign. It seems that Austen Bracker was working from Norwich for a time, and that he acquired his type from the foundry there. After his departure, it seems likely that there was a break in the founding tradition at Norwich; since a bell of 1559 at Reepham was cast in Bury St Edmunds, from which town the Wymond-ham churchwardens bought a new bell between 1554 and 1556.[46]

Even though it is difficult to attribute particular bells to their makers with certainty, it is probably worth drawing together some of the features which may be used to analyse the work of early Norwich founders. Much printed material relies on L'Estrange's researches, completed over 100 years ago, but more recent work on documents allows us to re-interpret some of his findings. It is now possible to pick out various details which help to distinguish bells cast at different periods, and to suggest a few groups of bells which may be attributed to their founders.

Alphabets, crosses and stops

It is easiest to begin by considering the types of lettering used on bells, many of which may be compared to those found in contemporary stained glass and on monumental brasses. It is clear that the designers of bell inscriptions had access both to scholarly sources and to professional calligraphers. There is little doubt that the style of lettering was influenced by the work of the scriptorium of the Norwich Cathedral Priory; and one has only to look at the Ormesby Psalter,[47] for example, to see the inspiration for the fine decorated capitals used by local founders over a long period. The black-letter parts of inscriptions on many bells use the conventions employed by scribes from the late 13th century onwards: such as the consistent use of a short 's' at the end of a word and a long 's' elsewhere. The apparently peculiar use of variants of the letter 'r' in bell inscriptions reflects the work of Norwich scribes, as does the distinction between the joined and free-standing letter 'a'. It is also worth noting that the contractions of words often found on bells (such as 'Johis' for 'Johannis', 'nuc' for 'nunc' and 'Dns' for 'Dominus') are almost always made according to proper convention.

Some of the earliest bells attributed to Norwich founders have inscriptions in capitals alone, and it is worth remarking that in Norfolk the fashion for inscribing bells entirely in capital letters persisted perhaps from the 13th century through to the Reformation and beyond. The Lynn founders used capitals for all their inscriptions, as did Simon Severey, the

[46] Wymondham churchwardens' accounts, copy at Colman-Rye Library, Norwich.
[47] Bodleian Library, Oxford, Ms. Douce 366.

probable founder of the 15th century 'Crostwight type' bells found in north-east Norfolk. Although the earliest black-letter on bells appears c.1380, the preference of some Norwich founders for mixed lettering did not prevent other contemporary founders, such as John Magges, from continuing to set inscriptions solely in capitals.

The wax patterns for the lettering, which were fixed to the model of a bell during the moulding process, were made in pottery matrices. These seem to have been part of the permanent equipment of the bellfoundry premises, used by a variety of tenants and passed on to successors in much the same way as the 'instruments of my craft' mentioned in the will of Richard Brasyer I. The pottery matrices used to form the wax patterns for individual letters were arranged in long strips with the letters in alphabetical order, as can be seen on bells at Bedingham and Fritton where the inscriptions consist of sets of consecutive letters from the alphabet. The Bedingham inscription shows both variants of 'r' and 's' on adjacent matrices, and at Fritton the two types of 'a' can be found.

Since it appears that several other founders were either employed by the chief founding family, the Brasyers, or were in partnership with them, it is to be expected that they would be using the same matrices for letters and ornaments: it comes as no surprise to find a bell bearing the name of Richard Brasyer (at Tacolnestone) inscribed in the same letters as bells cast by Richard Baxter (at Fundenhall, Ketteringham and Trimingham). Nor can it be assumed that a founder would restrict himself to one particular type of lettering when he was designing a ring of bells. At Toft Monks the tenor bell is differentiated from the contemporary second bell by the use of a much larger and more ornate set of capitals and black-letter; and early rings at Norwich Cathedral and St Michael at Coslany have their tenors distinguished in the same way.

At least ten different sets of capitals showing a high degree of individuality in design and decoration were used at various times by Norwich founders. Only three types of black-letter have been noticed, one of which was clearly designed to go with the large capitals used on big bells. The types recognised as belonging to pre-Reformation Norwich founders are described below.

NORWICH CAPITAL LETTERS

TYPE A.

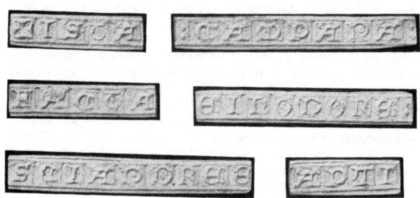

From a bell at Norwich. St Peter Hungate Museum. This fine set of capitals, which is never found with black-letter, can be unequivocally associated with William de Norwyco, whose name appears on bells at Barford and Bintry. He probably worked during the second half of the 14th century.
Photograph by the author, by permission of the Norfolk Museums Service.

TYPE B.

Thomas Potter's larger capitals. A highly ornamental type is found on some larger bells, such as the Salle tenor. It sometimes appears with the distinctive founder's mark of Thomas Potter (as at Boxford, Suffolk); and most writers refer to this type as 'Potter's larger capitals'.
Casts by Ranald Clouston, photograph by Christopher Dalton.

TYPE C.

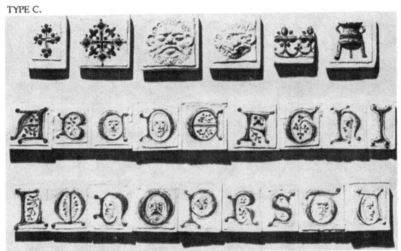

Thomas Potter's smaller capitals. Used on bells bearing the names of Thomas Potter, Richard Baxter and Richard Brasyer (of which there are good examples at Erpingham, Fundenhall and Tacolnestone).
Casts by Ranald Clouston, photograph by Christopher Dalton.

TYPE D.

Brasyer's larger capitals. This large type-face, which is found on bells such as the tenor at Toft Monks, is often called 'Brasyer's larger capitals'. *Casts by Ranald Clouston, photograph by Christopher Dalton.*

TYPE E.

Brasyer's smaller capitals. There are good examples of this relatively
common type at Geldeston and Tacolnestone.
Casts by Ranald Clouston, photograph by Christopher Dalton.

TYPE F.

Taken from a bell by Thomas Derby at Ampton, Suffolk. This rather slim
type, used to form neat inscriptions without black-letter, appears on some
bells which bear Thomas Potter's distinctive mark. These capitals also
appear on bells at Ampton, Suffolk and Burnham Overy, Norfolk which
seem to have been cast by Thomas Derby, who was working at Lynn
from c.1450. It seems likely that Derby initially worked with Thomas
Potter from the Norwich bell-foundry, where he probably cast the bells
for Besthorpe and Framingham Earl; and that he subsequently removed
to King's Lynn, taking some of the letter matrices with him.[48]
Photograph by the author.

[48] The small lozenge stop, which is found on the Besthorpe and Framingham Earl

TYPE G.

'Burlingham' type capitals, used by John Magges. Shoulder
and cannons of bell at North Burlingham, St Peter. Capitals of
this kind are universally referred to as 'Burlingham type',
after their appearance on the very fine ring of three bells at
North Burlingham, St Andrew. They appear on a number of
excellently cast and inscribed bells, some of which can be fairly securely dated to the second half of the 15th century. The
design of the bells, and the appearance of Brasyer's mark on
a bell at Newton by Castleacre, suggest close association with
the mainstream of Norwich work; and it is likely that John
Magges, a founder contemporary with Richard Brasyer I, cast
them. *Photograph by the author.*

---

bells, appears at Ampton, Suffolk on the third bell of four. The distinctive 'royal
head' marks which appear on both the third and tenor bells at Ampton show
that they were cast by the same founder. Ampton third has 'THOMAS FECIT'
as part of the inscription, while Ampton tenor has the word 'DERBY'. J. J.
Raven (*Church bells of Suffolk*, 1890, p. 157) states that: 'The occurrence of fig. 6
(The royal head) on a Norwich and London bell in the same tower is remarkable.' He was following Stahlschmidt's false identification of Derby as a
possible London founder (J. C. L. Stahlschmidt, *Surrey Bells and London bell-
founders*, London, 1884, p. 35).

TYPE H.

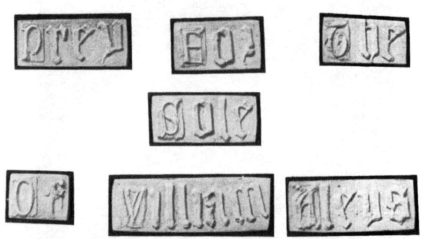

From the former clock bell at Cratfield, Suffolk; here used with smalls of
type 'b'.
Photograph by the author.

A set of capitals, clearly designed for inscriptions on small bells, is found
on a 15th-century bell at Cratfield; and is associated with Austen
Bracker's cross on the Long Stratton clock bell, probably cast in the
middle of the 16th century.[49]

[49] Cratfield clock bell is inscribed 'Prey for the Sole of William Aleys', whose
name appears in the Cratfield churchwardens accounts several times, and last
in 1498 (J. J. Raven, *Cratfield parish papers*, London 1895, pp. 29, 109). Stratton
clock bell, inscribed 'SANCTA CATERINA', was not mentioned in the 1552
inventory; but the dedication to a saint who had an altar in the church is
significant. A possible explanation is that it was cast during the Marian
counter-Reformation.

TYPES I and J.

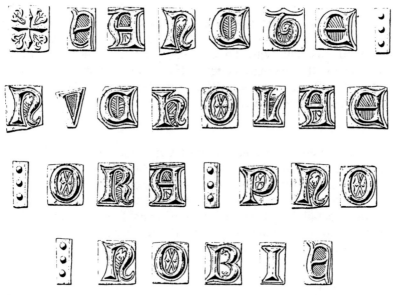

TYPE I.

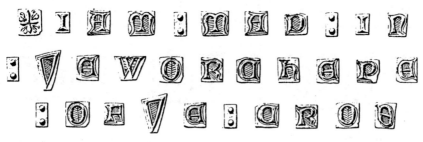

TYPE J.

Drawings of Type I and Type J by William Kimber at the Whitechapel Bell Foundry, reproduced by kind permission of Alan Hughes.

Two matching types of different sizes were to be found on a bell at Gorleston before the new ring was cast in 1873. A relatively small number of early bells which have these capitals can be identified by their profiles and distinctive mouldings; those at Mundham, Gillingham and Wramplingham, for example, are probably the work of 13th-century or 14th-century Norwich founders.

Black-letter types

Type 'a'

This particularly fine black-letter set is used to complement large initial letters of types 'B' and 'D' at Toft Monks and Salle, for example. Thomas Potter used this type with the smaller capitals of type 'C' to form the inscription on the Erpingham tenor (formerly at Norwich St John de Sepulchre), probably because neither of the larger types 'B' or 'D' was to hand when the bell was cast.

Types 'b' and 'c'

Type 'b' is a smaller black-letter alphabet of similar quality and design to type 'a'. It is found on a large number of excellently-cast bells such as the Fundenhall tenor and the Trimingham service bell. Type 'c' is thinner and less neatly formed than type 'b', to which it is similar in size although different in detail. It is found on bells of variable quality, ranging from excellent castings at Burnham Norton and Geldeston, to less praiseworthy efforts at Colton and Southburgh.

TYPE 'a'   TYPE 'c'   TYPE 'b'

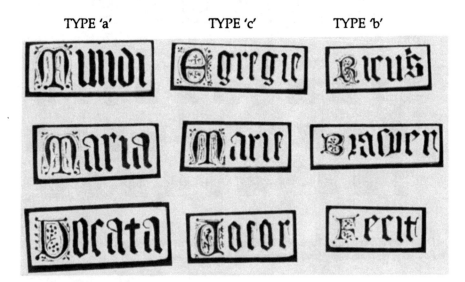

NORWICH BLACK LETTER TYPES a, b and c.
Type 'a' (left), the largest set, was probably introduced in the early fifteenth century. This example *'Mundi Maria Vocata'* from the tenor bell at Norwich Cathedral, is badly pitted by the action of noxious fumes from the old gasworks, which was close to the Cathedral.
Type 'c' (centre) was probably introduced c.1500. This example *'Egregie Marie Vocor'* from Tacolnestone.
Type 'b' (right) was probably current from c.1380 to c.1500. This example *'Ricus Brasyer Fecit'* from Tacolnestone.
Casts and photograph by the author.

While the capitals 'A', 'F', 'G', 'I' and 'J' are never accompanied by black-letter, most inscriptions are set in mixed type. It is exceptional to find inscriptions set in the alphabets 'C', 'D' and 'E' alone, most inscriptions being formed of capitals and black-letter in various combinations. A useful classification of early Norwich bells can be made by considering the common combinations of lettering which are set out in the table below.

	Type B	Type C	Type D	Type E	Type H
Type a	B–a		D–a		
Type b		C–b		E–b	H–b
Type c				E–c	

It is worth observing that black-letter type 'c' is found on 'Alphabet' and 'English' bells at Bedingham, Colton, Fritton and Southburgh for which documentary sources suggest a 16th century date;[50] and that types 'a' and 'b' are found on the very few bells which bear the names of founders working during the first half of the 15th century. This suggests that black-letter types 'a' and 'b' appeared first, followed by type 'c'; and since types 'b' and 'c' are almost identical in size, it seems likely that the latter was intended as a replacement for the former, rather than an alternative. The fact that there are probably four times as many surviving bells with type 'b' suggests that type 'c' was a comparatively late introduction; and it is worth noting that type 'b' was still in use in 1481, when the Gild of Corpus Christi had its bell cast for Oxborough (now hung at Salhouse). It is suggested that black-letter type 'b' supplanted type 'c' towards the end of the 15th century.

Whilst black-letter type 'b' is found with capitals of both types 'C' and 'E', black-letter 'c' never appears with capitals of type 'C', implying that the style of black-letter was changed from type 'b' to type 'c' during the currency of the type 'E' capitals. Although the inscriptions on the Mund-

[50] The alphabet bell at Bedingham might be dated approximately by a bequest in 1513 (Agnes Goslinge, 1513, ANF Sparhawke 322). A date for the Colton bell is suggested by bequests to bells in 1505 (specifically to the 'great bell') and 1518 (Walter Jowell, 1510, ANF Batman 40, and William Bloker, 1518, ANF Batman 281). The second bell at Fritton has the letters 'ER' on the crown, probably referring to Edward VI. It appears that there was work on the church tower, including the construction of a new octagonal belfry, during the first quarter of the 16th century, and the bells could well have been hung after 1547. The date of the Southburgh bell seems to be fixed by a bequest in 1522 to the smaller bell of the pair (Thomas Karr, 1522, ANF Gedney 81). It is possible that all these bells were cast by inexperienced hands, since they lack the fine qualities normally associated with the earlier Norwich founders.

Cross 1.1

Cross 1.6

Stop 2.1

Cross 1.2

Cross 1.7

Stop 2.2

Cross 1.3

Cross 1.8

Stop 2.3

Cross 1.4

Cross 1.9

Stop 2.4

Cross 1.5

Cross 1.10

Stop 2.5

Classification of crosses, stops and founders' marks used by Norwich bell-founders.
Initial crosses and stops introduced c.1350–c.1550.

The small foliage mark '2.2' found on Norwich
bells: and the two similar crosses contrasted.
The crosses shown are (right) Thomas Derby's
cross '1.2', and (left) the thicker version '1.3'
introduced by earlier Norwich founders.
Photograph by the author.

ham bells show that both types 'C' and 'E' were in use at the same time,
the overlap may have lasted for only a few years.[51] Capitals of type 'E'
eventually supplanted type 'C' as the standard for smaller bells, before
the black-letter 'c' was introduced.

Thus the sequence of mixed lettering appears to start with 'C-b', perhaps introduced c.1380 by Robert Brasyer, and also used by both Richard
Baxter and Thomas Potter. Type 'E' capitals – certainly current when the
bells were cast in the late 1440s for Ipswich, St Lawrence[52] – were probably introduced by Richard Brasyer I, who seems to have used types 'E-b'
as the standard for mixed lettering, a combination which is often associated with the large ermine shield. The change to type 'E-c' must have

[51] The two larger bells at Mundham have an unusual monogram scratched into
the mould near the cannons. The initials are apparently 'IB', suggesting that
John Baly may have cast the bells.
[52] The back three bells at Ipswich St Lawrence may be relatively positively identified with a bequest in 1449 to the 'new bells already bought' in the will of Alice
Greenhod, (NCC Alleyn 17).

happened after the casting of the Oxborough bell in 1481; and this latest combination of type is found on a fair number of very good bells, as well as some very poor ones. This suggests that black-letter type 'c' was introduced by Richard Brasyer II, and after his death continued to be used by successors, some of whom were not particularly skilled founders. An arbitrary date c.1500 seems to be the best available estimate for the change to type 'E–c'.

Although large capitals of type 'B' are found with Potter's trademark at Boxford, they were apparently not available when he cast the Erpingham tenor: so he may have introduced type 'B' during the period 1403–1428 for use on larger bells. Type 'B' capitals are found on several bells which, because thay lack the Brasyer shields, are usually attributed to Richard Baxter. The large capitals of type 'D' were probably introduced rather later by Richard Brasyer I.

Almost all inscriptions have an initial cross, and many of the rhyming hexameters are subdivided by a stop. It appears that particular crosses and stops were specially designed to accompany each of the sets of upper case letters, where they appear with reasonable consistency. There are variations, however, as well as a number of additional ornaments which appear more randomly; and in some cases unusual crosses or stops may indicate the work of particular founders.

The cross '1.1' appears only on bells with type 'A' capitals, cast by William de Norwyco and no others; while 1.8 is used exclusively by the founder of the 'Burlingham' group of bells, probably John Magges. A few bells with 'Burlingham' capitals have the cross '1.9', which is also found with the name of Austen Bracker and the date 1556 at Shouldham; at Long Stratton the small clock bell has 'H' type capitals with the cross '1.9'. The cross on Hardley tenor, '1.10', is also found on bells cast by Thomas Lawrence, probably in London, before his arrival in Norwich in 1541. The cross '1.7' is very uncommon, appearing with Norwich capitals 'C–b' at Great Glemham (Suffolk) and Mundham; it is noted as being in the hands of the London bell-founder Richard Hille and his successors perhaps as early as the 1420s, and it may have come to Norwich around 1470.[53]

The crosses '1.2' and '1.3' have been confused by some writers on bells, largely because they are so similar. The stouter cross, '1.3' appears almost exclusively with the type 'C–b' lettering, an exception being its combination with both 'C' and 'H' capitals on the small clock bell at Cratfield. Bells bearing the names of Richard Baxter (at Fundenhall, Ketteringham and Trimingham) and Richard Brasyer (at Tacolnestone) have this cross, which seems not to have found favour with Norwich founders after the introduction of type 'E' capitals; it does, however, reappear in the 17th

---

53 H. B. Walters and H. T. Tilley, *Church bells of Warwickshire, 1910*, plate XIII. See also: G. P. Elphick, *Sussex bells and belfries*, 1970, pp. 45, 46.

Marks used by Norwich bell-founders.
Casts by Ranald Clouston, photograph by Christopher Dalton.

century on bells cast by William Brend. Cross '1.2', a very slender version, is found only with type 'F' capitals: its association with the stop '2.2' suggests that Thomas Potter used it, and it appears on a bell by Thomas Derby (later of King's Lynn) at Ampton (Suffolk).

The cross '1.4' and stop '2.4' appear frequently with type 'E' capitals, accompanied by either of lower case 'b' or 'c'. Cross '1.5', which is only found with type 'E' capitals when accompanied by black-letter 'b', is also found with type 'B' capitals, as at Boxford and Salle: this suggests that '1.5' was originally intended to go with the larger alphabet 'B', but was used with 'E' before the cross '1.4' came into use.

The rebus '2.1', which sometimes appears as a stop on the inscription band and at other time takes the place of a founder's mark on the shoulder of a bell, is clearly associated with the name of Thomas Potter on the tenor bell at Erpingham. Other occurrences of '2.1' with type 'F' indicate that Potter was, perhaps, working independently of the contemporary Brasyers, probably with Thomas Derby. The foliage stop '2.2' occurs on the Erpingham tenor, thus associating it with Thomas Potter; and its occurrence on several early bells with the cross '1.3' and founder's mark '3.2' suggests that Robert Brasyer, and founders working with him, used this mark. The grotesque face with prominent ears, '2.3' appears with the early type 'C–b' (and with Richard Baxter's name at Fundenhall), as well with type 'F' capitals.

The stop '2.4' was used for a long period with types 'E–b' and 'E–c'; and the larger stop '2.5', which was designed for use with the larger lettering and cross '1.6', seems to have been in use at the same time as '2.4'. The simple diamond stop, which appears either singly or in pairs like a colon, helps to establish the link between Thomas Derby's earlier work at Norwich and his later work at King's Lynn. The 'Burlingham' type 'G' alone lacks a distinctive stop, the founder being content to simply to use full points in pairs or triples.

The bell-founders' shields

While lettering, accompanied by crosses and stops, is almost universally confined to the inscription band below the shoulder of the bell, a number of other marks are more usually found on the shoulder itself. Three common founders' marks take the form of shields, having an ermine or a sprigged ground charged with three bells and a coronet. A fourth type is charged with three crowns and an arrow, and some bells carry a representation of the arms of the city of Norwich.

A record of the monumental inscriptions remaining in St Stephen's Church, Norwich confirms the ascription of the shield charged with bells and a coronet to the Brasyer family. While the small ermine shield (3.2) is found with the three types of mixed lettering 'C–b', 'E–b' and 'E–c', the larger shields (3.1 – ermine) and (3.3 – sprigged) never appear with type

'C–b'. Neither of the two ermine shields appears on the apparently late group of 'Alphabet' and 'English' bells, although '3.2' appears on a clock bell apparently cast c.1555 for Long Stratton. The fact that the Norwich bell-foundry was known by the sign of 'The Three Bells' for a very long period during the 15th and 16th centuries suggests that the personal arms of the Brasyer family became a more general trade-mark for the Norwich bell-founders, typified by the common use of the small ermine shield.[54]

The Brasyers' small ermine shield (3.2)

The design of bells with the shield '3.2' is far from consistent, although there are a number of well-defined subgroups; and their likely casting dates appear to be widely distributed through a range from the 14th century to the 16th century. Probably introduced by Robert Fuller *alias* Brasyer shortly after his arrival in Norwich in 1377, it seems likely that the small shield with an ermine ground, '3.2', is the earliest of the three. Since Robert Brasyer was involved in business with other founders (we know that he employed John de Ryston as an agent at Lynn, and was associated in business with the Suttons at Norwich) it is likely that this shield was first used on bells cast during his ownership of the foundry, by founders who worked for him. This small shield later became the distinctive 'house-mark' of the foundry which continued in use through to the 16th century.

The Brasyers' large ermine shield (3.1)

The larger ermine shield '3.1' appears c.1449 on the three heavier bells of the ring of five at St Lawrence's church, Ipswich. It also appears on three of the bells at Norwich Cathedral, which apparently remain from the ring of five installed after the fire of 1463.[55] A further pair of bells bearing the shield '3.1' at Toft Monks is probably

---

54 See the will of Richard Brasyer II, NCC. Coppynger 81, and Mackerell's 18th-century account of the monuments in St Stephen's church, which is kept in the parish chest there. The property known as 'The Three Bells' is well described in NED. roll 24, membrane 6.

55 See note 52, above. See also: DCN. Sacrist's roll 299 for repairs following the

related to bequests in 1464 and 1470.[56] The shield seems to have been used only occasionally with type 'c', and has not been found on any of the late group of 'Alphabet' and 'English' bells. With very few exceptions the bells with the mark '3.1' are of similar design and of excellent quality, and it seems likely that the larger ermine shield may have been used to distinguish bells cast under the direct supervision of Richard Brasyer I from those cast by his tenants at the foundry. The shield '3.5', which sometimes accompanies '3.1', is a representation of the arms of the city of Norwich; very suitable for the work of a bell-founder who was also an Alderman.

The Brasyers' sprigged shield (3.3)

There is no doubt, from the inscription on the service bell at Tacolnestone, that the large sprigged shield '3.3' was associated with one of the Richard Brasyers; it also appears on four bells cast for Banham church at about the time of bequests in 1470 and 1478.[57] Several bells bearing shield '3.3' have the later lower-case type 'c', and the shield is found on all bells of the 'Alphabet' and 'English' type. This shield seems, therefore, to belong to Richard Brasyer II, probably first used to distinguish bells cast by him during his father's lifetime, and continuing in use at Norwich after his death.

---

fire; and DCN. Sacrist's roll 300, Michaelmas 1469: '*In ij cereis pro exequiis Roberti Brethenham vij d.* The tenor inscription asks for prayers for his soul.

[56] See the following wills: John Stroude, NCC Brosyard; and Richard Gaye, ANF Grey 299.

[57] See wills: Bartholomew Canne, ANF Grey 290; William Ploughman, NCC Gelour 206.

The 'crowns and arrow' shield (3.4)

The shield '3.4' appears in Norfolk and Suffolk only on bells with type 'G' capitals, and is nowhere found with mixed lettering. Several bells inscribed with type 'G' capitals have been found in Kent, two of which (at Patrixbourne and Postling) have the shield '3.4'. Stahlschmidt suggests that these bells were cast by William le Belleyetere, a founder whose name was found in a Canterbury deed of 1325; and the simple text of the Kent inscriptions, as well as the design of the bells would support a 14th-century date for them. A date c.1467 proposed for the larger bell at Colney, however, supports the suggestion that the shield was used very much later by a Norwich founder.[58] It is surprising that the shield and lettering should have survived virtually unused for perhaps 125 years before reappearing in Norfolk; but there are definite indications of a 15th-century date for East Anglian bells of this type, not least in the variety and sophistication of their inscriptions. Circumstantial evidence from known 15th-century towers such as Burlingham St Andrew, Norwich St George Tombland and Athelington (Suffolk), is also strong. It is very likely that this shield and type belonged in the 15th century to a founder, most probably John Magges, who used the Brasyers' premises as an independent craftsman rather than as an employee.

Arms of the City of Norwich (3.5)

A few inscribed bells have no shields on their shoulders, but use lettering associated with the Brasyers. One bears the name of Thomas Potter, and three others the name of Richard Baxter. It is possible that these men used the plant at the Brasyer's foundry as partners who expressed their independence by placing their own names on some of their bells, rather than as employees who would be bound to use the foundry trade-mark.

---

58 J. C. L. Stahlschmidt, *Church bells of Kent*, 1887, p. 13. Grateful thanks to Mr Richard Offen for confirming details of the William le Belleyetere bells from churches in Kent. The Colney bell can be probably dated c.1467 by the will of

3.6 The monogram of Alice and
William Brend

3.7 Arms of the City of
Norwich

Founder's marks used on bells by William Brend: the monogram on the names
Alice and William Brend, and the Norwich city arms (different from those used
by the Brasyers).

John Brend I
Casting bells by 1564, will proved 1582

The earliest references in wills[59] suggest that the Brend (or Brand) family
may have originated in the Waveney valley, although other members may
have come from Fulmodestone, Knapton and Coltishall. John Brend,
Robert Brend and Thomas Brend made wills in South Elmham between
1488 and 1509; and Alice Brend of Bungay wrote her will in 1524. John
Brend, the bell-founder first appears in Norwich documents[60] in 1565,
when the baptism of his son, Robert, appears in the register of St
Stephen's Church; and his name appears in parish rates for 1567 and 1577.

The initials 'IB' appear on bells at Merton and Southburgh, both of
which are dated 1564; but Brend did not take up the freedom of Norwich
until 1573. He may have been casting bells outside the city before then,
since the bell founder who made new bells for Snettisham in 1563 seems
to have cast them in Walsingham, while having the indentures made and

---

William Amy, who left 5 marks towards the larger bell in the steeple, to be
raised at a rate of 13s. 4d. per year. NCC. wills, Jekkys 64.

[59] See NCC wills Hubert 69 and 77, Spyltimbre 174 and Groundesburgh 12, for
example.

[60] See St Stephen's, Norwich register, also the rates recorded in the churchwardens' accounts (both kept at the church).

signed in Norwich. The churchwardens' accounts at Tilney All Saints[61] show that bells were cast for that church in Norwich in 1575 and 1576. The initials 'RB' (which occur with John Brend's initials on bells at Southburgh and Colton in 1564, and at Knapton in 1565) possibly represent Ralph Brend who, was living in All Saints' parish in 1577, when his son was baptised.[62] About 30 bells by John Brend I remain, most of them good castings, if rather untidily inscribed. His two bells at Little Walsingham are good examples of his work; and his lettering is best seen at Kimberley, where the larger bell in inscribed: 'FILLEI DEI VIVI MISERERE NOBIS ANNO DOINI 1578 I B.' The small number of his bells found in Lincolnshire most probably arrived there secondhand as a result of the business activities of John Mallows, an 18th-century Dereham bell-founder.

John Brend's will of 1582 makes no mention of bell-founders' premises or tools; and it is very likely that he worked as a tenant at the old bell-foundry, referred to as 'Brasyer's Workhouses' in Landgable assessments of 1549 and 1558, which was in the hands of Mr Symond Bowd and called 'The Workhouses' in the assessment of 1570. His burial is recorded in the register of St Stephen's Church, Norwich on 31 July 1582, and his will mentions two sons, Robert and William, neither of whom had come of age.[63]

William Brend
Born c.1563, died 1634

Although his brother Robert's baptism[64] is recorded in the Norwich, St Stephen's, register in 1565, William Brend must have been baptised elsewhere; and since he had not come of age when his father wrote his will in 1582, he must have been born after 1561. The fact that he was sufficiently competent to cast a bell for Framlingham church, Suffolk, in 1583 suggests that he had worked at the foundry with his father for some years before; and it is remarkable that his name has not been found among the lists of Norwich freemen. William and Alice Brend had moved from St Stephen's parish by 1586, when the burial of their eldest son, John, is noted in the register of All Saints' church;[65] and it would appear that it was in 1588 that

[61] See A. O. Stallard, *The transcript of the churchwardens' accounts of the parish of Tilney All Saints, Norfolk*, 1922, pp. 224–229; also Snettisham churchwardens' accounts NRO PD 24/1. See p. 209 for an explanation of bells by John Brend I in Lincolnshire.

[62] See NCR Landgable rent books, Case 18d, and All Saints' register NRO PD 70/41.

[63] St Stephens's register; and his will at NCC Moyse alias Spicer 434.

[64] *Ibid.*

[65] NRO PD 70/41.

TASBURGH 4th bell dated 1593

TASBURGH 2nd bell
Date stamp

TASBURGH Tenor bell
Monogram of William Brend
with Alice, his wife

Lettering used by William Brend at Tasburgh. The initials of Thomas Baxter of
Rainthorpe, patron of the living, who probably subscribed to the making of the
bell. The capitals are from Brend's large set, and Baxter's shield is cut from a
sheet of wax.

they acquired property in All Saints' parish which was described as the
bell-foundry in a deed of 1597.[66]

William Brend was working in Norwich at a time when there was a
rapid expansion in bell-ringing in East Anglia, and he was often required
to replace older rings of three or four heavy bells by lighter rings of five
and six bells. The output of the foundry was enormous, and approximately 300 of William Brend's bells remain in Norfolk and Suffolk churches.
The quality of these bells varies considerably: from very poor castings at
Tasburgh and Yelverton (dated 1613) to excellent bells at Saham Toney
and Oulton (dated 1618). William Brend's son, a second John born in 1594,

[66] See NED Roll 30, membrane 48; and CBN p. 35.

ANNO DOMINI 1603

Lettering used by William Brend at Forncett St Mary 1603. The letters
and date are cut from strips of wax.

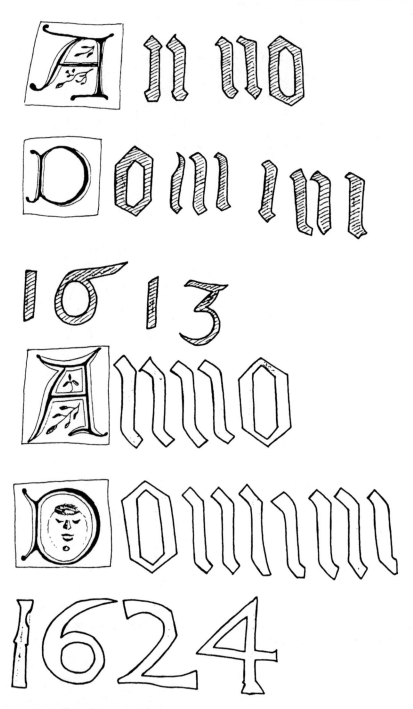

Lettering used by William Brend at Yelverton 1613 and 1624. The small capitals are cast in pottery matrices, while the irregular smalls are formed from wax strips.

Inscription at Ludham on a bell cast by William Brend.

was closely involved in the work of the bell-foundry; and his initials first appear with those of his father in 1610, the year of his 16th birthday. During his father's later years, John Brend took an increasingly more prominent part in the business, and the improvement in the design and consistency of bells between 1625 and 1630 is probably due to him.

A number of lettering types are found on William Brend's bells, many being inscribed in rough, ungainly capitals, found as late as 1615 on a bell at Arminghall. From time to time he used patterns cut from sheets of wax to form inscriptions in neat Roman Capitals, and stylish Arabic numerals. Occasionally he used wax capital letters very similar to those on bells by earlier Norwich founders; but despite many similarities with the earlier lettering, the moulds appear to have been newly made for William Brend. A large set of these capitals was used in 1593 at Tasburgh, and there are many bells with a smaller version. Plain die-cast Roman capitals of various sizes are also found, ranging from the large letters on Ditchingham

MΛRKETSTEED
REΛDER

Lettering used by William Brend at Attleborough in 1617.

THVRLETON

ΛO DNI 16ƺ2

Lettering belonging to William Brend used on a bell at Thurlton in 1632.

tenor to the very small alphabet found at Thurlton. Some bells have a monogram on the initials of William Brend and his wife, Alice: a rough form used at Forncett St Mary in 1603 was later developed as the neat shield found on many of their bells. A number of other foundry marks appear to have been handed down from earlier founders, among them the well-known sprigged and ermine shields of the Brasyers, and the lion's head stop used by Richard Baxter.

Noteworthy bells from the Norwich foundry under William Brend include the following:

1610   Ketteringham. A ring of five (tenor 9 cwt) was completed, splicing in two pre-Reformation bells. William Brend's bells are particularly neatly inscribed.

1613   Wingfield. A ring of five bells (tenor 13 cwt) was completed, the bells bearing dates 1596, 1602 and 1613: a treble was added in 1742.

1614   Aslacton. A ring of five (tenor 8 cwt) was completed, probably by bringing together stock bells dating from 1604, 1607 and 1614. The contemporary bell-frame remains.

1615   Great Ellingham. Four bells with interesting inscriptions remain, probably from a complete ring of five with a tenor of about 14 cwt.

1617   Attleborough. A ring of five with a tenor of about 14 cwt was completed by casting four new bells from three old ones, and splicing in a bell of 1581. Only one bell of 1617 now remains in the present ring of six.

1618   Shropham. Three fine bells remain as 1, 3, and 5 of a ring of five (tenor 12 cwt).

1618   Oulton, Suffolk. The back three of an excellent ring of five (tenor 11 cwt) remain.

1619   Ludham. The ring of five, cast from the metal of an earlier ring of four, must have been William Brend's most remarkable work. The 18 cwt tenor was recast in 1627, and the treble in 1825.

1619   Hingham. The tenor bell (16 cwt) of the present octave is a fine bell.

1621   Norwich St Andrew. The 15 cwt tenor bell (which according to the inscription on a bell at Ingham, spoils this ring of bells) is inscribed 'LET US TEWNE AND SOUND TOGETHER INGLANDS SWETE PEACE FOR EVER.'

1622   Worlingham. The rather doleful ring of five (tenor 12 cwt) was completed, including bells dated 1608, 1621 and 1622.

1622   Shotesham All Saints. The ring of five (tenor 11 cwt) was completed, splicing in two pre-Reformation bells. Although the tenor is rather thin (sounding F natural), the bells are a good ring of five.

1623   Acle. A complete ring of five (tenor 9 cwt) was cast, of which two remain.

1623	Paston. A complete ring of five bells (tenor 12 cwt) was cast, of which four bells remain.
1623	Tittleshall. William Brend's ring of four bells (tenor 12 cwt) hang from their contemporary fittings in a frame which was adapted for them in 1623. They are now derelict.
1624	Halesworth, Suffolk. The 18 cwt tenor is probably William Brend's largest surviving bell.
1629	Stratton Strawless. A complete ring of five (tenor 11 cwt) was probably provided, of which four bells remain in the present ring of six.
1630	Catfield. A complete ring of five (tenor 10½ cwt) was cast from the metal of four old bells. Four of William Brend's bells remain in the present ring of six.
1630	Claxton. A very fine ring of three bells (tenor 8 cwt) was cast: the bells are now derelict.
1632	Thurlton. The ring of five bells (tenor 11 cwt) was probably cast in the village under the direction of either William Brend or his son, John.
1633	Walcot. Four excellent bells (tenor 12 cwt) were cast and tuned as the front four of a ring of six. The treble added in 1878 puts them into the unusual Phrygian mode.

William Brend seems to have lived in All Saints' parish for most of his working life, and the parish register records the baptisms of two sons and two daughters to Alice and William Brend between 1589 and 1601,[67] as well as the burials of his eldest son John in 1586, and two infant daughters on succeeding days in 1591. There is no doubt that William Brend retained his interest in the bell-foundry to the end of his life, since payments for bells were made to him as late as 1634, the year of his death.[68] It seems that in their last years William and Alice Brend lived with their daughter, Elizabeth Draper, in Thetford; since the payment for rehanging and recasting a bell for North Barsham[69] was made to 'ould Brand of Thetford'. William Brend's will, written on 27 September 1634, makes it clear that he considered his son John as a partner in the business: leaving him all the working tools and other implements belonging to the bell-foundry, although requiring that John's mother, Alice, should retain an interest in the foundry. The probate inventory attached to the will gives a record of the contents of a 'mansion house' rather less splendid that that bequeathed by Robert Brasyer two centuries earlier. There were three principal rooms: kitchen, buttery and parlour; and the tableware consisted of two pewter basins, six pewter dishes, six pewter cups, six trenchers, four wooden

---

[67] NRO PD 70/41.
[68] *Ibid.*
[69] See the Barsham Tithe Book, NRO PD 177/35.

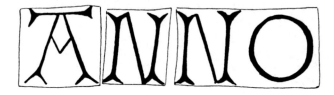

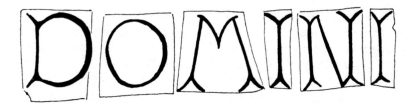

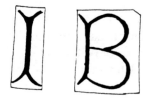

Lettering used by William Brend at Kirby Bedon, and by his son at Taverham.
The Roman capitals are cast in pottery matrices, as is the date.

dishes and six wooden spoons.[70] William Brend was buried in All Saints' church, Norwich on 1 December 1634.

John Brend II
Born 1594, died 1658

John Brend was the fifth child of Alice and William Brend, baptised[71] at All Saints Church in 1594 with the same name as a brother who had died in 1586. His initials first appear on bells cast by his father in 1610, the year of his 16th birthday. As has already been noted, his influence can be detected in the improvements to bells cast after about 1625, and seen in bells like the excellent ring of three at Claxton (1630). His widowed sister appears to have married John Draper, the Thetford bell-founder in 1630. Elizabeth Brend was baptised in 1595; and there is a record of the marriage[72] of John Draper, widower to Elizabeth Taylor, widow, in 1630 at All Saints' church. This relationship is confirmed in John Draper's will[73] of 1644: in which he makes his wife, Elizabeth, his sole executor; and 'my brother John Brend of Norwich' his supervisor. The initials 'IB ID' appear on bells at Great Witchingham (1630) and Hindringham (1636), and formerly Sculthorpe (1630); and a number of other bells were cast jointly by John Brend and his brother-in-law, as is confirmed by a bond which related to the bells at Aylsham.[74]

Under the combined influence of John Draper and John Brend II, bells from the Norwich foundry reached their highest standard since the early 16th-century, when bells of superlative quality were being cast by the Brasyers. The distribution of bells cast in Norwich (which occur mainly in central, and east Norfolk; and east Suffolk) and from Thetford (found mainly in west Norfolk, west Suffolk and Cambridgeshire) suggests agreement rather than competition between Brend and Draper. Competition with other founders, and especially those at Colchester, can be seen in the inscription[75] on the second bell at Wickham Market: 'THE MONVMENT OF GRAY IS PAST AWAIE IN PLACE OF IT DOTH STAND THE NAME OF IOHN BREND 1657.' Inscriptions such as this are few and far between, the simple formula 'IOHN BREND MADE ME' being used on most bells. A large number of bells cast by John Brend II date from the years before the Civil War, which was a difficult period for bell-founders working in East Anglia. No bells in Norfolk bearing dates in the years 1643, 1644 or 1645 have been

---

[70] NCC Moyse alias Spicer 434. See also NRO INV 41/184, and NRO PD 70/41.
[71] NRO PD 70/41.
[72] Ibid.
[73] CBN p. 47.
[74] CBN p. 94.
[75] CBS p. 252.

noticed, and only one in 1646.[76] Major works by John Brend II include the following bells:

1635   Hanworth. A ring of five (tenor 9 cwt) completed by either recasting or adding the treble and tenor to bells dated 1612.

1636   Hindringham. A ring of four bells (tenor 11 cwt) cast in association with John Draper. A treble was later added, but the ring of five is now derelict. Two of the 1636 bells are badly cracked.

1637   Happisburgh. A complete ring of five (tenor 11 cwt) cast, two of which remain in the present octave.

1637   Cratfield, Suffolk. Fine 18 cwt tenor bell recast.

1641   South Repps. A complete ring of five bells (the fourth later replaced by a pre-Reformation bell brought from Thorpe Market) of very good quality (tenor 13 cwt), now forming the back five of the present ring of six.

1641   Woodton. Five small bells (tenor 8 cwt) remain from an early ring of six.

1653   Wymondham. The 25 cwt tenor bell was recast, probably John Brend II's heaviest bell. Although of quite respectable tone, the bell was recast when the new ring of ten was installed in 1967.

1656   Yoxford, Suffolk. Five bells cast in 1655 and 1656 form the front five of a ring of six, whose tenor (11 cwt) was recast or added in 1685.

1657   Buxton. Four bells of this date remained in the ring of five until 1874, with a treble cast or recast in 1707. In 1910 the tenor was recast and and the bells increased to six.

1657   South Elmham St Margaret, Suffolk. Three smaller bells recast or added to complete a ring of five in the Dorian mode, which included bells of 1596 and 1627.

The registers of All Saints' church, Norwich record the baptisms of eight sons and four daughters born to John and Frances Brend between 1621 and 1649. Five of them are named in his will, written in 1654, in addition to Elias Brend whose baptism has not been traced. The bell-foundry and working tools were left in the hands of six children (his wife having died in 1650): Elizabeth, Ellen, Daniel, Elias, Francis and Hester were to receive in turn the annual rent raised by letting the foundry and its equipment, which they were bound to maintain in good repair. John

---

[76] H. B. Walters, 'The church bells of Worcestershire', *Transactions of the Worcestershire Archaeological Society for 1925–1926*, Worcester, 1927, p. 33, gives the inscription on the 7th bell at Droitwich, St Andrew: '+ GOD SAVE OVR KING IOHN WHEELER G EDWIN BARRETT G BAYLIES 1645 I M'. One cannot imagine such an inscription on a Norfolk bell of the same date.

Brend's burial[77] is recorded in the register of All Saints' church on 18th September 1658.

Thomas Brend
Born 1627, died 1665

Thomas Brend was baptised[78] at All Saints Church, Norwich in 1627; where four of his children were also baptised between 1651 and 1665. Although most of his bell-founding work was done in conjunction with his brother, Elias, their initials appearing together on bells cast between 1658 and 1664; two bells in east Norfolk appear to be the work of Thomas alone. The old fourth at Martham[79] (recast 1868) was inscribed: 'GOD AMEND WHAT IS AMES AND SEND LOVE WHER NON IS 1660 R B'; and the smaller bell at Ingham is inscribed: 'MY TREBLE IS WHEN I SHOULD SING ST ANDREWS TENNER SPOYLE THAT RING 1661 T B.' The latter bell was treble in the old ring of five at Ingham (reduced to two bells in 1779); and the inscription doubtless refers to the problems experienced years before, when William Brend found it difficult to please the churchwardens of St Andrew's Church, Norwich in casting a new tenor bell for them. When Thomas Brend died in 1665, two of his children had predeceased him; and his son Elias, baptised shortly after his father's death, died of the plague in 1668.[80]

Ralph Brend
Born 1625, left Norwich c.1666

Ralph Brend, third son of John Brend II, was baptised[81] at All Saints Church, Norwich in 1625. He and his brother Thomas entered into a bond with the churchwardens at South Elmham St James when they cast a bell for them in 1662. This bell, bearing the initials 'RB' survives as the only example of his work. Three of Ralph's children died of the plague in 1666; and since his own burial is not recorded, it is likely that he left Norwich with his remaining family to avoid further tragedy.

Elias Brend
Born c.1639, died 1664

Elias Brend's baptism has not been traced, but it appears from his father's will that he came between sons Daniel (baptised in 1637) and Francis

---

[77] See CBN p. 38 and NRO PD 70/41.
[78] NRO PD 70/41.
[79] CBN p. 171.
[80] NRO PD 70/41.
[81] *Ibid.*, and CBN p. 39.

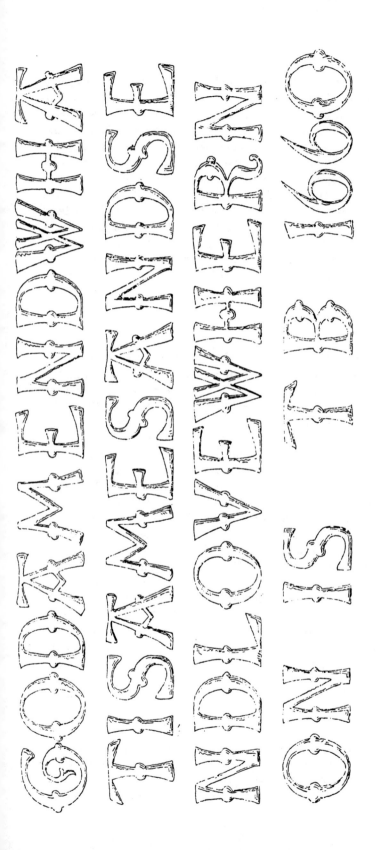

Unique inscription by Thomas Brend on a bell formerly at Martham.
Drawing by William Kimber at the Whitechapel Bell Foundry, reproduced by kind permission of Alan Hughes.

(baptised in 1642). Perhaps Elias was born when his father was working away from home, and had his family with him. Three of Elias's children were baptised[82] at All Saints' Church, Norwich, between 1661 snd 1666, and their burials, together with their father's, are recorded in January and February 1667, at the height of the plague. About 20 bells of reasonable quality remain from the hands of this young founder, the last of a family which had been casting bells in Norwich for four generations.

The plague having, to all intents and purposes, wiped out the Brends, we find Norfolk churches turning to John Darbie of Ipswich for bells required during the next few years. The Loddon churchwardens had a bell recast by him in 1669, a bell was cast for Ranworth and the Gissing ring was remodelled in 1670; a ring of four was cast for Snetterton in 1672, the year that Litcham completed its ring of five.

Michael Darbie and Thomas Slow
Working in Norwich in 1661

The names of both Michael Darbie and Thomas Slow appear in an agreement with the churchwardens of St Andrew's church, Norwich for recasting four bells of the ring of six in 1661. They describe themselves as bell-founders of Norwich, and it is likely that they were operating independently of the Brends, since they agreed 'from time to time fetch & take at the said Church of St Andrew all & every such defective bells to be new runn as aforesaid & the same carry to his or their workehouse without St Stephens gates in Norwich to be by them artificially new made as aforesaid'. The Brends, it will be remembered, had their foundry in All Saints' parish. One of Darbie's bells remains at St Andrew's, and two others were cast in the same year, for Mileham and Feltwell. There is also an entry in the Norwich, St Peter Mancroft accounts for new brasses made by 'Mr Stowe', which may be a mistake for Thomas Slow.[83]

Michael Darbie's career[84] began in Kent in 1650 from whence he had moved to Oxford by 1654, where he cast a number of bells, including Great Tom at Christchurch (later recast by Christopher Hodgson). His brief appearance in Norfolk has left only the record of the three bells listed above, and he is next traced to Southwark in 1670. He visited Cambridgeshire and Essex in 1671, and by 1674 was working at Windsor and in Sussex. His latest recorded bell is dated 1675 at Yatton Keynell, Wiltshire.

---

[82] *Ibid.*

[83] NRO P 163 A. A transcript by Mr D. Cubitt was published in the *Ringing World*, 1977, p. 559. See St Peter Mancroft churchwardens' accounts, NRO PD 26/71.

[84] Michael Darbie's career as a founder, beginning in Kent in 1650, has been traced by F. Sharpe in his *Church bells of Oxfordshire*, Brackley, 1953, p. 474.

Edward Tooke
Working from 1671, died 1679

Edward Tooke's name first appears on bells dated 1671 at Norwich, St Peter Parmentergate and Aldeby. He seems not to have inherited the strickles and patterns used by the later Brends, although he initially used the moulds employed by Elias Brend before producing his own fine letter stamps. About 40 of his bells remain, some cast in conjunction with Samuel Gilpin: although they do not look particularly impressive, many of them sound very respectable. Tooke added two trebles to complete Norfolk's second octave at Norwich St Peter Mancroft[85] in 1675; and his finest surviving bell, the 12 cwt tenor at Filby, was cast in the same year. His burial is noted in the register of All saints' church in 1679, and his will[86] makes no mention of his family in connection with the disposal of the bell-foundry, which he leaves in the hands of his executor, Richard Johnson.

Samuel Gilpin
Working from 1677, died 1705

Samuel Gilpin seems to have learned his craft under Edward Tooke and had risen to a position of responsibility by 1677: it was perhaps as foreman of the bell-foundry that he was paid[87] by the Aylsham churchwardens for recasting two bells bearing Edward Tooke's name. His own name appears only only on bells at Toft Monks (recast in 1963) and Langley, but documentary evidence[88] shows that uninscribed bells cast by him in 1682 remain at Norwich St Catherine Mile Cross. These bells, formerly at St Mary Coslany, closely resemble the uninscribed bell at Shelton (which dates from 1683); and another bell cast by Samuel Gilpin for Tharston in 1699, which remained until 1976. The similarities in design appear in the moulding wires and in the unusual rectangular cannons. Samuel Gilpin is also known to have increased the Loddon bells to five in 1680, recasting the old tenor into two trebles; and in 1700 he cast four bells for Aylsham,[89] of which two remain as 5th and tenor in the ring of ten. It is probable that Samuel Gilpin took over the business when Edward Tooke's death caused the bell-foundry to fall into the hands of his executors; since the Loddon churchwardens had agreed to 'deliver or cause to be delivered to the said Samuell Gilpin at his workhouse in the parishe of All Saints in the Citty of Norwich the great bell belonging to the parishe church of Loddon'. By 1683 it appears that Samuel Gilpin had moved from Tooke's foundry to a

---

85 CBN p. 183.
86 CBN p. 39.
87 *Ibid.*
88 CBN p. 81. See also NRO MC 78/96/21 for the Loddon material.
89 CBN pp. 93, 94.

site outside the city, when the Shelton bell was collected from Trowse. In 1698 Gilpin was asked to estimate the weight and value of two bells which the Denton parishioners were keen to sell,[90] and the price of £3. 10s. 0d. per cwt gives some idea of the value of bell-metal at that time. Samuel Gilpin's burial[91] is recorded in the register of Norwich St John de Sepulchre in 1705.

A number of later Norfolk founders cast bells in various places: using Norwich as a base, but spending significant periods out in the county, and further abroad. Some of these should properly be classed as itinerants, but they are more conveniently dealt with under the heading of the place where much of their work was done.

Henry Pleasant
First recorded at Sudbury in 1691, working from Norwich in 1705, died at Sudbury in 1708.

Although Henry Pleasant's earliest bells were cast at Colchester,[92] his main centre of operations from 1691 onwards seems to have been at Sudbury, where bells for Brockdish (1697) and Bunwell (1699) were probably cast. We find, however, that the Besthorpe churchwardens collected three bells from Thetford[93] in 1702, where he may well have cast the Thetford St Cuthbert treble, and four bells for Euston in the previous year. His visit to Norwich was brief, and he was probably working from Samuel Gilpin's bell-foundry in 1704/05 when he cast the trebles for the octave at St Andrew's church, Norwich, as well as the small bell at Earlham. He returned to Sudbury in 1705, where he was buried[94] in 1708.

Charles Newman
First recorded at Lynn in 1684, probably working from Norwich with his son c.1705, died at Bury St Edmunds 1709.

Charles Newman cast bells at various places[95] in the Eastern Counties between 1684 and 1709; and one of his main centres of operation was Haddenham, Cambridgeshire, to which both he and his son Thomas returned at intervals. In a document[96] of 1691 we hear of 'Charles Newman of Hadenham in the Ile of Ely in the County of Cambridge Belfounder', and the suggestion that this was the family home is confirmed

90 NRO FCP/1 (fragile).
91 CBN p. 42.
92 CBE p. 121.
93 Besthorpe churchwardens' accounts, Colman – Rye Library, BES 274.2.
94 CBE p. 123.
95 CBC, CBE, CBN, CBS *passim*.
96 Warranty for a bell at Diss, NRO PD 100/77.

by the record of the baptism[97] of his son, Thomas Newman in 1682, who returned there to be married in 1707. Many of Charles Newman's bells are found in Norfolk, Suffolk and Essex churches which would not have been easily served from a foundry near Ely; and it is quite clear that he travelled in search of work. It seems likely that he used various centres, returning to the same premises at intervals to cast a few bells before moving on elsewhere.

The earliest bell bearing Charles Newman's name is the tenor of the ring of four at St Michael's church, Cambridge dated 1684, where the churchwardens accounts[98] show that three bells were cast at Haddenham by Christopher Graye in 1683, and that the tenor was cast at King's Lynn. Bells cast for several churches near the Suffolk-Essex border between 1686 and 1696, may have been produced at Bury St Edmunds; since the church-wardens' accounts[99] at St Mary's church, for 1696 suggest that his foundry was then in that town. He probably returned to Haddenham once or twice during that period to cast a few bells for Cambridgeshire churches: Cambridge St Clement (1691), Fen Ditton (1692), Orwell (1694) and Wilburton (1695).

Newman was also working from a temporary foundry at Botesdale[100] during 1691, where he probably cast a ring of five for Redgrave church; and the Diss churchwardens took advantage of the bell-founder's presence in the area to add a treble to their ring of five. The details of the undertaking are worth recording. In a document dated 21 September, 1691, the churchwardens 'are prevailed upon to undertake the charge and trouble of Running and Hanging an other bell in Diss Steeple to make the number of Bells there six, which new bell is to be a Treble under the five already hanging there'. A total of 27 names were subscribed and a sum of £16. 17s. 8d. was promised. The articles of agreement with the bell-founder are dated 27 October, 1691, and require Charles Newman 'at his Furnace at Bootsdale in the County of Suffolk to Cast and runn A good treble bell and make the same Tunable for a Treble under the five bells . . . without skirting, opening or Chiping any of the bells already hanging by the Judgment of Mr Francis Gibbs of Eye, Suffolk and John Kett Junior, Turner, of Diss'. Since an itinerant founder would have no large store of bell-metal with him, the churchwardens agreed to purchase and deliver to him a suitable quantity of good quality metal. The bell metal was acquired from redundant bells at Gasthorpe and Coney Weston (for the disposal of which there are extant faculties at Norwich), and duly delivered to Botesdale. The new bell was adjudged, and proved satisfactory, on 18 January 1692, after which the founder guaranteed his work for a

---

[97] CBC p. 96.
[98] CBC p. 93.
[99] CBN p. 66.
[100] See proceedings at Diss, NRO PD 100/77.

year and a day in the sum of £20. The completed accounts show that the work cost a total of £22. 18s. 2d.

Charles Newman probably made his first contacts in Blakeney[101] in 1696, in which year he cast bells for Helhoughton and South Raynham, and he was definitely working at a foundry in north Norfolk between 1699 (when the Bessingham churchwardens collected a bell from Blakeney) until 1703, when operations were transferred to Horstead. During this period he seems to have returned to both Bury and Haddenham to cast bells at various times.

Thomas Newman may have been sent to learn his trade at Norwich from Samuel Gilpin, before returning to help his father at Blakeney in 1702; and from 1704 onwards Charles Newman's name occurs on very few bells, probably because he was helping his son to reorganise the business, first at Horstead and later in Norwich.[102] It is likely that father and son moved in 1705 to Norwich, working from the Bracondale foundry after the death of Samuel Gilpin.

Most of Charles Newman's bells are additions or recastings of individual bells, and his ring of five at Redgrave lasted only until 1736 when his son recast[103] them. The back five at Scarning is his most significant surviving effort; the tenor was cast in 1703, probably at Horstead, and the other four in 1697, probably at Blakeney. Towards the end of his life Charles Newman returned to Bury, where he probably cast the treble bell for Kennett, Suffolk; and his last bell, inscribed 'C N 1708' hangs on the west gable of the Reynolds Library at King Edward VI School/Norwich. In his will,[104] dated 10 September 1709, 'Charles Newman of Bury St Edmunds, Bellfounder' bequeathed to his son, Thomas all his working tools.

Thomas Newman
Born 1682, working in Norwich from 1702, died 1745

Born in 1682, Thomas Newman would have been closely involved in his father's activities from an early age.[105] It seems very likely that was sent to learn his craft with Samuel Gilpin at Norwich, where he cast a bell for Howe church in 1702. The bell is inscribed 'THOMAS NEWMAN AT NORWICH MADE ME 1702', and its general design suggests that he was using Gilpin's plant. The characteristic square cannons, probably from Samuel Gilpin's patterns, appear on a number of Thomas Newman's early bells. Later in 1702 Thomas Newman had returned to his father's foundry at Blakeney,

---

[101] See Bessingham churchwardens' accounts PD 222/14. Fragile (1985), thanks to Miss Susan Maddock at NRO for reading them. See also CBN p. 178.
[102] See notes on the career of Thomas Newman.
[103] CBS p. 226.
[104] CBE p. 118.
[105] See note 97, above.

where he received the old bells from Tunstead[106] to be recast into a new ring of five. There were problems with the work, and various recastings were needed before the churchwardens were satisfied. The Tunstead accounts show that the foundry moved to Horstead in 1703 when the churchwardens paid 'for the carriage of the bells three times to Blakeney and twice to Horstead and thrice fetching the scales and weights to Tunstead church to weigh the bells and other things by a bill of particulars £5-04-03'. Newman appears to have worked from Horstead with a blacksmith named Simon Otes and a bellhanger named Richard Field.

As well as casting bells for Tunstead and Bacton at Horstead, Thomas Newman was employed at churches near Bury St Edmunds and Haddenham in 1703 and 1704. In 1705 he cast complete rings of five bells for Cambridge Holy Trinity and Fowlmere, probably at Haddenham, from which town a bell was supplied for Wyton in Huntingdonshire.

Following the death of Samuel Gilpin in 1705, it would appear that Thomas Newman occupied the Bracondale foundry. The 17 cwt tenor at Worstead which has Thomas Newman's initials on it, is inscribed: 'I TELL ALL THAT DOTH ME SEE THAT NEWMAN AT BRAKINDEL DID NEW CAST ME 1706.' After a period of almost frantic activity in 1706 and 1707, only one bell by Thomas Newman has been found for the year 1708, and none for 1709. Charles Newman died in 1709, and it is possible that his last illness caused this dislocation of his son's bellfounding activity.

Thomas Newman spent a large part of 1710 working in west Norfolk, setting up a temporary foundry at Swaffham, according to an advertisement[107] which he placed in the Norwich Gazette on 21 October 1710.

This is to inform the Publick, that CHARLES NEWMAN [recte THOMAS NEWMAN], Bellfounder of this City has ever since January last been at Swaffam in Norfolk a Casting of Bells, where he has had the good success of Casting a compleat Peal of 6 Bells for the Parish of Snetsham, and another Peal of 5 bells for the Parish of Castleacre, and 3 to make up 5 for the Parish of Hilborough, which are now a Hanging up, besides others to the number of 29 since January last; but now is returned Home to his Office in Norwich, where he is ready to serve any Parish that has the like Occasion to new cast broken Bells, or design to make any Alteration in their Rings, and he will perform the said Works as well as any Pretender to that Art in England, and with as much Expedition as can be desired. This is also to inform the Hotpressers of this City that have their Boxes out of Order, That they may have them new cast to Perfection, he having had better Success in that

---

[106] NRO PD 285/38.
[107] Much of this account is based on extracts from Norwich newspapers kindly communicated by Mr D. Cubitt of Norwich. to whom the writer is very grateful. They were included in a series of articles published by Mr Cubitt in the *Ringing World* between 12 March, 1971 and 19 November, 1971.

> Business than any that ever yet took them in hand to do. Likewise any sort of Brasses either for Wind or Watermills, or any other Engins, are new cast by the said Thomas Newman, at his new erected Office without Bear-street Gates.

It seems likely that on his return to Norwich Thomas Newman moved the foundry from the Trowse end of Bracondale to a 'new erected Office' near Ber Street Gates, where it remained until 1758. The next few years saw considerable activity, including a complete new six for East Dereham in 1711, which the Society of Ringers in Norwich were 'invited to ring and give our Approbation of'. They were able to 'allow and approve of them to be a good harmonious Peal', according to the Norwich Gazette of 22 September, and an advertisement in December announces that: 'The Five Bells at St James's in St Edmunds-Bury in Suffolk are now made a Peal of Six, by casting the old Tenour and making a new Treble by Thomas Newman, Bell-founder of this City; and are now Fixing up, in order to ring for the welcome News of Peace when it comes.' He cast several more bells at Norwich, including a complete ring of five for Scottow in 1713, before returning to Cambridgeshire in 1716. Bells for Bluntisham, Harston and Milton were probably cast at Haddenham in 1718, as were several others for churches in west Norfolk, but the tenor bell of the four at Berden, Essex is inscribed: 'THO NEWMAN AT CAMBRIDGE MADE ME 1723 WILLIAM HOY CW.' Probably Newman's largest bell, the tenor at Newmarket St Mary, was cast in conjunction with Thomas Gardiner in 1719.

After 1728 Thomas Newman seems to have settled in Norwich, where, apart from excursions to Cambridge in 1729 and to Bury St Edmunds in 1735, he remained until his death in 1745. As well as a large number of individual bells, Newman cast complete fives for Honing (1730), Lawshall, Suffolk (1735, probably at Bury), Redgrave, Suffolk (1736) and Brome, Suffolk (1737); also a ring of six for Palgrave, Suffolk (1737). There was a great deal of interest in bell-ringing in Norwich during the first half of the 18th century, and a newspaper item in November 1737 states that: 'Two new Trebles are cast by Mr Newman of this City, to make a Peal of 6 Bells at the Parish Church of St Laurene [recte St Lawrence]: he is also going to cast Two Trebles for the Parish Church of St John at Madder Market, in order to make a Peal of Six Bells there: The Parish of St Giles too are about Bettering their bad peal of Six, which it is hoped will in Time be done by making a good Peal of Eight, as it is the most commanding Steeple in this City.' By the end of the year the St Lawrence bells were 'allowed by all to be so compleat and agreable a Peal of Six, that they now talk of getting 2 more to make a peal of 8'. Talk was not enough, and the bells at St Lawrence's remain as Newman left them; nor was he entrusted with the trebles for St Peter Mancroft, which were cast by Samuel Knight at Holborn, London in 1737 to complete a ring of ten. According to the Norwich Gazette of 30 September, 1738: 'The Two new Trebles for St

Giles's here are so curiously hit by Mr Newman the Founder, and the rest so greatly improved by the Direction of Mr Willam Goddard, that Every body must acknowledge them to be the most Tuneable Peal of eight in this City'

New octaves in the county were completed by Thomas Newman at Diss (1741), Hingham (1742) and Kenninghall (1743). At both Diss and Kenninghall he supplied secondhand bells as well as his own castings. His last bells were cast in 1745, the year of his death, and burial[108] at Norwich, St John Sepulchre.

John Stephens
Working in Norwich from 1717, died 1727

The departure of Thomas Newman to Cambridgeshire in 1716 left the way clear for another founder to occupy the Bracondale bell-foundry, and the following advertisement[109] appeared in the Norwich Gazette in July 1717:

> This is to give Notice that John Stephens from London, Church Bell Fonder [sic], who casteth all sorts of Bells, and also all sorts of Brasses, (he served his Apprenticeship with Mr Abraham Rudhall in Gloucester City, the Ablest Bell-Founder in England, to the Judgement of Norwich Ringers, who have sent for him from London) is now come to Norwich to live: and all Gentlemen shall have good Security for their Bell or Bells, he having perform'd the Business these 18 or 20 Years. He is to be spoke withal at Mr John Baist's at the Sign of the Castel, by the Hall's End in the Market-place in Norwich, at any Time.

It seems that Thomas Newman's sudden departure had prompted the Norwich Ringers' invitation to John Stephens, and they must have travelled far afield to gain their opinion of Abraham Rudhall's work. Stephens's background at Gloucester would explain the change in design of Norwich bells which coincided with his arrival, as well as their generally good quality. Abraham Rudhall,[110] to whom he was apprenticed, was able to advertise in 1705 that he had cast 'one ring of 10 bells, ten rings of 8, and 32 rings of 6, and 25 rings of 5, with several bells into peals of the

---

[108] CBN p. 42.
[109] See note 107.
[110] For an account of the Gloucester bell-foundry under the Rudhalls see M. Bliss and F. Sharpe, *Church bells of Gloucestershire*, 1986, p. 59. I am also grateful to Mr C. J. Pickford for information on the Rudhalls and their bells, as well as suggesting that the Norwich ringers could have heard the rings in London and Newark. Mr D. Cubitt has also pointed out various occasions when the Norwich ringers travelled long distances to ring on celebrated rings of bells, not least their visit to York Minster in 1765.

number of 547; besides others which he hath not been so careful as to remember, as not being aware so exact account might be required of him'. John Stephens would have have been working at the Gloucester Foundry during its most productive period, and it is not unlikely that the Norwich ringers would have heard Rudhall bells in London. A heavy octave was hung at St Dunstan in the East in 1700, and St Bride's ring of ten was cast in 1710. Another possibility is a visit to Newark, whose ring of eight was hung in 1713. It is worth noting that Abraham Rudhall I gave up control of the Gloucester bell-foundry c.1717, and the advent of his son, Abraham II, may have precipitated Stephens's departure to London and eventually to Norwich.

By the middle of 1718 Stephens was firmly established[111] near Ber Street Gates, and had cast a number of bells, including those which augmented Martham and Redenhall to six, and Framlingham, Suffolk to eight. Other excellent bells followed, including rings of five at Burgh and of six at Tunstall in Suffolk. It appears from the Norwich Gazette of 25 July 1724 that two trebles were cast and added to complete a ring of ten at St Peter Mancroft: 'Yesterday Morning the Two new bells for St Peter's Church were successfully run by Mr Stephens; they are now putting up in the Steeple, and all Ten are designed to be rung this Afternoon by 3 a clock. The 2 new Bells are admirable good Notes, and 'tis generally believ'd will nick the other 8 to the Satisfaction of all Judges.' A later issue of the paper proclaimed that the 'Two new Bells prov'd incomparably good, and being Tun'd to the Approbation of several Great Masters, they are now beyond all Question as good a Ring of Ten Bells as any in England'. The bells appear to have been a speculation[112] by Stephens, to which subscribers were not sufficiently forthcoming; and the bells were removed from the tower before October of the same year. Hessett's heavy ring of five, and a six for Pulham Market were cast in 1725; and Stephens was successful in adding trebles to complete the octaves at Norwich St Michael at Coslany and Great Yarmouth in 1726. Fives were cast for West Harling and Sparham in 1726, and his largest bell, the tenor at East Bergholt, was cast in the year of his death. John Stephens's burial[113] is recorded in the register of St John Sepulchre, Norwich in 1727.

An advertisement[114] in March 1728 refers to John Stephens's intestacy; and that the administration of his estate, initially granted to Mr Thomas Wright of St Stephen's parish, had been revoked in favour of Mrs Elizabeth Rainsdon, at the King's Arms, near Ber Street Gates.

---

[111] See note 107.
[112] *Ibid.*
[113] CBN p. 42.
[114] See note 107.

Thomas Gardiner

Working from Sudbury in 1709, Norwich 1745 to 1758, returning to Sudbury where he probably died in 1762.

Thomas Gardiner had been casting bells for churches in the Eastern Counties at Sudbury for some years before moving to Norwich,[115] and his earliest bell is dated 1709. He is known to have cast bells at Benhall, Suffolk in 1718, and to have collaborated with Thomas Newman in casting the tenor bell for St Mary's church, Newmarket in 1718. Gardiner seems to have come to Norwich soon after Newman's death in 1745, casting three bells for Tilney All Saints in that year; and in 1746 he cast six bells for Wells, returning to complete the octave a few years later. The last complete ring of bells from the Norwich foundry was made for Field Dalling in 1750, and the advertisement[116] in the Norwich Mercury of 11 August records 'That THOMAS GARDINER, of the City of Norwich, Bell-Founder, did cast an entire new Peal of Five BELLS, for the Parish of Field Dawling in the County of Norfolk (the Tenor of which is in B. mi flat of old Concert) and that the said Peal is Strong and well executed, and was opened the Day above written to all Approbation'. The Field Dalling bells remained almost as Gardiner left them until they were rehung for chiming from a clavier in 1985. All the contemporary ringing fittings were complete, including a blacksmith-made spanner designed to fit the nuts on the cannon-straps, but the bells are no longer ringable. The Foxley bells were (until one was recast in 1902) a ring of six by Gardiner, probably completed in 1753.

The latest date for a bell cast in Norwich appears to be on the small clock bell[117] at Felbrigg Hall, inscribed: 'THO. GARDINER NORWICH FECIT 1756'; and the end of the foundry is notified in an advertisement[118] in the Norwich Mercury of 2 September 1758: 'To be LETT immediately, A House just out of Bear street Gates, with a compleat Foundery for a Bell-Founder, late in the occupation of Thomas Gardener, Bell-Founder. There is a Quantity of Metal and some useful Tools, to be disposed of. N.B. There is not one of the Trade in this City. Enquire of the Printer of this Paper.'

KING'S LYNN BELL-FOUNDERS

The situation of King's Lynn on a navigable arm of the Wash, with river communication through the Fenland rivers to parts of Lincolnshire, Northamptonshire, Cambridgeshire, Norfolk and Suffolk, made it an ex-

---

[115] CBE p. 124.
[116] Norwich Mercury, 11 August, 1750, communicated by Mr D. Cubitt.
[117] Information from Mr R. W. M. Clouston, who visited the house in 1984.
[118] Norwich Mercury, 2 September, 1758, communicated by Mr D. Cubitt.

cellent centre for heavy industry, and it has been noted that bells and brass pots were among the merchandise on which levies were made at the Lynn Tolbooth as early as c.1240. The dues payable are detailed in a roll of 1286/87, at 4d. per cwt.[119] It is also known that when the new bells for Ely cathedral were cast in 1345, the bell-founder, John of Gloucester, was able to obtain suitable clay, copper and tin at Lynn.[120]

Master John, alias John de Lenne
Mentioned in a document of 1299

No record of entries to the freedom of Lynn[121] survives before 1292, but L'Estrange[122] quotes a subsidy roll of 1299 which refers to '*Magister Johannis, fundator campanarum*'. A bell at West Somerton with identical lettering to that on 14th-century bells at Salle and North Tuddenham bears the name of '*IOHANNES DE LENNE*'; and it seems more than likely that the Master John of the Tallage roll is the man who cast the Somerton bell.

Thomas Belleyetere alias Thomas de Lenne
Mentioned in a documents of 1322 and 1344

The admission of Thomas Belleyetere to the freedom of Lynn has not been traced,[123] but L'Estrange discovered an entry relating to him in a Subsidy roll of 1322/33. His name also appears in a Lynn Chamberlain's account of 1343/44. A number of bells which appear to be of 14th century design carry the name Thomas, including those at West Newton (formerly at Babingley), North Tuddenham and Long Stratton. Bells recorded by L'Estrange at Wood Rising and Trunch, which also named their founder as Thomas de Lenne have now gone.

---

[119] R. Howlett, 'Tolls levied at the King's Lynn Tolbooth in the 13th century', *Norfolk Antiquarian Miscellany*, Norwich, 1887, vol. III, part 2, pp. 603–609.

[120] D. J. Stewart, *On the architectural history of Ely cathedral*, London, 1868, p. 117. See also p. 391.

[121] W. Rye, *A calendar of the freemen of Lynn, 1292–1836*, Norwich, 1913, see the introduction.

[122] CBN p. 22, CBS p. 8. Raven suggests that this 'Master John' should be identified with John de Ryston, whose name appears on a bell at Bexwell; and goes on to surmise that John de Lenne, alias John de Riston, is also identical with John Godynge, whose name appears on bells at Wendling and Worlington (Suffolk).

[123] See Rye, *op. cit.*, 1913; also CBN p. 22; and D. M. Owen, *The making of King's Lynn*, 1984, p. 30.

Edmund Belleyetere alias Edmund de Lenne
Made a freeman of Lynn in 1344 and mentioned in a document of 1353

The admission of Edmund Belleyetere to the freedom[124] of Lynn took place in 1344/45, and L'Estrange quotes the record of money owed by the Chamberlain of Lynn for an old bell purchased from Edward Belleyetere in 1353. It is very likely that he cast Salle 6/8, which is inscribed 'EDMVNDVS DE LENNE ME FECIT', and is of very similar design to the bells at Long Stratton and North Tuddenham.

William Silisden
Made a freeman of Lynn in 1376 and wrote his will in 1409

William Silisden, who was admitted to the freedom[125] of Lynn in 1376/77, is the likely founder of the three bells at Great Walsingham, the largest of which is inscribed 'WILLMVS SILISDEN ME FESID'. The design of the bells differs greatly from that of bells ascribed to earlier Lynn founders, as does the alphabet employed by William Silisden. The Red Register of Lynn has a number of references to William Silisden[126] who was elected one of the four chamberlains of the town in 1384, and a return of the taxes collected by him appears in the town accounts for 1386. In 1394, however, he was found to have made a false declaration to the king's collectors of taxes for the half-hundred of Freebridge, and was made to pay a fine of 20 shillings towards building the chapel of the Holy Trinity at St Margaret's church. An entry in the roll[127] of the Master of the Cellar at Norwich Cathedral Priory for the year 1400–01 shows that metal to the value of £12 was purchased from one William de Sylesden. His will, dated 6 February, 1409, shows that he was successful in business and was not completely disgraced by misleading the royal officers in 1394. He left the large sum of 40 shillings for tithes and oblations at the altar of St Margaret's church, as well as 20s. to the fabric fund there and 13s. 4d. to St Nicholas's Chapel. He requested burial in the chapel of St James, Lynn; and left money for the friars to pray for his soul. Properties in West Lynn and in 'Stonegate', as well as 'Tylekilns' lying in Watlington, were bequeathed to his son John. The latter are very significant, since there are many similarities between the crafts of bell-founding and tile-making, not least in baking clay moulds. It is, therefore, possible that he cast his bells in Watlington.

---

[124] See Rye, op. cit., 1913, p. 8; and CBN p. 22.
[125] Rye, op. cit., 1913, p. 21.
[126] See H. Ingleby, The Red Register of Lynn, King's Lynn, 1922, fos 121, 126d, 130, for example; also his will at NRO. KL/C12/9.
[127] DCN 1/1/68.

John de Ryston
Made a freeman of Lynn in 1385 and mentioned in a document of 1390

John de Ryston's admission to the freedom[128] of Lynn, where he is described as a bell-founder, is dated 23 July 1385, and his name occurs on a
bell at Bexwell. As well as casting bells in his own right, he appears to
have acted as an agent for the Norwich bell-founder, Robert Brasyer; and
a lawsuit[129] in 1390 shows that he was not then thought to be fulfilling his
obligations faithfully. Robert Brasyer may well have worked with John de
Ryston before moving to Norwich, since his admission to the freedom of
the city shows that he came from Stoke Ferry, a few miles distant from
Ryston.

John Godynge alias John de Guddinc
Probably c.1411–1454

The name of John Godyng appears as a representative of the *inferiores non
burgenses* in a settlement of disputes concerning the finances of Lynn in
1411/12; so it is likely that his foundry was situated outside the borough.[130] The records of the Trinity Gild, who owned a staithe and ware-
houses, record receipts for winching bells in the period c.1410–1423; and it
seems very likely that John Godyng was shipping bells out from Lynn at
that time. The type employed on the bell at Bexwell is identical to that on
bells at Wendling and Worlington (Suffolk), both of which bear forms of
the name of John Godynge; and it would appear that he took over the
foundry plant of John de Ryston. Judged by the bells at Wendling, his
work was of the finest quality. The will of one John Godyng of Sedgeford,
which is relatively near Lynn, was proved[131] in the peculiar jurisdiction of
the Dean and Chapter of Norwich in 1454.

---

[128] Ingleby, *op. cit.*, 1922, fo. 122 d, where the entry appears as 'John de Biston'. The
original register was examined at Lynn by Miss Susan Maddock, of the Norfolk
Record Office, who reports that the entry should read 'John de Riston'.

[129] PRO CP 40/519 (1390) where the entry reads '*Robertus Brasyer civis Norwici per
Nicholaum de Charwod attornatum suum obtulit se iiij die versus Johannem de Ruston
de Lenn, Belleyetere, de placito quod reddat ei rationabilem compotum suum de tempore quo fuit receptor denariorum ipsius Roberti. Et ipse non venit et preceptum fuit
vicecomitate quod summoneatur. Et vicecomes modo mandat quod nichil habuerit et
ideo capiatur . . .*'

[130] Owen, *op. cit.*, p. 393. See also NRO KL/C38/1–16 *passim*, for entries in the Gild
records (the series is incomplete).

[131] NRO DCN Q232C, small book without folio numbers. Date 9 October 1454.

Thomas Derby
Made a freeman of Lynn in 1450

In his admission to the freedom[132] of Lynn, Thomas Derby is described as a bell-founder, and his name appears on a number of bells. Two at Ampton (Suffolk) have similar founder's marks; but their inscriptions are set in different types of capital letters: the smaller bell bears the name 'Thomas' and the larger has 'Derby'. Other bells with this surname have been noted at New Houghton, Burnham Deepdale, and Chippenham (Cambs); while the lettering is noted on bells at Wimbotsham and West Lynn. The founder's marks[133] which are common to all bells in the group are impressions of crowned heads; and one of the two alphabets employed, together with a matching stop and cross, was probably in the hands of Norwich bell-founders during the early years of the 15th century. The alphabet in question appears at Wacton with Thomas Potter's marks, and on the fine bells at Framingham Earl and Besthorpe; so it seems likely that Thomas Derby learned his craft at Norwich, probably working with Thomas Potter at the Westlegate foundry before removing to King's Lynn.

Edmund Belleyetere, son of Thomas Belleyetere, was admitted to the freedom[134] of Lynn in 1364/65, but the account rolls of the Trinity Guild of Lynn show that he was a wealthy merchant engaged in trade of all kinds. In 1384/85, when an aqueduct in the Tuesday Market was reconstructed, the chamberlains bought 20 'waynescotes' and 4 'rigoldes' from him; and in 1385 he is among the Lynn timber merchants who had grievances against the Hanseatic merchants, to whom he had lost the huge sum of £108 by what appears to have been an act of piracy. Neither his admission as a freeman of Lynn, nor those of his known apprentices suggest any connection with bell-founding; nor does his will, dated 1417.

No record of the admission of any later bell-founder to the freedom[135] of Lynn has been found. Local church records[136] show that major work on the bells at St Margaret's Church and at St Nicholas' Chapel was undertaken by a variety of founders in the late 15th and 16th centuries, and that

---

132 Rye, *op. cit.*, 1913, p. 51.
133 J. C. L. Stahlschmidt, *Surrey Bells and London Bellfounders*, London, 1884, p. 35, notes the group of bells and, having conveniently omitted the smaller of the two bells at Ampton from his list, ascribes them to one Henry Darby of London, in the period 1362–1390 (*op. cit.*, p. 74).
134 See Rye, *op. cit.*, 1913, p. 16, and NRO KL/C38/ rolls 1 – 7, for example.
135 Rye, *op. cit.*, 1913, *passim*.
136 NRO PD 39/74, St Margaret's accounts 1592–1673. There is also a manuscript index, with extracts from the accounts, by E. M. Beloe (NRO PD 39/72 and PD 39/73).
NRO PD 39/355, St Nicholas chapelwardens' accounts, 1616–1719. These have been partly transcribed and printed: E. M. Beloe, *Extracts from the Chapel Wardens' Accounts of St Nicholas' Chapel, King's Lynn*, King's Lynn, 1928.

business was mostly with the Thetford bell-founders between 1598 and 1626. In 1617 the chapelwardens[137] of St Nicholas' chapel agreed with 'James Edberry bell fownder that he should newe cast one bell at the Towne of Jermans and we should delyver the said bell there at our chardge for castinge whereof we were to paie vj lb. x s'. James Edbury, who had previously worked from Bury St Edmunds with John Driver, was unsuccessful, and the metal was brought back to Lynn for the bell to be recast in a furnace set up in the Common Staithe yard. Edbury's bell was found to be 'untuneable' and was finally recast by John Draper of Thetford in the following year. Other founders from Stamford, Ipswich and Bury St Edmunds were subsequently employed at the Lynn churches at various times, and in 1684 a bell was recast[138] for St Nicholas' chapel by Christopher Graye at Haddenham. Closely associated with Christopher Graye was Charles Newman, who probably worked as an assistant before taking charge of the business in 1684. The records[139] of St Michael's church, Cambridge, show that Charles Newman recast the tenor bell in 1684 at King's Lynn; and it is not unlikely that, having worked on the St Nicholas' bell with Graye, he decided to remove the business to the more convenient centre at King's Lynn in the same year. He cannot have remained long at Lynn, since he was working[140] from a foundry at Botesdale, Suffolk by 1691.

THETFORD BELL-FOUNDERS

Thomas Draper 1
Working at Bury St Edmunds c.1574, and at Thetford from 1579 to 1595

It seems very likely that Thomas Draper began his career as a bell-founder at Bury St Edmunds, and that he later removed to Thetford. Thomas Draper's initials are first noted on a bell dated 1574 at Wissington, Suffolk, where they appear with those of William Land, Stephen Tonni's foreman at Bury St Edmunds.[141] The Thetford Hall Books contain many references[142] to Thomas Draper, including his admission to the freedom of the borough in 1578. Various assessments for taxes shortly after 1578 show that he was one of the wealthiest merchants in Thetford when he was elected to serve as one of the 'Twentymen', who with the Mayor and Burgesses formed the corporation of the borough. He was elected mayor

---

[137] Beloe, op. cit., 1926, see under year 1617.
[138] NRO PD 39/144, the agreement for the work.
[139] CBC p. 95.
[140] See warranty for a bell at Diss: NRO PD 100/77.
[141] CBS p. 254.
[142] At the King's House, Thetford, indexed at NRO T/TC1/1, fos 1, 30, 55 and T/TC1/2, fos 196, 214, 215.

of Thetford on 17 October 1592, an occasion which he celebrated by casting a bell for St Cuthbert's church.

It appears from the Wattisfield churchwardens' book[143] that Tonni and Land were also working from Thetford in 1578, when 'the belfounders did dyne, thre of them.' His earliest works are the two former trebles at Illington (transferred to Gaywood and Happisburgh when Illington church was abandoned): both are inscribed: 'PRAYS GOD THOMAS DRAPER ME FECIT 1577'. Thomas Draper's bells are generally of good quality, and his largest surviving bells are inscribed in excellent black-letter. The sixth bell at Redenhall, inscribed *'coeli solamen nobis det deus thomas draper me fecit 1588'*, has also the initials 'ID' in small capitals, presumably those of his son, John. As well as using simplified versions of the Bury St Edmunds founders' marks, Thomas Draper adopted a fine large shield bearing his own initials and charged with three bells. His finest lettering appears on the treble at Thetford St Cuthbert, where excellent capitals and black-letter smalls have much of the character of pre-Reformation founders' alphabets.

In his will,[144] dated 1595, Thomas Draper leaves his business to Margaret Draper his wife, to revert to his sons after her death. The widow certainly retained an interest in the foundry, and her name appears as a party to a bond for newly cast bells at North Lopham; her will[145] was proved in 1622.

Thomas Draper II
Working between 1593 and 1598

Thomas Draper II cast at least one bell before his father's death in 1595: as is recorded in an inscription[146] on a bell formerly at Hepworth: 'THOMAS DRAPER THE YOUNGER MADE ME 1593.' Two bonds[147] among the Banham parish papers relate to the recasting of the tenor bell of the ring of five there. In September, 1597, Thomas Draper promised to 'take down, yote and make perfect and substantial with harmonye in everye respect answerable unto the fower bells which are in Banham steple the great Bell their att his proper cost and charges and also shall place the same conveniently and sufficiently in the oulde rome and place wheare beefore it was placed and shall so perform his worke in perfecting therof as it shall continue sownde and perfet the space of one wholl yeare after the perfecting therof'. The Banham people were not entirely inclined to trust his goodwill, and they bind him 'that he shall honestly and truely preserve

---

[143] CBS p. 99.
[144] CBN p. 44.
[145] NRO ANF wills Hill 105.
[146] CBS p. 201.
[147] Seen at Banham church.

and keepe to the best profet the overplusse of mettle that shall arise of the sayde bell without perloyninge or feltchinge any therof'. The bonds at Banham show that Thomas was collaborating with his brother John in the work. No bell now remains by Thomas Draper II, and his latest date was recorded on the old second bell at Cranwich:[148] 'THOMAS DRAPER ME FECIT 1598'.

John Draper
First mentioned in a document of 1597, will proved 1644

John Draper's initials appear on a bell cast by his father for Redenhall in 1588, and he appears to have been in partnership with his brother Thomas when they cast[149] a bell for Banham in 1597. He and his mother, Margaret Draper were parties to a bond[150] with the North Lopham churchwardens in 1600. The earliest bell which can be ascribed to him is at Little Massingham, cast in 1599; and his few bells dated between 1600 and 1605 are widely scattered. He cast[151] a bell at Wells for Beeston-next-Mileham in 1606; and the distribution of his bells suggests that he may have worked from both Thetford and Wells for a number of years.

John Draper married[152] Sarah Stibbard at Fakenham in 1609; and seems to have spent most of his time at Thetford, although with an excursion to cast[153] bells at Cambridge in 1618. The parish records[154] at East Bergholt, Suffolk show that when the 26 cwt tenor bell was recast at Bury St Edmunds in 1621, payment was made to 'Andrew Gerne of Berre St Edmunds, by the apoyntment of the M[aste]r workman John Draper of Thetford'. The initials 'AG' and ID' appear together on bells in west Suffolk dated between 1621 and 1630, and it is possible that bells bearing John Draper's name alone may also have been cast at Bury during that period.

The Shipdham accounts[155] show that John Draper gave them advice when the bells were recast under the directions of the churchwardens in 1616. The relevant entries are as follows:

> To Nicholas Ewren for woode to runne the bells – xxv s. iiij d.
> To Michael Wightman for cc bricks – iij s. ij d.
> Laid out by John Rawlinge at the shooting of the iiij belles – xv s. ix d.
> To Peter Frost for xxv li. and a halfe of pewter – xix s.ij d.

[148] CBN p. 119.
[149] Bond remains at Banham.
[150] CBN p. 45.
[151] CBN p. 99.
[152] NRO Bolingbroke's index to the Consistory Marriage Licences.
[153] CBC p. 64.
[154] CBS p. 164.
[155] NRO PD 337/85, 1982.

Laid out for Draper the day after the twelf day – xviij d.
Laid out more by Jo. Rawlinge at the shooting of the great bells –
iij s.
Laid out by Stephen Dannye when the bell was sent to shooting
– x d.
To Wiskard for keeping the bells – viij d.
To him for going to Thetford [no amount recorded].

The purchases of wood and bricks show that a furnace was set up in the village for casting the bells, and the suggestion that John Draper was called in as a consultant is confirmed by the appearance of his numeral stamps to record the date on two of the surviving bells of the ring of six.

The marriage of the widowed John Draper to Elizabeth Taylor in 1630 has been noticed above,[156] and this liason with John Brend's sister seems to have been the occasion for a number of joint efforts at casting bells. A large number of bells by John Draper remain in churches throughout the Eastern Counties – many of them excellent in quality – but no complete ring of five or more bells has survived. His latest bells are at Thuxton and Yaxham, dated 1642, and his will[157] was proved in 1644.

Henry Draper
Mentioned in a will of 1595, cast a bell in 1602

Thomas Draper's will of 1595 mentions six sons, two of whom have already been mentioned. The only reference to another bell-founder in the family is found at North Elmham,[158] when the tenor bell was recast in 1602:

Paid the bellfounder in earnest – ij s.
Paid to Raby for takinge down the bells – ij s.
Paid for hanginge upp the bells – vj s.
Paid fo cariinge a lod of billet for the bell founder – viij d.
Paid for cariinge of the bell to wayinge and stones to waye it
with all – ij s. vj d.
Paid to the bellfounder for castinge of the great bell and for in-
crease of mettell – viij li.
Paid for cariinge brick and claye to the bell founders – iij s.

The bell was clearly cast locally, since the churchwardens provided the materials for firing and moulding, and a bond[159] dated 12 June 1603 identifies the founder as Henry Draper, Bellfounder of North Elmham who 'hathe lately cast anewe the greate bell hanging in the steple of North

---

156 See notes on John Brend II.
157 CBN p. 46.
158 NRO PD 209/154.
159 NRO PD 209/41.

Elmham'. The bell probably survived until Joseph Mallows cast the new octave for North Elmham in 1757; and no specimen of Henry Draper's work is known to remain.

THE EAST DEREHAM FOUNDRY

Joseph Mallows
Working between 1750 and 1760

Little can be gathered from the East Dereham parish records concerning Joseph Mallows whose earliest recorded bells (dated 1750) hang at Dersingham,[160] although his activities as a bell-tuner are noted in the East Dereham churchwardens' accounts for 1748.[161] His first major work was to cast a unique ring of five for Beetley in 1752 whose inscriptions were formed in a cypher where the numbers 1, 2, 3, 4, 5, 6, 7, 8, 9 represented the letters A, E, I, O, U, L, M, N, R: thus the tenor bell was inscribed: 'JOS MALLOWS F2C3T 1752 H289Y W93GHT TH471S B92172 CHW'. Sadly this bell was sold to help pay for repairs to the tower in 1907; and two more (one of them cracked) were lost in 1974, when a very light ring of six was formed, using the second bell of the old five as the tenor. Bells were cast for Colkirk and Whinburgh in the next year; and in 1754 a single bell was recast for Holme-next-Sea, while three trebles completed a five for Reymerston.

Joseph Mallows's bell-founding career seems to have a curious gap in the middle; and it may not be a coincidence that in March 1754[162] 'Mr Catelyn, thought to be the greatest Artist in England for hanging bells, is just come from London to East Dearham, on purpose to hang a new Peal of Eight fine large bells, very lately cast by Mr Lister, of Whitechappel, Successor to the ingenious Mr Phelps, deceased'. It is not recorded whether Mallows assisted in the work; but it has been pointed out to the writer how much the hangings and fittings (especially the 'half-cheese' clapper-heads) of the four bells cast for Fundenhall church by Thomas Lester in 1754 resembled those on the old bells at Beetley. Perhaps Mallows occupied some of his time hanging bells cast at Whitechapel; a possibility further supported by the design of the clapper hanging in Lester's tenor of 1751 at Bressingham.[163]

An advertisement in the Norwich Mercury of 31 July 1756 invites

[160] CBN p. 124.
[161] NRO PHI 610.
[162] Once again the writer is indebted to Mr D. Cubitt for permission to use his transcripts of extracts from the Norwich Mercury. All quotations in this section are from this source.
[163] The Reverend D. L. Cawley and Mr R. W. M. Clouston have pointed out the peculiarities of the bell-gear installed by Mallows, and commented on the clappers at the churches mentioned.

'Gentlemen RINGERS and others' to 'The Day of Opening of the Peal of six Bells at Shipdham in Norfolk, now lately hung, tun'd, and compleated by Joseph Mallows of East Dearham in the said County, Bell Founder'. The present ring at Shipdham includes three bells which may have been supplied and tuned by Mallows, although probably not cast by him since they are uninscribed. Like Thomas Newman of Norwich, who was working a few years earlier, Joseph Mallows seems to have provided a number of rings which consisted of secondhand bells spliced in with others of his own making; and it is worth remembering that the middle of the 18th century was a time when many churchwardens were raising monies for church repairs by selling bells. One of his speculations in 1756 was to purchase the complete and excellent ring of five which had been cast in 1726 by John Stephens of Norwich for West Harling church, to which he added a treble of his own casting. The ring of six was hung in Caston tower, where they were opened in March 1757.

Some of the metal for the new octave which Joseph Mallows cast for North Elmham church in 1757 came from Longham church; and other parcels has been acquired from various scrap metal dealers in Norwich and Walsingham. Although Mallows himself provided none, we find that 17 cwt 2 qrs of metal had been purchased from Mr Hewitt, who appears to have been a close business associate. The total cost of eight bells, frame and fittings was £403. 5s. 2d., of which sum £102. 10s. 0d. was paid to 'Mr Hewitt and Mallows for Casting the s[ai]d Peal of Eight Bells'. This heavy ring was Mallows's most significant achievement, and those who rang on the North Elmham bells before they were replaced by the present light octave remember them with affection. Brooke bells are now Mallows's most important surviving work, where he cast four bells in 1758 and spliced in two older bells to complete a ring of six.

The churchwardens' accounts at Benington, Lincolnshire show that when Mallows cast a new bell for them in 1758 he also supplied a second-hand bell which had been cast by John Brend I of Norwich in 1572. In 1759 he returned to Benington to add two trebles and recast the tenor; and towards the end of the year there was opened at Hethersett a light five 'now lately cast and compleated by Joseph Mallows, Bell-Founder in East-Dereham, in Norfolk'. There are a few Lincolnshire churches which have bells cast by the Brends of Norwich; but it seems more likely that they were bought secondhand from Joseph Mallows, than that earlier founders supplied them new. His latest bells appear to be the two trebles at Upwell, and a bell at Wainfleet St Mary in Lincolnshire, all cast in 1761.[164]

---

[164] CBN p. 229. T. North, *The church bells of Lincolnshire*, 1882, *passim*.

DOWNHAM MARKET FOUNDERS

Thomas Osborn

Born 1741, working at St Neots from 1773 and from Downham Market from 1779, died 1806

Thomas Osborn was born at Downham Market[165] in 1741 and seems to have started his business career as a carpenter. When his father, Richard Osborn, joiner of Downham Market, died in 1762, Thomas Osborn seems to have carried the business on. Ten years later he had risen to the position of foreman at the St Neot's foundry of Joseph Eayre, and continued there in partnership with Edward Arnold after Eayre's death in 1772. A few bells cast by Osborn and Arnold remain, including five of a ring of six cast for Outwell in 1778, the year in which Osborn returned to Downham Market. The earliest bells from the Downham foundry seem to be the eight at Hilgay, four of which are inscribed 'THOS OSBORN DOWNHAM FECIT 1779'. He was still at Downham in 1781 when he cast the bells for Finchingfield, Essex, but seems to have moved to London in 1782.

Bells cast by Patrick and Osborn 'of London', dated 1782 include the fine octave at London St Botolph Bishopsgate and seven of the octave at Hatfield Broad Oak, Essex. The two founders cast the tenor bell for Norwich St John Maddermarket in 1782, but the partnership seems to have dissolved before 1783, since the Hatfield tenor bears the name of Robert Patrick alone. Fine rings cast by Thomas Osborn include the heavy ten at Bury St Edmunds Cathedral, and the octave at Woodbridge.

William Dobson seems to have joined his grandfather at the Downham foundry in 1798, when he apparently cast a ring of five for Crimplesham. He can have been no more than 18 years old when he completed the Crimplesham bells, and the 1803 five at Wisbech St Mary is the only example of a complete ring bearing the joint names of Thomas Osborn and William Dobson. Thomas Osborn's will[166] was written on 13 March 1804, in which he makes the following bequest to William Dobson:

> I Give and devise all that my Messuage or Dwellinghouse situate in Downham Market aforesaid wherein I now live with the Workshops Outhouses and Appurtenances thereunto belonging as also those two pieces of Land lying in Downham Market now in my own occupation which I lately purchased from the Trustees of Mr William Cleasby deceased unto my grandson William Dobson his heirs and assigns for ever I do also give and bequeath unto the

---

[165] Much has been printed concerning the Downham Market foundry, and little can be added to the material published by L'Estrange (CBN pp. 48–49), Mr D. Cubitt (Ringing World July/August 1976) and Dr J. Eisel (Ringing World January 1986).

[166] NRO NCC wills, Halfhide 330.

said William Dobson All my Stock in Trade and Utensils relating
to and concerning the Trade or Business of a Bellfounder as also
all such Horses that I may have in my possession at the time of
my decease for his own use and disposal I likewise give and
bequeath unto the said William Dobson the sum of one hundred
Pounds.

Osborn died on December 6th, 1806; and his will was proved on 23
December 1806, when the Downham Market foundry passed to William
Dobson.

William Dobson
Working at Downham Market from 1798, foundry sold 1832, died 1842

Having learned his craft, and inherited the Downham Market bell-
foundry, from his grandfather, William Dobson built up an extensive
business which sent bells to many parts of England and Wales, as well as
to Dublin and the West Indies. His largest ring of bells was the twelve at
St Nicholas, Liverpool, which were said to be uncharacteristically poor in
tone, since many of his smaller rings are excellent. The eight bells at Diss,
the last complete ring cast at Downham Market, are first class; and
numerous smaller rings such as those at Grimston, Heveningham (Suffolk) New Buckenham and Wiveton are very good indeed. Dr John Eisel
has traced a bell of 43 cwt cast in 1817, surely one of the heaviest ever
made in Norfolk, to its present home in the west of Ireland, and it is
accepted that the 29 cwt tenor bell at St Neots, Huntingdonshire was the
last bell cast at Downham Market.

William Dobson sold the bell-foundry to Thomas Mears of Whitechapel in 1833 and moved to London at about the same time. There is no
record of his having worked for Mears, and he died at the Charterhouse,
London in 1842.

THE REDENHALL FOUNDRY

Captain A. P. Moore, Gervas Holmes, Esq., and Mr H. A. O. MacKenzie
Working from 1878 to 1885

The foundry was set up during the summer of 1878[167] by two accomplished ringers, Captain Arthur Penistone Moore and Gervas Holmes,
Esq., who were joined by H. A. O. MacKenzie, an engineer who designed

---

[167] Most of the material in this section is derived from the Candler Mss. belonging
to the Norfolk and Norwich Archaeological Society, and housed in their Library at Garsett House, Norwich. A brief account of the foundry appears in C.
Candler, *Notes on the parish of Redenhall with Harleston*, 1896, pp. 147, 148. The

Captain Arthur Penistone Moore, bellringer and bell-
founder of Redenhall.
From a photograph in the belfry at Redenhall.

one of the first Brougham carriages[168] to work by steam power. A notice in
Church Bells, dated 13 September, 1879, remarks that: 'It has long been
contemplated by the two first-named gentlemen to revive the art of cast-

---

other major source is Moore, Holmes and Mackenzie's letter book, now among
the archives of the Whitechapel Bell foundry who took over the goodwill of the
firm in 1886. For a full and interesting account largely based on this source see
D. L. Cawley, 'M. H. M. the last Norfolk Foundry', *Ringing World,* 1983, pp. 159,
179, 199.

[168] Information from Mr Richard Adamek of Stratton Strawless.

ing church bells, and they secured the assistance and co-operation of Mr MacKenzie, a gentleman of great engineering and musical knowledge.' The foundry was established at the premises of Messrs Knights and Stacey at Harleston, who were well-known as agricultural engineers and ironfounders; and the bells were cast on a site in Wilderness Lane on the outskirts of the town. Harleston forms part of the large ecclesiastical parish of Redenhall, at which church both Moore and Holmes were ringers; and the premises were known as the Redenhall Bell-Foundry.

The firm adopted a number of unorthodox designs for bell-frames and ringing gear, and were anxious to cast bells which came from the moulds without requiring subsequent tuning. While it was easy to cast single 'maiden' bells, there were many problems in producing a complete ring of bells in tuneful accord, whose notes would require no further adjustment after casting. Bells were cast with a large mushroom-shaped stud in place of the traditional cannons, and specially designed cast-iron headstocks were made, in which the bells were fixed by a single large nut. This supporting nut also holds an independent crown-staple in such a way that it would be a very simple process to quarter-turn bells when they became worn by the blows of the clappers. The stays were also placed in the centres of the headstocks, working against a rolling bar (as at Surlingham and Winterton), or against a curiously suspended pendulum bar (as at Weybread). The principle underlying the design of MacKenzie's patent clapper was for the clapper ball to lift clear of the soundbow of the bell immediately after striking, thus preventing any damping of the vibrations. The 'Redenhall Patent Clapper' was fitted to several bells which the firm hung for full-circle ringing, including the rings at Blofield and Tunstead, as well as to the 27 cwt tenor bell at Great St Mary's church, Cambridge. The iron bell-frames produced 'on Mathematical principles' at Harleston aroused some criticism from traditional bell-hangers, as did the ringing gear fitted to some bells.

Remarkable, and characteristically Victorian confidence is shown in the letters sent to churches where the firm was asked to estimate for work. After reporting to the Rector that the quality of the Morningthorpe[169] bells was extremely poor, and that the bell-frame was in imminent danger of collapse, they go on to remark: 'Of the quality of tone and accuracy of intonation of our bells as well as of our system of hanging and fitting, we had much rather that the inhabitants of Morningthorpe (before placing the work of restoring their bells in our hands) should form their own judgement, than that we should say anything on the subject. At the present time we have, standing in our fitting shop, a peal of eight bells complete and ready for ringing; these we shall be most happy to show to any one interested in the matter, who will honour us with a visit to our Foundry.' They were, however, more sympathetic to the craftsmanship of

[169] NRO PD 56/13.

earlier founders when they restored the ring of four bells at Surlingham, which contained two fine pre-Reformation, London-cast bells. When a new frame was fitted in 1883 and the bells were rehung using the firm's patent fittings, the cannons were not removed as was the current practice; and the cast-iron cannon-retaining headstocks are among the earliest of their kind.

The first complete ring of bells cast at the Redenhall Bell Foundry was the six at Weybread, Suffolk (1879), where the attempt to produce a 'maiden' peal was almost sucessful: only two of the bells had been slightly tuned. The bells were very favourably received, although The Reverend W. W. Hutt of Hockwold wrote to Captain Moore: 'My impression is that the Weybread peal slightly tuned by such a man as old Haley would be almost a none-such.' A number of single bells were cast after the success of the Weybread bells, including a bell for St John's church in the centre of Harleston in 1881. The Norfolk News of 30 April, 1881, comments:

> When the Redenhall Bell Foundry was first started, most of the inhabitants of this neighbourhood looked upon the scheme as a wild one, and few indeed were those who ever expected that the company would ever succeed in casting a bell, let alone a good one. These expectations have, however, been completely set aside, and if there still remained in the minds of any a doubt, it must now have vanished, for within the past few days these gentlemen have placed in the turret of St John's church, Harleston, a little bell, which, for brightness and purity of tone could not well be surpassed. The old bell on which the town clock strikes, is one of unusual power and sweetness, so that the inhabitants have for many years been accustomed to the sound of a really first-class bell. It is now, therefore, all the more pleasing to find that the new church bell gives such universal satisfaction, and in no way suffers when compared with its older sister. The proprietors of the Redenhall Bell Foundry are heartily to be congratulated on the issue of their enterprising efforts.

The two trebles at Southwold were recast at Harleston, and rehung in 1881; and three old bells for Westmeston, Sussex were recast later in the same year.

The octave referred to in the letter to Morningthorpe had been completed in July 1882, when the Norfolk Chronicle remarked on the sweetness of tone demonstrated in a carillon recital performed by Mr MacKenzie in the foundry yard at Wilderness Lane. A number of distinguished ringers called at Harleston to hear the new bells, the first octave cast in Norfolk for half a century, and the Reverend F. E. Robinson, having heard the bells chimed, wrote on 22 August 1884: 'Before I heard the ring of 8 bells cast by you for Thorpe church I always preferred the tone of the

Whitechapel bells to that of any others by whomsoever made – But now I am inclined to give you the palm, and to describe the tone of the above bells as <u>Mears improved</u>.' The bells were hung at St Andrew's church, Thorpe Episcopi, in the most unsuitably designed new brick tower, which proved too weak for them to be rung in full circles. This must surely have been a most bitter disappointment to Messrs Moore, Holmes and Mac-Kenzie. Their rings of six at Winterton and Stanford-le-Hope in Essex were more successful, although the latter bells were recast in 1936.

The Redenhall Bell Foundry closed in 1885, passing on the goodwill to the Whitechapel Bell Foundry, who took over a number of schemes inaugurated by Moore, Holmes and Mackenzie. With the closing of the Redenhall Bell-foundry, the craft of bell-founding finally disappeared from Norfolk.

OTHER NORFOLK BELL-FOUNDERS

Simon Severey
Died at South Repps in 1454

There is a group of fine bells, found mainly in north-east Norfolk which are markedly different from apparently contemporary bells cast at Norwich and Lynn. Their characteristics include extremely high casting quality with neatly formed inscriptions, and strong cannons of plain and functional design. The only indication of a date for this group of bells appears in the inscription on the single bell at Crostwight: '+ ASLAK : IOHES : ME : IOHEM : NOIAVIT'. One cannot argue with L'Estrange's identification[170] of the man who gave the bell its name as John Aslak, Lord of the Manor and Patron of Crostwight, whose will was proved in 1434. He left bequests to the monks at Bromholm (20s.), Wymondham (13s. 4d.) and Hickling (6s. 8d.) for their steeples, as well as 20s. to the emendation of Crostwight church. The tower at Crostwight[171] was under construction in 1438, when Thomas Norton left 4s., to the work, and it is very likely that a new bell would have bought at about the same time, either provided by John Aslak in his lifetime, or possibly commemorating the recently deceased patron.

Two bells of this type are found at Norwich, St George Tombland, but the distribution of the rest suggests that the founder was operating from Aylsham or North Walsham. In his will[172] of 1454, one Simon Severey of South Repps described himself as a brasier, as did all of the contemporary Norwich bell-founders, thus providing reasonably strong circumstantial evidence for the authorship of what L'Estrange has called the

[170] CBN p. 83.
[171] C&C.
[172] NCC wills, Betyns 16.

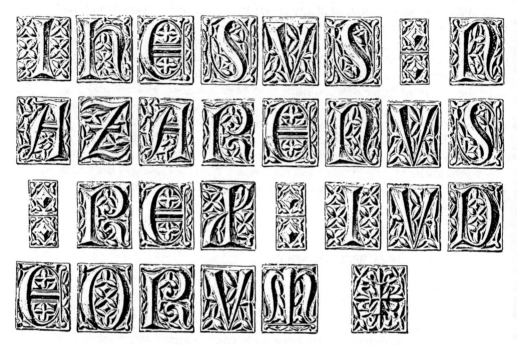

JHESUS : NAZARENUS : REX : JUDEORUM +

Lettering of the 'Crostwight' type, probably used by Simon Severey of South Repps. Here copied from a bell formerly at Haveringland.
Drawing by William Kimber at the Whitechapel Bell Foundry, reproduced by kind permission of Alan Hughes.

'Crostwight' group of bells. Simon Severey's will gives no further clues or confirmation that bells were a specific product of his brasier's craft. His executors were Lawrence Brinklee of Aylsham and Martin Nark of Knapton; and there were bequests to four of the gilds in Aylsham, as well as to the fabric fund of South Repps church.

Walter Blowere

An old bell[173] hanging in the small tower at Spixworth bears this founder's name, but no documentary evidence has been found for him.

[173] CBN p. 76.

William Eldhouse

Blomefield records his name on a bell which hung at Itteringham[174] during the first half of the 18th century, but which has now gone.

Robert Plummer

Blomefield records the name on a bell which hung in the ruined church at Wolterton[175] during the first half of the 18th century, but which has now gone.

BELLS POSSIBLY CAST BY ITINERANT FOUNDERS

Henry Yaxley
Possibly at Fritton, and certainly at Thrandeston in 1671

Two known bells are inscribed with the name of Henry Yaxley. Fritton 1/3 is dated 1671 and Wyverstone (Suffolk) 1/3 is dated 1674,[176] and both bells carry a distinctive shield charged with a chevron between three mullets. Raven confuses the identification of Yaxley's work by wrongly stating that the Brasyer's three-bell shield appears on the Fritton bell, and adds that he may have cast some of the bells for Horham, Suffolk, church in 1683.[177] The Horham bells are the earliest surviving ring of eight in existence, and the octave was completed in 1672, two bells being dated in that year and one, presumably a recasting, dated in 1673. The bells of 1672/73 have similar lettering to that on the Fritton bell, and a small stamp in the form of a pentagonal rosette appears in both towers thus apparently confirming Raven's supposition. Deedes and Walters[178] ascribe a bell dated 1684 at Great Sampford to Henry Yaxley on the strength of a shield which also appears on the Wyverstone bell.

The churchwardens' accounts at Bressingham[179] show that Henry Yaxley was paid for recasting their fourth bell at Thrandeston in 1671, which bell is inscribed: 'MILES GRAYE MADE ME 1671 HENRY MALLOWES & WILLIAM ROWT CHURCH WARDENS.' Although the lettering is larger than that employed at Horham, the design is similar; and it would appear that Yaxley was acting as a foreman for Miles Graye III of Colchester. In the context of other contemporary bells by Miles Graye III listed by Deedes and Walters,[180] all of which are in churches in north Essex and south-east Suffolk, the Bressingham bell is an anomaly. It may well be the case that Graye

[174] *Ibid.*
[175] *Ibid.*
[176] CBS p. 258.
[177] *Ibid.*
[178] CBE p. 111.
[179] NRO PD 111/70.
[180] CBE pp. 101–104.

sent a competent foreman to work on his own in north Suffolk, who subsequently went into business independently of his former employer. He may have cast bells in various localities, possibly working at Fritton before moving on to Thrandeston.

Thomas Doo
Named in documents of 1674 and 1677, cast a bell in 1687

Very little is known of Thomas Doo, apart from a few references in documents and a single bell bearing his name. The churchwardens' accounts[181] at Martham record payments in 1674 to 'Thomas Doo Bellfounder in Yarmouth', who supplied new gudgeons for s bell, and provided a clock with a dial for the church. He is probably identical with the supplier[182] of new chimes and quarters at Norwich, St Peter Mancroft who was paid £39 for work which probably took place after the completion of the octave in 1675–1676. In 1677 the bells at both Garboldisham churches[183] were repaired by Thomas Doo and Robert Lowdell. The only bell known to have been cast by Thomas Doo is the single small bell[184] which hangs above the roof of the parochial chapel at Botesdale, Suffolk.

[181] CBN p. 161.
[182] CBN p. 184.
[183] NRO PD 197/64.
[184] Information from Mr R. W. M. Clouston, who reports that this bell was described by C. H. Hawkins, whose notes are in the Library of the Society of Antiquaries at Burlington House, London.

GENERAL INDEX

Appropriation of churches by religious houses 68, 72
archaeological evidence for bell-founding 140, 141, 145
Augmentations, Court of 13
authorities quoted: see Index of names
Aylsham Collection 22

Bede-roll 71, 73
bedesmen as ringers 7
bells and bellfounders 138 *et seq.*
   accounts for casting 88, 139, 152, 194, 206, 207, 209
   alphabet bells 167
   bad workmanship 155, 204
   bass bell 155
   bell-metal, cost 157, 192
   bellyeter 142
   black-letter 159, 166
   bond for casting 11, 90, 153, 188, 190, 193, 205, 206, 207
   cannons 89
   capital letters 158, 167
   cast by churchwardens 207
   changeringers, founders' encouragement of 22, 35, 198
   clay 139, 200
   competition between bellfounders 186
   cope 139
   crosses 158 *et seq.*
   design 139, 140
   diversification of crafts 149, 150, 151, 155, 201, 212, 218
   equipment for founding 153, 159, 184
   fire-risk 142
   founders: see Index of names
   founders consulted by churchwardens 207
   foundries: see Index of places
   innkeeper 148, 151, 153
   inscriptions 30, 36, 71, 139, 188
   itinerant 140, 190, 192, 207, 217
   letter moulds 139, 159
   lettering 158 *et seq.*

levy on bells shipped at staithe: 141, 200, 202
'maiden' bells 213, 214
metal 139
monumental brasses 153
mould 153
moulding 139
multiple occupation of foundry 140, 143, 150, 152
ornament 158 *et seq.*
recasting 35
running (= casting) 198
secondhand bells 39, 157, 177, 193, 209
shooting (= casting) 206
spoiled in casting 145
stock bells 28
stops 158 *et seq.*
strickle 139, 153
subscriptions for new bells 26, 32, 34
summoned from Gloucester 197
tenor bell 11, 188
treble bell 11, 188
tuneable (= melodious) bells 11, 12, 29, 197, 205
wax letters 139, 159
bells, uses
   Ascension Day 8
   civic occasions 30
   commemoration of benefactors 8
   Corpus Christi 8
   early ringing 7
   funerals 9
   half-muffled ringing 4, 41
   invasion warning 1
   monastic offices 1, 5
   processions, ringing during 8, 66
   royal occasions 10, 12, 17, 30, 31, 42, 92
   sacrist at Cathedral 6
   sanctus bells 15, 44
   secular timekeeping 10
   service ringing 6, 8, 11
   victories 30
   weddings 10, 17

INDEX OF NAMES

INDEX OF PLACES

Lightning Source UK Ltd.
Milton Keynes UK
UKOW031416201212

203955UK00005B/27/P